D0753931

VISION QUEST

Other Sun Bear Books

The Medicine Wheel
by Sun Bear and Wabun

The Path of Power
by Sun Bear, Wabun, and Barry Weinstock

The Bear Tribe's Self-reliance Book
by Sun Bear, Wabun, and Nimimosha

THE BOOK OF THE

VISION QUEST

Personal Transformation in the Wilderness

REVISED EDITION

STEVEN FOSTER
with Meredith Little

Prentice Hall Press

New York   London   Toronto   Sydney   Tokyo

Grateful acknowledgment is made to the following for permission to reprint material copyrighted or controlled by them:

The Bollingen Foundation, Inc., for an excerpt from *Hero With a Thousand Faces* by Joseph Campbell. Doubleday & Company, Inc., for an excerpt from "Once More, The Round," copyright © 1962 by Beatrice Roethke, Administratix of the Estate of Theodore Roethke, from the book *The Collected Poems of Theodore Roethke;* and for excerpts from *Technicians of the Sacred* edited by Jerome Rothenberg, copyright © 1968 by Jerome Rothenberg. Harper & Row, for excerpts from *Seven Arrows* by Hyemeyohsts Storm, copyright © 1972 by Hyemeyohsts Storm. New Directions Publishing Corporation, for an excerpt from *Paterson* by William Carlos Williams, copyright © 1948 by William Carlos Williams. Sierra Club Books, for an excerpt from *The Unsettling of America* by Wendell Berry, copyright © 1977 by Wendell Berry. *The Pacific Sun,* for excerpts from "Surviving Vision Quest," by Steven Foster. Natalie Rogers, for excerpts from her book, *Emerging Woman, A Decade of Midlife Transitions,* copyright © by Natalie Rogers. Rites of Passage, Inc., for excerpts from *A Vision Quest Handbook* by Gift Bearer and others, copyright © 1980. Princeton University Press, for an excerpt from *Hero With a Thousand Faces* by Joseph Campbell, Bollingen Series XVII. Copyright 1949 by Princeton University Press. Copyright © renewed 1976 by Princeton University Press.

Prentice Hall Press
Gulf + Western Building
One Gulf + Western Plaza
New York, New York 10023

Library of Congress Cataloging-in-Publication Data
Foster, Steven, 1938-
  The book of the vision quest: personal transformation
in the wilderness / Steven Foster with Meredith Little.
    —Rev. ed. p. cm.
  Bibliography: p.
  ISBN 0-13-080144-5 (pbk.): $9.95
  1. Spiritual life. 2. Rites and ceremonies.
3. Vision quests. I. Little, Meredith, 1951- . II. Title.
III. Title: Vision quest.
BL624.F67 1988
291.3'8—dc19   88-19180
                                                    CIP

Designed by Victoria Hartman
Manufactured in the United States of America
10 9 8 7 6 5 4 3 2 1

Revised Edition

For M, in memory of
Κιονιον Ιθαχη
and
For Tom Pinkson, in memory of
The Yosemite

Contents

Preface to the Revised Edition

Returning from the Last Chance Mountains with a group of vision questers, we were presented with the news that Prentice Hall Press would accept this new, expanded edition of *The Book of the Vision Quest* for publication. The season is fall. The leaves of the cottonwoods are turning the bright golden glow of death. It seems entirely appropriate that winter should be almost here.

Soon the dark of the year will come. What will keep the people warm through the long, cold nights when the trees stand bare and the aching wind sows seeds of yearning to the iron earth? Some say the wheels of war will carry us back again to the Dark Ages. Others say that Armageddon is at hand. Still others, preferring to make no further effort to swim upstream, turn away from the global realities of human survival, and endlessly contemplate themselves in mediamirrors that lie, that tell them they will never grow old, that they will never want or suffer, that no matter how they treat her, the Earth will always be technicolor green. Of course, there are always the legions who say, "Follow like sheep and you will escape the slaughter."

Here is our contribution to the survival of the people through the coming winter. Here is a fire, fueled by human hearts, ignited by dreams of human wholeness. Here is a warming flame from which light may be drawn to illuminate the cold hearths of the world.

We have been especially pleased to learn that this book has penetrated the Iron Curtain and found an audience among Soviet citizens who, like Americans, are looking for ways to revive the power of ancient rites of passage within their culture. Requests for the book have also come from Germany, Sweden, the Netherlands, South Africa, Zambia, Mexico, Honduras, New Zealand, Australia, England, and Wales. The interest of diverse peoples suggests the relevance of passage rites such as the vision quest to diverse cultures. This relevance is not surprising. The archetype is a prominent feature of the human collective unconscious.

For this revised edition we are especially grateful for the help of Wabun Marlise James, Sun Bear, and the Bear Tribe.

—Steven Foster
Meredith Little
The School of Lost Borders
Big Pine, California
1987

Second Preface

Four years have elapsed since the first printing of *The Book of the Vision Quest*. During this time the work has been blessed by the spirits of wind and rain, lightning and thunder. Individuals come from all over the country to participate and be trained. Many others are also doing the work. Today, there is hardly an isolated range of mountains in the American West that has not heard the voice of a modern vision quester crying for a vision.

Meredith and I continue to go with people to the "sacred mountain." Faced by steadily increasing numbers of participants, however, we felt the necessity to go into semiretirement and to move our family to the Eastern Sierra where we currently operate a small school for individuals seeking to be trained in the ways of fasting, vision, and dream quests. Here, at the edge of the northern Mojave Desert, we keep close to our family and study at the feet of *las sierras desiertas*.

When Island Press changed its editorial focus, the book faced oblivion. A note from Wabun (and the Bear Tribe) expressing interest in the future of the book arrived the very day we were told by Island Press that the rights were reverting to us. We particularly want to thank Wabun and Sun Bear for agreeing to take on a second edition. We are learning to take such miracles as a matter of course. The vision is not under our control—and never was. We are but two of its many earth-appointed custodians, as are Wabun, Sun Bear, Shawnodese, the Bear Tribe, and so many others. The spirit of Mother Earth is moving in our hearts and in the world at large to get her word out. The vision quest is good for all of us—as individuals, families, communities, culture, and land. This rite of passage must be set free. It has been trapped behind culturally conditioned fears for too long. Let the river flow freely through the

thirsty canyons of the modern world. There is a way to heal ourselves and our land.

With these brief remarks we want to honor the contributors to
this book who subsequently became vision quest guides. They have
served their people well, without a single serious injury or death.
Mark Stillman, Linda Gregory, Virginia Hine, Patricia Burke,
Marilyn Riley, Steve DeMartini, and Jack Crimmins—we salute
you! We also want to honor those who guided Rites of Passage,
Inc., in the years after we left: Jennifer Hine-Massey, Drew Pratt,
Michael Bodkin, Miguel Batz, Theresa Koke, John Morris, Tim
Garthwaite, Howard and Sue Lamb, Frank Burton, and others.
Above all, we want to publicly express our loving gratitude to
Virginia Hine, grandmother and teacher, who went on her last
vision quest in January 1982.

—Steven Foster
Meredith Little
The School of Lost Borders
Big Pine, California
1984

Preface

This book is about the re-creation, in modern times, of an ancient rite of dying, passing through, and being reborn. It is also the story of the efforts of a small group of individuals to assist urban and suburban people to go into the wilderness to enact this ancient rite of passage—the vision quest.

This book is the first of its kind. It speaks with a collective voice and a single voice. It speaks not only from the local universe of individuals but from the common universe in which we all live, and in which we have lived since time began. The words are in the English language, but the expression is panhuman.

The experience of fasting alone in the wilderness of which these voices speak is the indirect outgrowth of teaching methods that I began to practice as an assistant professor in the School of Humanities at San Francisco State University during the tumultuous years of 1969–1971. Research into American mythology led me to the rites of passage of the first people of America. Other research into the roots of mythology led me to various other wilderness rites of initiation, some of them ancient, others not so ancient.

Idealistically, I envisioned a school that would perform a maieutic or "midwifely" function, Socratically preparing people in transition or crisis to enact a meaningful, symbolic rite of passage in a natural setting that formally confirmed the resolution of the crisis or passage. The classroom, a wilderness womb, would provide nourishment, learning, and preparation for reentry into the stream of human time, engendering in each candidate a personal mythic mission to serve society in some meaningful way.

The channels through which such concepts could be taught, however, did not exist within the institutional framework. I was baffled and frustrated by seemingly insurmountable obstacles.

There was simply no place for the experiential study of the vision quest in the college curriculum. Not only that, but the vast majority of my colleagues had been educated and conditioned to view a course called The Vision Quest from an "academic" perspective. It was too "far out," too idealistic, too risky, too "flaky." In a frustrated turmoil, I left college teaching.

At that point, I went into the desert on my own search. I was stimulated by the recent appearance of a strange and powerful new book—Hyemeyohsts Storm's *Seven Arrows* (1972). This man wrote in clear, urgent tones: "The Vision Quest, or perceiving quest, is the way we must begin this search. We must all follow our Vision Quest to discover ourselves, to learn how we perceive of ourselves, and to find our relationship with the world around us."

When I returned from the desert I was lost for a while. Finally, one rainy day, I found a man—or he found me. His name was Edward L. Beggs and he was the director of a federally funded adolescent drug abuse family service agency known as (like a bolt of lightning!) Rites of Passage.

I remember the day well. I met Edward at a meeting, and afterward we walked back to our cars together and talked. Our talk continued absurdly in the rain for an hour or so, while I shivered from excitement and the cold. Later, in 1973, I went to work for Edward (and the "Feds") at Rites of Passage, which in those days offered a variety of services to young people: therapy, counseling, education in the processes of severance from home and family, even a sex-information hotline. Much went on in the name of drug abuse treatment that was not specifically such. For three years I was paid for doing something different from what my job description prescribed.

It was at Rites of Passage that the vision quest, as we now conduct it, first began to take form. It could not have existed without the encouragement of Edward Beggs or the pioneering efforts of Robert Greenway, professor of "wilderness psychology" at Sonoma State University. Others appeared also: Tom Pinkson and Vern Muhr, the director and instructors of the Marin Open House Wilderness Project. This program, conceived by Tom to help rehabilitate junkies and speed freaks, was imaginative and courageous. Before long, an exchange of ideas and enthusiasm resulted in the creation of a vision quest wilderness rite, a formal ceremony of passage.

In 1974, I went to the Tiltill Valley of the Yosemite with a dozen other people to reenact my first naive attempts at a vision quest. This act culminated three years of seeking my own vision amid the despair and frustrations of my own life and the lives of many I lived with. I was volunteering at Suicide Prevention at the time and seeking some way to quell my deepest fears that I had nothing worthwhile to give away. I could not have known that I had actually completed a passage and that my ship had landed on the shore of a new world. Nor could I have known that my Suicide Prevention "shift partner" would become my wife and life partner–sharer two years later.

Before my work in the original Rites of Passage was terminated, I had participated in a dozen vision quests, mainly involving young people on the verge of leaving home. The more involved with the concept I became, the more convinced I was that the vision for my life lay in teaching rites of passage and reintroducing ancient birth ways into the wastelands of American culture.

But the "Feds" said no. They decided, somewhere in the dim halls of the National Institute for Drug Abuse, that funds were being misappropriated on crazy stuff called "vision quests." In June of 1976, Rites of Passage ceased to be, and I was footloose with my life myth, with no cultural socket to plug it into.

For a year I tried to ignore the vision. I was in love with Meredith, elated by my incredibly good fortune to have found her. We went to Europe and then to Greece, to a tiny village on the island of Ithaki, legendary home of Odysseus, the "wide wanderer." Amid the romance and simple reality of life on Ithaki I almost forgot the vision quest. My love and I walked in the moonlight above the ancient village of Annoghi and, drawn by the dark and fertile sea, decided to make a baby.

Only then, when Meredith was pregnant with Selene, did we begin to face the dare that lurked in our homeland, in our old neighborhood, in our hearts. As the vision grew again with a new urgency between us, we began to feel the increasing tension between our Greek home and our Marin County home. We made plans to return and take up the vision quest work.

But how? We had just enough money to fly back and rent a

house for a month. Meredith was looking like a pear. It was probably not the best time to set out on the trail of a star. We returned to America from our island of love-without-a-care, certain about what we sought, uncertain about the means to go about it.

Then the little miracles began to occur: money from unexpected sources, the realization that people were willing to pay us to prepare them for the vision quest, Edward Beggs agreeing to relinquish his rights to the use of the name, Rites of Passage, to us. His beautiful gift was followed by powerful encouragement and support from Dr. Tom Pinkson, my old vision-questing friend. Tom has since shifted much of his visionary energy to people who face life's greatest passage: death itself.

Many friends have come to help. Some have helped materially, others spiritually. Constant through it all has been the presence of Meredith. Her insight, imagination, and labor infuse every page of this book. The rigors of our life quest have led us through the Slough of Despond to the drawbridge of the Castle of Despair, but she has borne herself calmly, courageously on.

A man who at the age of seventeen participated in that first Yosemite vision quest, a poet-teacher named Jack Crimmins, came to work with us many years ago and codirected our youth program. Now a Ph.D., he works with cancer patients and heads an organization called Dream Quest, serving the greater Los Angeles area with his own version of the quest. His life testifies to the power of the ancient processes through which he leads his "clients."

For a long time, Virginia Hine, noted anthropologist, and Marilyn Riley, youth vision quest teacher, contributed their intelligence, energy, beauty, and unique gifts to further the work and to encourage the fruition of this book.

Other people throng to be mentioned, people who, for one reason or another, have been as the salt of the earth to this book: Derham Giuliani, Enid Larson, Louise Malfanti, Tim Garthwaite, Char Horning, Natalie Rogers, Philip and Elizabeth Little, Ron Pevny, Barbara Dean, Jan Duncan, Howard Voskuyl, Sam Wilcox, Pat Nalley, George Rideout, Del Rio, Georgia Oliva, Steve DeMartini, Wabun, Hyemeyohsts and Rocky Storm, Grandpa Eagle, Coyote, Rattlesnake, Bighorn Sheep, Kangaroo Rat, the Inyo County Mountain Rescue Unit, Keenan, Chris, Selene, Warren and Winifred Foster, and many others.

Nor should I forget to mention a man whom I know as Rolling Thunder on the Mountain, of Imlay, Nevada, who pointed up to the steep ridges of Thunder Mountain and said: "See up there? Two canyons. One is Sacred Canyon and the other is Thunder Canyon. Go up there, and don't come back until the voices have stopped."

—Steven Foster
Meredith Little
Forgotten Creek
Death Valley
1980

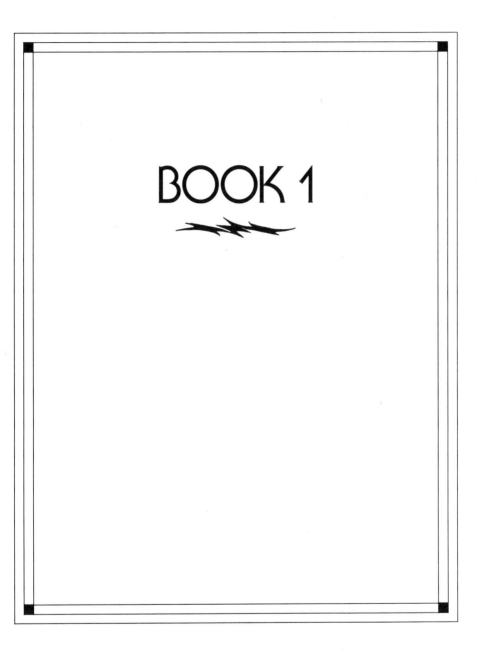

BOOK 1

THE QUEST

What can be known? The unknown.
My true self runs toward a Hill.
More! O More! visible.

Now I adore my life
With the Bird, the abiding Leaf,
With the Fish, the questing Snail,
And the Eye altering all;
And I dance with William Blake
For love, for Love's sake. . . .
—Theodore Roethke, "Once More, the
Round"

Many years ago, haunted by guilt, pursued by images of freedom, persistently, relentlessly believing that I had to acquire experiences at the risk of all, I left my vocation of college teaching and went into the world. Though I lived with great appetite, and seemed, even to myself, suicidally bent on my own destruction or the destruction of anyone who loved me, I found myself drawn into the land of my father's childhood and early manhood: the vast stretches of loneliness called Nevada, and the remote, desolate regions of the desert called Mojave.

I went into the desert alone, not knowing why, searching for something I had lost, or could find: something, someone, some revelation waiting for me at the bend of the dry river bed, some face-to-face encounter with what I feared, and desired, most.

At the time I did not realize I was seeking death. That is, I was not seeking to die, but to reap the fruit of death, to reenter the womb of things, the matrix of unknowing, and to be born anew, severed from old distinctions and limitations, to induce, by sheer force of will, self-transformation.

But self-transformation is a gradual, painstaking process won at the expense of joy and sorrow, or so it has been for me. Nevertheless, certain power events, or growth events, blaze out from the background of my life. These events mark the juncture at which my restless heart touched the timeless, transforming heart of the universe. The year I spent in the desert was filled with many such events.

Was it because my mother had told me I had been conceived at Shadow Mountain, within view of the mountains of Death Valley, that I went into the desert? Was it because my childhood had been steeped in the stories of the Old Testament, the tales of the desert prophets, Moses, Isaiah, Elijah? Was it because, even when I was very small, I felt a deep affinity with the spirit of the desert? Something lured me. I responded with instinctive faith in a feeling that quickened me to the core, a shuddering, shivering, passionate feeling.

I packed an old VW bus with a few essentials, said goodbye to my children, my friends, and my life, and drove away. I headed east toward Reno, gateway to the far-flung deserts of the Great Basin. I came back, eventually, to pick up the threads of my "civilized" life, a life that had changed because I had changed.

But when I got into my car and took off down the road, I gave no thought to returning. I had reached a point where desperation overshadowed responsibilities. I could not continue living as I had been living. Something more was waiting. Surely, if I actively sought it, the answer would be revealed to me out there, in the trackless waste. I drove away with such deep excitement. I had not thought I was capable of such emotion.

What happened to me in the desert? I cannot exactly say. My lips are sealed by the inadequacy of words. I am convinced that the Great Mother eventually led me to heights and depths of being that are akin to "visionary." But much of the time my memory only coughs up facts, events, and places. I was not prepared to understand all that came to pass. Much of the time I was bored—either having nothing in particular to do or attending to the basic needs of my own survival. Sometimes I had to deal with the consequences of my own ignorance, such as not knowing how to start a fire with wet wood, not knowing how to adequately protect myself from the cold or searing heat, or not knowing how to perform simple but critical repairs on the engine of the bus.

Though for years I had made pronouncements about "nature" to students from my egotistical ivory tower, I knew very little about the process of truly living on the land. I understood very little about the rhythms and elements of our Great Mother. The night I finally took leave of Elko and turned my face to the Ruby Mountains I realized how inadequately I had prepared myself. I trembled with fear and considered going back. What if I died out there? It might be a long time before somebody found me. What if I got lost? I would have nowhere to go, no one to come home to, no one to help me find myself. I feared insanity. I feared flash floods (though I had never seen one), rattlesnakes, tarantulas, the dark, the cold, the bad roads, car trouble, dying of thirst, and physical illness. Most of all, I feared loneliness. All my heroic myths about myself came down like the walls of Jericho when I first heard, really heard, the awesome trumpet sound of the loneliness of the wilderness—the sound of *silence*. Against that absence of sound I was nothing but a cipher. My ego withered, as pages of a book thrown to a fire.

How little I knew about survival, or myself, or death! Having rejected other teachings, I had unwittingly apprenticed myself to the most exacting teacher of all. But I did not understand her language. Her voice was the roaring of silence in my ears. She taught, not with words, but through my body, with light and darkness, rain and wind, snow and fire. She pierced my virgin ears with bird calls. And the words and sounds she caused me to utter were not the words of the world I knew. Some of them were cries that came from my stomach and bowels, strange to my ears, more like those of an animal: howls, moans, grunts, and growls. And the actions she taught me were animal actions, almost forgotten: eating, sleeping, eliminating, creeping, burrowing, hiding, listening. The learning of these gestures marked the beginnings of change in my life.

Is it the vulnerability of loneliness that drives us to love and to be loved? The implacable stars and the horned moon ride the night sky, leaving the ache and emptiness of another morning without love in their wake. Thus we learn to live with loneliness, to curse and accept it, to fill it with the rituals of survival. But finally loneliness would break me down into rigid insistence: My body *craved*, as dry leaves crave the wind, the presence of another. I would go into Winnemucca or Austin or Goldfield or Goodsprings or Lone Pine or Furnace Creek, looking for someone to talk to. In a way, loneliness is a way of preparing for death. Once, as I drove a long, desolate stretch of highway between Wells and Ely, I overtook a young woman walking beside the road, without pack or water, twenty-five miles north of Currie. Imagining she was in trouble or needed a lift, I stopped and asked her if I could be of help.

She looked at me from a face blistered by the sun. She saw a wild-looking man, dirty, unshaven, horizons gleaming in his eyes. I saw a weary woman with a wasted longing in her eyes.

"No thanks," she said.

Curious, I asked her what she was doing here, out in the middle of nowhere.

"Nowhere is somewhere," she replied curtly and kept on walking.

So I drove on. Her toiling form shrank in the rear-view mirror, until she was just a speck, which then vanished. I sometimes wonder about her. She reminded me of myself. Surely she was one of those lonely, lost people learning how to die.

Many a night I spent watching unidentified lights move on the horizon. Sometimes they seemed to approach. The optical phenomenon so frightened me one night that I sat up all night by the fire, reluctant to close my eyes in sleep against the possible unknown terror the moving lights represented. Many a night I spent frightened, uncomfortable, anxious, restless, in a vague dread that calamity would befall me. Many a night I lay awake, remembering my children, my women, my family, my friends. Many a morning I awoke to the bitter taste of emptiness in my coffee, and for several days the pangs of unrequited love would keep me from food. Spasms of self-pity would come and go. Sometimes I heard the strange sound of a man crying for himself.

One early summer day in Dry Lake Valley, west of Caliente, Nevada, surely one of the most desolate regions of the earth, I ingested enough LSD for a dozen people. Reasoning that if I was to seize the fire from the altar, this was the way to do it, I entered the morning with high expectations. By noon the temperature had risen to intolerable limits, and I had no shelter but my car, which had become a furnace. At 4:00 P.M. I got into the furnace and drove all the way to Lake Mead, camping that night in the Valley of Fire. What had occurred had not included a self-transformation. I had walked several miles along a bad jeep road that only led me deeper into burning, infernal regions. A lizard slipped across my path, and I jumped a country mile. I wrote in my journal some time during the day: "If I am God, then why is God afraid of his own shadow?" I was badly sunburned and in some pain through the night. The next day God drove into Las Vegas and bought a hamburger and a chocolate malt, never to drop LSD again.

Nevertheless, I persisted in believing that eventually I would attain a vision. I sought places in the earth that were haunted by the ghosts of Native American souls, isolated springs and mountain tops, canyons crawling with rattlesnakes and cats, stone quarries where percussion flakes of obsidian, agate, and chert lay on the ground like unmelted snow for hundreds of years. I drank from the creeks of the Toiyabes and the Inyos, slept in the arroyos of the Funerals and the Paradise, climbed the ridges of the Black, Ruby, and Last Chance ranges. Everywhere my Teacher surrounded me with beauty and terror. She assailed my senses with the smell of sage, the taste of native trout, the scatter and gather of little birds. The coyote chilled me with calls that imitated the crying of my children. The rattlesnake hissed from the damp reeds. The half-rotted carcass of a wild burro grinned up at me from Crystal Spring.

I learned that Nature spoke to me when I emptied my ears of my own internal dialogue. I saw many powerful teachings, when my eyes were not distracted by my brain. I prepared my heart through fasting and attention to detail, watching by the hour as the leaves of the cottonwoods collected the solar wind. I thought every now and then about dying.

Many strange and wonderful instances of the Great Mother's creation were revealed to me. But I never had a vision, if by "vision" is meant that which Black Elk or Jacob or St. John saw.

When the time came to return to civilization, the same man returned who went forth. His Teacher had worked profound alterations in his heart, but he was the same man.

I knew more about this soul system, this cocoon. I knew I was an eye with two blind feet. My emptiness craved motion; my fire craved fuel; my ears craved the music of silence; my arms craved the rough, red earth; my feet craved miles; my thirst craved more deeply than any desert spring could satisfy. "Who are you?" the unshielded sun roared at me, tearing away the letters of my name from the being who crouched inside. The sun made me write a poem about him, tear it out of my journal, and fling it on the wasteland for the scorpion to read. He made me know myself then.

The desert, my Mother, taught me that the flash of a mockingbird's wing was more precious than the finest sapphire. She taught me that the smell of sagebrush after a rain was more lush than the words from a poet's mouth. Through her I came to know my belly when it was hungry, my eyes when they were wide open, my voice when it was chocked by my heart, my ears when they filled with alkali dust, my genitals when they were forgotten, my breast when it was emptied of loneliness by loneliness, my legs when they were called on for another mile.

Above all, I learned that my way would be hard; that my way would require courage, endurance, independence, and all the wits I possessed; that my way was narrow, dangerous, precise, spiraling ever upward, skirting the edge, threading the shuttle of my heart between the warp and woof of birth and death. I learned that it did not matter what others thought so long as I kept to the inner path that led to the final, ecstatic assimilation of contradiction in death; that my path was lonely, that death walked with me—he the body, I the shadow—into high noon. I learned to submit to my mortality, but never to my death.

The decision to return to civilization came suddenly one afternoon while I was in the laundromat in Elko, Nevada, the town where my quest had begun. It occurred to me, as I watched the locals and tourists do what I was doing, that I was not truly afraid of being alone anymore. In fact, I preferred it. My real problem was that I was afraid of being with people.

All at once I remembered my children. The life I had exiled myself from crashed in on me. I was overwhelmed by the reality of my situation. Aside from being a hermit, I really did not know what to do with my life. I was nearing middle age; my children were scattered; I had no mate; I had no money; I had no home.

I did have a civilized name: Steven Foster. The making of the sound of it was foreign in my mouth. The idea that the name was connected to the being who had been wandering the earth, scouring his body with sun and moon and wind, was confusing and disheartening. I wanted to remain with my spiritual ancestors, the Paiute ("water-people"), and dance the Ghost Dance. I gave myself a name: Heart in His Throat.

As my clothes whirled in the dryer, I went over all the old contradictions between Nature and civilization. Never did I abhor the latter more. But my heart, which I had come to respect, said calmly: "Go back to your life and your loved ones. Work it out there. That which you fear most is the source of ultimate revelation and power. Go and learn to live with your people."

So I went back to live a life I was reluctant to lead, to take my place as a man in the adult world of Marin County, California. I went back to live alone, as a single male and a divorced father. It was shaky at first. It was difficult to imprison my shadow under roofs and artificial lights. I feared humans, the most dangerous of animals. I feared my own social reactions. I was self-conscious and deeply scornful of people who lived artificial lives.

Slowly the freeways claimed me. The beat of the clock parceled out my days. There was somewhere to get to, someone to see and feel emotional about, something to do or something that should be done. There were dollars to earn and an infinite number of places to spend them. Gradually, the memory of my desert life retreated, attenuated by the insistent need to survive in the wilderness of the city. I forgot to practice the lessons my Teacher had imparted: the lessons of patience, self-reliance, clear sight, and animal ease. I began to question the relevance of my wilderness education to the practical necessities of survival in a wilderness more savage than any desert.

The mother of my children needed money and my children needed their father. The rent had to be paid, the master cylinder replaced, the check-out stand endured, the feet well heeled, the body made respectable with clothing. This seemed no dark night of the soul I faced; this was an endless round of pseudoevents, a

9

whirl of routine deadlines. For a long while my heart of hearts would not accept the idea that money had anything to do with survival. When I finally had to accept this fact, I accepted it bitterly. Yet it *was* a dark night of the soul I had descended into. I pitied myself. The impregnating joys of the wilderness were gone. The sorrows of bringing forth had commenced. I was not to be granted the privilege of being taught by the Great Mother without the responsibility of carrying these teachings to others. For a long time I resented the burden. But the vision of my life began to grow, regardless, in the close, anxious darkness of despair.

Something was being born in me. The tenseness and dismay of my life were due to labor pains developing in the region of my heart and pushing upward into an aching void in my throat. My days were the placenta upon which fed the roots and tendrils of an unenvisioned dream. The uterine dream, call it a dream of destiny, kicked and stretched in the bland plasma of unuttered words, and silently mouthed.

As with any birth, death precedes release. I had to die before my mind could read the words reflected on the mirror of my heart. Exactly when I died I do not remember. It might have been one rainy afternoon when I walked out to the mailbox, only to find it empty again. It might have been the morning after another disappointing one-night stand. The actual time of death does not matter. What does matter was the fact that in dying I had to let go of the old ways of seeing myself and place my faith in the unknown.

I also had to let go of the desert, to stop being nostalgic about her silence and mystery, to let her go knowing that her mountains would always be there, exposed and impassive, waiting for pilgrims to impregnate her with human consciousness. If ever I was to regain her, fully and totally, as a man of heart, I must leave her to herself and cling to my birthing vision. If the trail led me deeper into the greedy stomach of the monster of civilization, then I would go. I would allow myself to be swallowed up, but only so as to discover how to cut my way out. I was not helpless. I was not without abilities. I could learn to love. I could learn to teach again. I could save myself.

I determined, therefore, to put in some time volunteering on the Marin Suicide Prevention and Crisis Intervention Hotline. I did so not because I believed it was immoral to commit suicide but because my heart tugged me to it. A friend had taken the time to suggest that I might benefit from doing such work. The idea appealed to me. I could cast my voice into the wasteland and from my loneliness touch another human soul with the gift of the heart in my throat.

I enrolled in the training program. How was I to know that the woman who trained me would eventually become my wife? Through her I was introduced to the first symbol of my birthing vision—the Hotline Room. It was in this room with the telephones, the red light, and the big log book, that the temper of my heart was tested, as though by fire. It was in this room, late at night or early in the morning, rubbing the weariness from my brain, that I learned to listen to the despairing voices of lonely people and the tragedy of their lives.

The Hotline Room was the last-resort center of the city. Into it poured the electrical impulses of the disembodied voices of lonely human souls in ultimate crisis. The telephone, like a synapse, plugged live voices into each other and catalyzed a human drama of love and despair. The Hotline Room was a big ear. It listened to the stories that were secret and hidden, stories about the darkness and the underside of things, stories of people who were dying and afraid.

But the ear had a voice and a myth. The voice was like a lighthouse beacon, a heartbeat in the dark, the regular, steady breath of a living organism. It sent out the reassuring myth: "We are all lonely. But life is good; it is worthwhile living it. Be here when tomorrow comes. Someday you will find love." I did not always personally believe in this myth. Many times I would rather have said, "Go ahead and get it over with. Die and be happy." It seemed absurd to me that suicide should be unlawful. I was not always able to love those who called, or believe that, given the difficulties they faced, they would ever find love. But there were others who challenged me to help them to see for themselves that their life was, indeed, worth living. Many reminded me of myself. I trembled inside when I talked to them. I was learning how to love.

The Hotline Room taught me many things. It taught me that hate was not the only enemy of love. So also were guilt and anger and self-pity and hypocrisy and greed and indifference and deceit and many other things. Love seemed to have more enemies than any other truth. And yet it seemed to be stronger even than death. The Hotline Room taught me to listen, to weigh, to be fair, to be patient, and yet it created an urgency in me to go deeper into this matter of loneliness, to venture another day into this wilderness of pain and sorrow and confront the monster in his lair.

One night I called Suicide Prevention myself, just to see what it felt like to be a caller, or so I told myself. Actually, I was depressed. I had been fighting with my girlfriend and was unhappy. I made up a fictitious name and acted myself. The person who spoke to me was tired, but he was patient and loving with me. He said, "If you're ever down again, give me a call." Did he really mean it? I think so.

Doubtless, all those who called had one thing in common: They were lonely. Living with a wife or husband in a crowded apartment building, they were lonely. The gynecologist, fearful that he was gay, was lonely. John Doe, fading out on an undisclosed number of Valium, was lonely. The eleven-year-old girl lying in bed with multiple fractures and no mother or father, was lonely. Josh, lying naked on the floor of his apartment, drunk as a skunk, cradling a shotgun in his arms, was lonely. Jane Doe, having awakened from two days and nights of semiconsciousness following a beating by her boyfriend, was lonely. The housewife, calling to say she was afraid she was battering her children, was lonely. The overweight young woman pretending to be talked out of dropping a dozen reds, who hung up and dropped them anyway, was lonely.

In the morning when our Wednesday late-night shift was over, my shift-partner-wife-to-be and I would walk into the streets of fashionable Marin County, looking into eyes. We would want to stop certain people and say, "Weren't you the one who called Suicide Prevention last night and told us you were dying of leukemia and that your boyfriend was cheating on you?" By the light of day all seemed changed and new. Another day had dawned. It was time to start afresh. I prayed that all those people who had called me the night before would have their miracles today. But loneliness had come to dwell in the city and to stalk the night streets. Next time we came on shift, the voices called again: "No, I don't have any friends. I'm fat and ugly. People think I'm crazy but I'm not. They just don't like me."

Many a night I had to drag myself to the Hotline Room, unwilling to face the challenge of another night. What was it that drew me? I was fascinated and frightened by loneliness. It seemed to me that God lived there in its cruel depths, that loneliness somehow was the soil in which sprouted the seeds of love.

"Loneliness is the teacher of giving," says Hyemeyohsts Storm. Every time I picked up the phone there was a touching, a giving. As I came to recognize this bridging of unknowing between two souls, I began to see. I began to see what I could do, as a man, in this world where belief and myth seem to have broken down into passivity, "follow-itis," and rabid cynicism.

The vision first took form as a decision to love people, that is, to care consciously about their loneliness, to care whether they died lonely and out of balance, to care about the fact that we are all out of balance and in imminent danger of self-annihilation. Later, as I became more relaxed and maneuverable within the driving force of that vision, I realized it was the *only* thing I could do, and I would do it because doing it meant I was on the trail. Even in times of great weariness and despair, on the trail, I would go to sleep and die, only to rise the next morning born anew, ready to get back on my feet and on the way.

I got back up because the desolate winds of loneliness still stirred the wildflowers growing in the springtime of my heart. Though I had often forgotten the Great Mother in the press and demand of city life, she was always with me. She continued to speak to me through rain and sun, through a patch of weeds in a back alley. She renewed me, challenged me to see my neighbors as manifestations of myself. She challenged me to look into the open wounds humanity had made on her body. She challenged me to consider how I might be a channel through whom she might heal these wounds. It was she who spoke into the telephone, when I could let her, into the ears of loneliness that called.

And so the vision came from my heart, where tears of joy and sorrow are born in the throat and hammered by language into words. The vision of my life was this:

I saw the distant peaks and barren ridges of a desert land. Above a nameless canyon, a raven cut out from the shadow of death coiled in the wind. In the canyon below was a man, his shoulder hunched against a great, unmoving wall of stone, his tin cup filling with a faint, seeping trickle of cool spring water. In such a wild, thirsty land he might have been anyone seeking to stay alive. He happened to be me.

I was in this desert place because my people and I were thirsty and had nothing to drink. I knew where this spring was, deep in the rock-bound desert, and had gone there to spoon the precious gift of life into my water jugs. But I had to work quickly, for night was falling, and I would not be able to find my way back to the others in the dark.

I saw that the desert land and the nameless canyon with its tiny seep was my heart. The water I collected in my jug was oozing tears. These tears, pure and from the Source of Life, came up from me because I was crying inwardly. Why was I crying? Because I had been given the opportunity by the Great Mother to find water and bring it back to the others, to be a water bearer.

I saw that my journey would be an inward one, into the wilderness of my heart, and a double-edged outward journey, into the wilderness of rock, sand, and water, and into the wild, tangled jungle of other people's lives. These wildernesses, so dissimilar, yet of the same Source, were bridged, connected, and made one, when I drew water from the rock.

It was then that I began to conceive of a means by which I could share this vision with others on a more personal level than through Suicide Prevention. I had learned, through many a long night, that many of my neighbors were on the threshold, as I had been. Among these people the vision quest was created, first as a concept yearning to be born, and finally as actual practice.

In the beginning there were few who cared or understood. But these few counted for a great deal. We came together finally to enact for the first time the rite of passage we called the vision quest. It was late spring in Yosemite. It was not my beloved desert. Everything was a riot of green. I found a glacial boulder from which gushed a tiny waterfall. Beside that waterfall, for three days and nights, I fasted and cried for a vision. The waterfall spoke to me. It said: "You must look within your heart and see what you have to give to your people. Then you must go back and give it away." I looked within and saw what I had to give away.

When I left everything behind and went into the wilderness, I did what people have done for generations in countless cultures. The process and the truth of the process are profoundly connected to the collective unconscious, of which I was but a discrete member. The force of all those who had gone before entered me, not because I was worthy, but because I was human.

This vision is not Meredith's and my vision. It is *our* (all Homo sapiens) vision. In a greater sense it is a vision from the heart of our Great Mother, the same heart that in ancient times spoke from human beings of many lands and origins, including the original Asian people of America. And all of us who have followed this vision have entered a suspended time, an archetypal river of collective, unconscious knowing, a time of being alone with the Great Mother. The vision has helped us to grow, to change ourselves, to transform our life stories. Above all, the vision helped us learn to love, respect, and cherish each other, to walk in balance between the two worlds, to give away, to worship the fire in the heart of our Mother Earth who brought us into being.

BOOK 2

THE PASSAGE

*I suspect it was . . . the old story of the implacable
necessity of a man having honour within his own
natural spirit. A man cannot live and temper his
mettle without such honour. There is deep in him a
sense of the heroic quest; and our modern way of
life, with its emphasis on security, its distrust of
the unknown and its elevation of abstract collective
values has repressed the heroic impulse to a degree
that may produce the most dangerous consequences.*
 —Laurens van der Post, Heart of the
  Hunter

Imagine that your life has brought you to the courageous decision
to experience a vision or fasting quest in the solitude of the wilderness. Given our cultural bias against such hardships, your decision
would indeed be a heroic one. Nevertheless, it would be important
for you to realize that wilderness fasts have actually been a part of
human culture for many thousands of years and that untold numbers of people have vision quested as a means of celebrating or
confirming a life passage.

In traditional cultures, changes in life station were marked by
regular ceremonies of passage, many like the vision quest. Everyone participated in these ceremonies. If they did not, they forfeited
entrance to the next stage of their lives. Without passage rites,
individuals could not have understood their life crises, nor could
they have been capable of confidently assuming the responsibilities
and privileges conferred by their new life station. Tribal units

would have become unstable and ceased to survive, for each person's passage affected the collective.

In modern times, the "old ways" are glaringly apparent by their absence. Dismissing native, indigenous, or "primitive" ways as mere superstition, or of little relevance to an automated life, large numbers of us suffer changes in life status like victims—a burden to ourselves and others. Lacking inner resources developed from living a meaningful life, we often nurture a negative picture of ourselves as helpless pawns in the hands of fate. We think someone else must heal us because we cannot heal ourselves. Someone else must be the hero or the heroine for us because there is nothing we can do; we are but the helpless victims of hapless life stories.

The sanest models of human growth regard crises, accidents, changes, and life transitions as challenges and opportunities of the highest order. If you can "pass through" your difficulties, you will find yourself enlarged and renewed, with direction and purpose, on the other side. The *I Ching* proverb says: "A hundred times you lost your treasure—and must climb the nine hills" (Hexagram 51). Down deep you know that if you refuse to climb, you will not grow, that if you refuse to "cross the great water," you will not know. Indeed, the truest of human teaching tells how necessary it is to climb, cross over, or pass through if we expect to fulfill the promise of our lives. How many times in your span of years will you be called on to uproot and transplant, to let go of the old and embrace the new, to end it all and begin afresh, to plow under and plant new seed, to cease being ignorant and find out?

It is difficult to assess the full extent to which the loss of meaningful rites of passage has impeded the progress of modern people through the impasses of their lives. The symptoms of crisis are seen everywhere. Panic, hysteria, shock, anxiety, uncertainty, anger, boredom, drug abuse, self-destructiveness, emotional breakdown, twistedness, helplessness, and "psychosomatic" illnesses of all kinds attend the experience of a life passage. How often is the modern American able to resolve the crisis with his or her inner strength and determination? And how often must he or she resort to minister, medium, medicine man, psychiatrist, counselor, healer, guru, doctor, or psychic for help?

Do you entertain fears that you do not have an adequate myth or value system? It may be that you have been fishing in troubled waters, unable to turn away from the past and look to the healing future. Perhaps you moved from one home to another and something of you got stuck in between. Perhaps you changed your occupation but cannot make a go of the new job. Maybe your spouse or a loved one has died, but you cannot put an end to the grieving. Perhaps you gave birth to, miscarried, or aborted a child, but you have not been able to live with the changes brought about by the event. Has a natural disaster left you emotionally devastated, unable to get back on your feet? Are you in danger of succumbing to suicidal depression rather than accepting the dangerous opportunity your situation represents? Has violence been done to you or have you hurt someone else with your anger or lust? Have you learned from your experience? Did you become a parent but never accepted the demands of parenting? Have you become enslaved to the thralls of drug or alcohol addiction? Can you find strong medicine within yourself to poison the demons on your back?

Those without a meaningful life story all too easily trap themselves in nets fashioned by others to ensnare them, or they are swallowed up in their own thrashings. Because the birth canal they are passing through is so focused on their pain and suffering, all they can see is blackness and their inability to carry on. Such people are "at risk" to themselves, others, and the Earth they live on. They need to see that they are not victims, that they possess the inner gumption to make meaning of the quandary they are in, that they *do* have a worthy life story. Wouldn't it be beneficial if they could realize that they did not need help, that they were perfectly able to help themselves?

Which brings us back to your hypothetical decision to fast alone for three or four days and nights in the wilderness on a vision quest. Why on earth would you want to do this? There must be a pretty good reason. That reason is the transition you wish to confirm. The ceremony will formally mark the end of the life crisis that has brought you to the threshold of this ancient fasting way. You must be very clear with yourself about why you are leaving everything behind and going alone and hungry upon the Earth.

Of course, you would also need to realize that many people in this culture no longer approve of such goings-on. How can the formerly wild human animal who has come to love and need his cage approve of those who opt for the freedom to find out what is happening outside? From the very start you must understand that you are, for the most part, on your own, and that any self-transformation that occurs will not be due to the validation of others or to society at large.

Doubtless, your decision would not be made lightly, or in the fervor of romantic passion. You would be forced to examine your motives, to look carefully at your expectations. Apart from the presence and teaching of Mother Nature, your experience would rarely be wholly uplifting, mystical, transcendental, and so forth. Highs/lows, excitement/boredom, hope/despair, sacred/profane would mingle to compose a flow of experienced events that would also include times when your gears were in neutral or your engine had fallen asleep.

Isn't it true that our ability to transform ourselves is directly proportional to the intensity of our desire to shed our old skins? From the vision quest you would receive exactly what you put in. You would have to *want* to change and then go about doing whatever was necessary to secure those changes. No amount of fancy talk would bring about the desired alterations. You would not get something for nothing.

Truly, this rite is not a magical formula. It is structured to draw upon the power of ancient archetype and symbol, but only in order to provide the participant with time-honored tools for the spontaneous creation of his or her own myths and ceremonies of passage and confirmation. Only the bare bones, the structural skeleton underlying this rite, would be made available to you. The vision or fasting quest is nothing but a circle drawn in the dust, an empty form filled by the perceptions and values of the candidate. It is a mirror in which one sees oneself reflected.

Woven through the fabric of your experience would be the threads of a priceless story about self-understanding and self-inheritance. One of the main themes of the plot would be your relationship to Mother Nature. The main protagonist in your story, she would bestow her favors, teachings, moods, signs, and symbols on your life, regardless of how you might perceive her. To be sure, she would cover you with dirt and shower you with light. You would hear her wisdom voice in hawk, fox, rattlesnake, beetle, coyote, raven, mosquito—in all her creatures. You would be confronted with the miracles she has wrought in the "stone eaters" or plants,

in the buckwheat, the bunch grass, the willow, the evening prim-
rose, the cacti. You would experience your body occupying her
space and her body occupying your space. She would "in-itiate"
("go into") you. She would blind you with the nakedness of light.
She would restore your eyesight with the falling dew of dawnrise.
Finally, you would be unable to resist her. You would take her
hand and go wherever she led you, for there would be no other
course of action. Civilized rituals would avail you but little. Witness
the attempts of a quester to brew a cup of tea on a windy day:

> I had a hard time with the fire and was somewhat dis-
> couraged at the fact that all I wanted was one cup of hot
> tea. I couldn't find the spoon. While looking for it the fire
> went out. The water was kind of warm. I was going to
> settle for warm tea when a gust came and the pot fell into
> the smoldering fire. I tried again, resorting to toilet paper
> [as tinder]. But the T.P. just smoldered. . . . I am sitting
> on this rock, drinking slightly warm instant tea, which is
> full of dirt, and there is a bug floating around in it. My
> fingers will have to do in fishing it out. My spoon is still
> gone. And, it is quite cold.

Mother Nature would show you other ways to get warm, to cool
yourself off, or to find shelter. You might not even want to learn.
You might try to hide from her by wrapping yourself up in
thoughts of misery or self-pity. But she would find you like a little
bird and sing to you from the bushes. You might try to ignore your
aloneness with her and give yourself a multitude of tasks, but she
would encroach on your noisy schedule with her perfect silence:

> I threw stones today and went hunting for wood and
> hiked to the far end of the hill and painted a picture of
> the valley there and it rained and thundered. I drank
> water . . . and sat in my circle and asked questions, played
> the flute and read Whitman. And after all this . . . I looked
> up and I was alone.

And so you might dance with the One many peoples call Grandmother. You would discover, in spite of the dirt, the blisters, the

biting wind, the searing heat, that you had formed an affectionate attachment to her—a love, a respect, an awe. You might begin to see her as Teacher.

As I sat on the rocks looking west toward the Sierra, my cry came to me. It went like this: "Mother Earth, please be patient with infant man. We are young and have much to learn. Teach us." . . . All the while I got all choked up and began sobbing. Afterward, I felt a mixture of feelings. The picture of this very old woman, who is very wise, patient, forgiving, sad, and lonely came to me. I think that is what made me cry.

In the Essene Gospel of John, Jesus speaks of the truth that every vision faster carries in his or her heart:

I tell you in very truth, Man is the Son of the Earthly Mother, and from her did the Son of Man receive his whole body, even as the body of the newborn babe is born of the womb of his mother. I tell you truly, you are one with the Earthly Mother; she is in you, and you in her. Of her were you born, in her do you live, and to her shall you return again. . . . For your breath is her breath; your blood her blood; your bone her bone; your flesh her flesh; your bowels her bowels; your eyes and ears her eyes and ears.

The gift of love for our Great Mother is given to us at birth. But we often forget to remember. That is why it is sometimes necessary to go to her, to fast, and be alone with her, so that we can fully remember the kin relationship between our bone and her stone, our blood and her rivers, our flesh and the body of nature.

The time you spent alone, fasting with your Earthly Mother, would symbolically depict your passage through the crisis or transition of your life. The supports on which your life story was built would stand out starkly for you to see. But there would be no judgment in that natural world. There would only be consequences. Mother Earth and all her denizens would not admonish you for your behavior as you negotiated the symbolic passage. If doubt, self-blame, self-denigration, or other negative feelings arose, they would arise from within you. Nobody would be there to impose their perceptions on yours. You would clearly see that the negative aspects of your life passage had a great deal to do with your own way of looking at your experience. You would have plenty of time to wrestle with your monsters. Whatever the outcome, you would have tapped your own power, your own waterhole, your own will. If you prayed and called out to God for help, you prayed in your own voice, using your own words. No other living being acted as your intercessor or high priest. You forged your own connection to the Source.

Finally your trial in the sacred world of the threshold would come to an end. You would emerge from the wilderness passage and by so doing confirm that your deathwarding birth contractions were at an end. The ordeal of the tomb-womb would be over. Your questing spirit would inherit the body of a new life, a changed circle of purpose. You would reenter the human mainstream at a new stage of growth, with a clearer understanding of yourself in relation to the natural environment and to others in your life.

If you were to commit yourself to this wilderness rite of passage, you would have to admit that you were no different than your ancestors. Though the cultural circumstances surrounding the modern vision quest have vastly changed, the experiential, human element has remained the same. We are still capable of communicating with the great heart of our Grandmother. It would be a mistake to assume that we live in a world too far removed from our real Mother to benefit from going to her and seeking vision for our lives. From the beginning of human time, the union of human and Nature has brought forth a healing mythos for the collective woes of the people. In the sanest perspective, you will remain incomplete if you deny yourself this ancestral legacy of empowerment. You would be helpless indeed if you completely ignored your ability to hear the roaring of the Sacred River—or if, in the company of other heedless ones, you aided in the destruction of our Earthly Mother, for we have no other to "give us, each day, our daily bread."

BOOK 3

THE RITE

*I received a letter containing an account of a
recent suicide: "My friend . . . jumped off the
Golden Gate Bridge two months ago. She had been
terribly depressed for years. There was no help for
her. None that she could find that was sufficient.
She was trying to get from one phase of her life to
another, and couldn't make it. She had been
terribly wounded as a child. . . . Her wound could
not be healed. She destroyed herself."*

*The letter had already asked, "How does a
human pass through youth to maturity without
breaking down?" And it had answered, "help from
tradition, through ceremonies and rituals, rites of
passage at the most difficult stages."*

—Wendell Berry, The Unsettling of
America

At this point, it does not serve the purposes of this book to continue
to speak to you in the conditional tense. We are going to make the
assumption that your interest is no longer hypothetical, that you
have indeed committed yourself to the vision quest. Now we can
consider information that would be vital to your participation.

The basic dynamics of a passage rite such as the vision quest are
described by a classic formula that underlies all initiatory ceremonies. In *The Rites of Passage*, Arnold van Gennep identified three
phases: severance *(séparation)*, threshold *(marge)*, and incorpora-

tion *(agrégation)*. These three phases can be likened to an opening of a door, a stepping across a threshold into a room, and a returning through a door on the other side of the room.

The first door you will open is called *severance,* or separation from parents, family, home, work, and the context of daily life. You will be asked to consider your former life to be at an end, to have "died" to your childhood, old ways, or former state. You will conclude your relationship to the temporal world. You will be taken to a place apart and undergo the second phase of the rite. But first you must prepare to sever by making yourself a worthy candidate to face the ordeal of the second phase.

The room into which you step is the *threshold.* It is the actual experience of the ordeal of passage. It takes place in the natural world, in a sacred, consecrated place set apart from the "profane" world. You will step across the margin of the threshold world, armed with symbolic tools of self-birthing. During your stay in the threshold, you will confirm the resolution of your crisis.

The final door you step through is called *incorporation.* You will return from the sacred world of empowerment and be united with the corpus of a new growth stage. In the mortal realm of civilization and the community you will carry out the terms of your life story or vision as it was revealed to you while you were alone in the wilderness.

Van Gennep's three-phase *schema* may be seen as a metaphor for the dynamic of life itself: severance from the mother at birth, sojourn in the sacred passage world of life, and incorporation into the Great Mother at death. All rites of passage, however, contain an esoteric or transformational formula that runs opposite to the flow of life as we tend to perceive it. Usually, we think of our birth as the beginning, our life as the middle, and our death as the end. But the rite of passage begins with death (severance, separation), moves through the stages of the death passage (threshold, margin), and ends with birth (incorporation, return to life). This "death journey" is the adamantine, symbolic kernel of all wilderness passage rites:

To make an end is to make a beginning.
The end is where we start from.
—T. S. Eliot, "Little Gidding"

Here is one more way to understand these three phases. Imagine you are a wave from the Great Ocean, breaking in, pausing, and returning to the deep. Note that, upon returning to the collective, you carry with you a residue, a part of the sacred shore.

To van Gennep's basic framework you can add the flesh and bones of your own creed or value system. By actually experiencing these ancient, initiatory phases, you will come to view your life from a transformational point of view. You will see that there is never a beginning without first an ending and a passing through.

You may wonder, "How can I leave it all behind if I am just coming back to it? How can I make a new beginning if I simply return to the old?" The answer lies in the return. You will not come back to "the same old thing." What you return to has changed because you have changed. Your perceptions will be altered. You will not incorporate into the same body, status, or world you left behind. The river has been flowing while you were gone. Now it does not look like the same river.

Severance

Waiting. If you are sincere,
You have light and success.
Perseverance brings good fortune.
It furthers one to cross the great water.
　　　　—I Ching, *"Waiting" (Hexagram 5)*

Referring to the Greek Mysteries, of which he was an initiate, Aristotle maintained that it was "not necessary for the initiate to learn anything, but to receive impressions and to be put in a certain frame of mind by becoming 'worthy' candidates" (Eliade, 1967). In other words, it is not as important for you to master a certain body of knowledge about the vision quest as it is for you to be open to "impressions" that engender an inner attitude that claims: "I am a worthy candidate." It is indeed necessary for you to become worthy of the next life stage. By the time you cross the threshold you must be capable of assuming the tasks and roles the new status will require.

From the moment you commit yourself, you begin to set your house in order, square yourself with friends and loved ones, and review your former life as if it had come to an end. From the standpoint of severance, your life story or value system will stand out in bold relief against the background of past events. You will recognize what is no longer meaningful to you—and what is. That which is still relevant will enrich the placenta, the yolk, upon which you will feed while you are in the "uterus" of the threshold passage. This placenta must have time to develop. We recommend that you spend at least six months getting ready to take the next step into the threshold phase.

You cannot participate in a formal vision quest rite without the aid of an instructor, initiator, or "midwife." This person will serve you by helping you to prepare, by standing watch while you are alone and fasting, and by accompanying you through the first steps of incorporation. If you are a member of a group of candidates, then all of you will meet with your guide(s) at least several times prior to the wilderness threshold phase. It is absolutely necessary that you attend such meetings. You will need to acquire pertinent survival information, including emergency procedures. You will need to discuss your intent and the meaning of your life passage with a person skilled in vision quest ways. You will need to talk about the real and mythical aspects of your life, about how your values affect your behavior. You will need to envision the world you are preparing to leave behind and the world to which you are returning. As one of the group, you will begin to feel the sense of shared commitment that binds candidates together in community and love.

Not all of your preparation, however, will involve meetings with teachers. Much of the severance phase will call for solitary preparations on the physical, psychological, intellectual, and spiritual planes.

FEAR

As the threshold time approaches, you will feel emotions akin to those with which you will ultimately have to face death. The former life, which you are committed to ending, begins to look more and more desirable. You may begin to wonder why you decided to do such a crazy thing. You may remember all the times you were weak or a "failure" at something. You may imagine the threshold to be horrible or boring. Demons set free by your imagination may throng about, demanding to be dealt with. If you become too frightened, you will abort your own "bringing forth."

Your preparations to sever will engender more genuine apprehension and anxiety than any other phase of the ceremony. The fear is real. This is not like going to a scary movie. You cannot simply walk out of the theater. Your fear may manifest itself as a slight sensation of nervousness at the pit of your stomach, or a full-blown feeling of panic. Accept the fear. The greater the perceived risk, the greater the potential for personal growth, and the more lasting the effects of the experience. Remember that fear is one of the marks of courage. Trembling hands can still rig a tarp. Shaking knees can still carry one to safety:

This shaking keeps me steady, I should know.
I learn by going where I have to go.
—Theodore Roethke, "The Waking"

Fear is also a sign of the onset of power. In this game, the power goes not to the one who can be most "macho" but to the one who is the most ready to surrender to the influences and impressions of the rite. Sometimes people will hide their fear. This can be dangerous if they are really afraid. Recognizable fear personae are the happy-go-lucky boy who will try anything if there is challenge in it; the strong, silent, capable man who is rugged enough to take the hardest knocks; the crazy little girl, out for kicks, who will do anything on a dare; and the caring, motherly type who looks out so hard for the others that she neglects to look inward. Usually, by the threshold time, fear masks have been dropped. If your guides know what they are doing, they will ask you to talk about your anxieties. You will be asked to look at yourself through the windows of fear. You must see yourself stripped of pretenses and pride, pared down to the bare bones of your will. Respect and accept your own way of dancing with your fears; take fear on as an ally and guide. Fear will teach you self-awareness and self-respect.

THE MEDICINE WALK
One step in preparation is to take a medicine walk, a day's journey upon the face of the Earth. A microcosmic form of the threshold trial, the walk is a mirror that reflects the signs and symbols of your inward quest. It will serve as an allegorical guide to your preparations.

Pack your knapsack with a few necessary items excluding food. Take water along if you will be hiking in an area where it is not available. Inform a friend where you are going and when you intend to be back. Then set out at sunrise in some natural area on a wandering, intuitive course, keeping to yourself and sticking your nose into whatever interests you. Though the walk does not necessarily exclude the presence of other people, your objective is to interact with no one until you return at the end of the day. If you are a tenderfoot, make your walk a conservative one, staying close to your vehicle or familiar landmarks. There is no need to endanger life and limb or to challenge the elements. Stop and rest whenever you wish.

As you wander, become aware of Nature's awareness of you. Signs and symbols indicating your life purpose, inherent gifts, personal values or fears, will present themselves. As you discern the beauty of life and the reality of death in the world around you, ask yourself: "Who are my people?" Pay attention to who you think about, worry about, wish was with you, and so forth. The spirits of these people may be important to you during your threshold trial. Find some natural thing that symbolizes your life quest or a quality in yourself. Bring it back and show it to your guide.

When the sun sets, return home. You may eat then, if you wish, or you may continue to fast through the twenty-four-hour period. This walking fast, of no physical harm to your system, will give you an idea of how you will react to a three- or four-day fast.

PREPARING TO FAST
One of the benefits of fasting is that it points out the profound role food plays in your life story. As the threshold looms you will probably wonder if you are strong enough to "go without" for several days in a wilderness place. Test yourself ahead of time. Practice going without food; skip meals. Some find it difficult to fast when surrounded by a multitude of goodies and a routine of three meals a day. Are you one of those? Find out. You can also help yourself by watching what you put into your body. Traditional preparation for a fasting quest includes abstention from alcohol, drugs, or other substances that poison or inhibit your body and mind.

During the last week of preparation, we recommend that you abstain from eating foods that your experience has told you are likely to build up undigested toxins in your organs, tissues, and blood. Beef, dairy products, nuts, and oily or fried foods are often hard to digest, and can be eliminated. Concentrate on the intake of fresh fruits and vegetables. Rice and fish are good sources of protein. Drink plenty of liquids. Supplement with vitamins. In the end, you are the best judge of what is best for you. We do not prescribe any particular prefast regimen except that you be in good physical shape. Get plenty of sleep. Various physical activities, practiced daily, can be considered ceremonies of preparation. They will enhance your sense of readiness and self-worth as a candidate.

DEATH LODGE

Imagine yourself to be at the verge of death. The word goes out to the village: "So-and-so is dying!" All your old friends (and enemies too) will come to visit you for the last time. The events of your life, good or bad, will pass before your eyes. You will remember with pleasure and regret. Now is the time to cleanly sever from your "days and ways" and to "make it good" with everyone who comes to say good-bye.

Set aside a formal time to visit with the persons and events that have composed your life karma. If you feel the need, write your will. Make provisions for the disposal of your body. Commemorate the events and crises of your life from the "detached" perspective of one who is about to die. Cut the cords attached to all the exhausted placentas of your past. Now that your former life is at an end, you will die cleanly and nobly, forgiving and forgiven.

THE JOURNAL

You might want to begin keeping a journal from the time you commit yourself to the vision quest ceremony. If you are utterly honest with your journal, it will serve you for many years to come. You will clarify your understanding of your participation and will attain new levels of insight regarding your life story. Your reasons for fasting will come to light, as will your names for the monsters who stand in the way.

Consider your audience. Are you keeping entries for yourself alone or do you hope that someday your children, parents, or friends may profit by reading them? Audience, to some extent, dictates style and legibility. You would not be megalomanic if you wanted to chronicle your experience of a life passage rite so that someone coming after you could read and profit by your experience. To that end, you might want to tussle with a few BIG LIFE QUESTIONS between the pages of your modest journal. We ask the following questions of young people who are marking their passage into adulthood by fasting for three days and nights in the wilderness. Adults might have a go at them too: "Why was I born a human being on this earth?" "Why must I die?" "Who are my people?" "What do I *really* want to do with my life?" "With what gifts/skills am I blessed? Am I using them?" "What is my name for God?" "What are the names of the great 'monsters' of my life? What must I do to face them?" "Who are my teachers?"

EQUIPMENT

As you collect your gear in readiness for the trip to the wilderness and the threshold phase, you will face many minor choices regarding what to bring and what to leave behind. Though you will walk as nakedly as possible to your rendezvous with the Great Mother, you must carry a few tools with you. You must decide what is essential *for you* and what you dare to let go. Your fully loaded backpack is symbolic of your attachment to the life you are leaving. The weight of it is like the weight of your karma. Do you really want to carry that much? Like the burden of fear, it may prevent you from getting to where you want to go. Recognize that as you prepare, you are involved in a life-changing act. You are selecting from your past those things that will make it possible for you to walk away from it.

EQUIPMENT LIST

backpack	water (at least two gallons per person)
sleeping bag	
sleeping pad (optional)	ground cloth or rain tarp
toilet paper	journal and pencil
75 feet of rope	warm clothes, stout boots, wool cap, good jacket
clasp knife	
matches	small day pack
bandanna	whistle

Optional Items:

dental floss	needle and thread
insect repellent	sun hat, sun glasses
candle/tinder bundle	musical instrument, camera, paints, etc.
small flashlight	
snake bite kit	insect sting kit
sunscreen	

(The list on the previous page is the distillation of fifteen years of experience with more than a thousand questers, each with his or her own idea of how much material culture was necessary for safety and well-being during the threshold phase.)

NOTES TO THE NEOPHYTE

If you have never worn a backpack or slept on the ground in a sleeping bag under the stars, you may be in for a pleasant surprise. To ensure that your surprise is pleasant, test the soundness of your equipment. Your most essential tool is your body and its mental, emotional, and physical health. Now is a good time to get it in shape. Load your backpack and carry it around on your back for a while. How does it fit? The load must be evenly distributed over your back and felt equally against shoulders and hips.

The adequacy of your sleeping bag is relative to the season of year. Make sure your bag is adequate to expected temperature ranges. The tarp can double as a ground cloth and rain shield: 7 by 9 feet is adequate; 8 by 10 feet is better. You want the lightest weight consistent with fabric strength; the wind will eat up a flimsy tarp. The rope is for fastening the tarp down securely. Matches should be kept waterproof. The bandanna should be large enough to serve as a sun shield, a sponge, a filter, a rag, a Lone Ranger mask against blowing dust, a tourniquet, a compress, a bandage, a signal flag, and a handkerchief. In most wilderness places, tennis shoes are not sufficient. Stout leather shoes or boots with tough soles are in order. A small day pack enables you to go on walking excursions carrying emergency items with you. The whistle should emit a noise loud enough to serve as an effective signaling device should you get lost.

Water is best stored in one gallon plastic bottles with screw-type lids. These can be made sturdier by fortifying their bottoms and sides with duct tape. Water is not an optional item. Although in some forms of the vision quest the candidate goes without both food and water, too many possible medical complications may arise among modern individuals not used to going waterless. Fasting without water may be a viable option if you are under the care of a respected teacher who has safely used this form for a long time— and if you are the only candidate he or she is responsible for. Otherwise, accept the benefits of drinking water. It will pulse through the clogged canyons of your body like a summer flood. Your urine will turn crystal clear.

SURVIVABILITY

Your fast in the wilderness will test your ability to physically survive. Nature is not a dangerous place, but there are potential hazards, especially to one who has little firsthand experience. The Great Mother will send you not what you want but what you need. If you expect a "trip," forget it. The Sacred World is profanely physical. You will be unable to find a soft place for your tender bottom. The stones will trick your feet. You will get stuck up some place from which you cannot get down. Hoping for a vision, you will receive uncomfortable lessons about how you are carrying yourself around in the personal world of survival.

It is absolutely necessary that you learn how to treat yourself or another person in the event of an accident, natural emergency, or illness occurring while you are dwelling in the threshold world. You must have at least a rudimentary conception of the nature and habits of talus slopes, flash floods, thunderstorms, sandstorms, rain, freezing wind, and searing heat. You will need to know how to get yourself out of bad weather; how, where, and with what to make a fire if you need to; and how to go about building rudimentary shelter. It might help to study the habits of rattlesnakes, scorpions, and bee and wasp species, and to know what to do if you are bitten or stung.

By the time you enter the threshold world you will have a good sense of the parameters and responsibilities of survival for three or four days and nights of solitary fasting. You will have learned and agreed to certain emergency procedures and guidelines necessary to your own and everyone's survival.

Threshold

Unless a grain fall into the ground and die
It cannot grow into an ear of corn.
Before you died, you had to be awakened.
This is the mystery of Elusis.
          —Mysteries of the Seed, *Anonymous*

You will go with your guide(s) to a wilderness place. All you have
will be the pack on your back. A base camp will be established on
the perimeter of the threshold area. Now you are at the border of
a land without borders. You are about to enter the hallowed cathedral of the Great Mother.

The last night, by the firelight, the faces of people in the group
have never seemed more honest. Defenses are down. Conversation
is real and full of truth. Like the others, you have come to the end
of a trail littered with old spoor. Soon you will walk away from it.
You are one sleepless night away from liberation. You lie in your
bag and look up at the stars. You toss and turn on your bed of earth
and wonder how you ever got yourself into this one. Tomorrow
the fast begins.

Before dawn, you must be up and moving. Reluctant as you may
feel, there is no turning back now. You pack your things. Without
the warmth of breakfast in your belly, you say farewell to everyone
and set off with your buddy.

You and your buddy will eventually separate at a mutually
agreed-upon place midway between your separate questing places.
There you will erect a cairn of stones, a boundary marker, where
you will invisibly communicate with each other once a day at
different times, leaving some sign of your well-being. Then you
will hug your buddy, turn your back on this last social contact, and
walk into the sacred world of the threshold. For the next three or
four days and nights you will see no one. In the silence of your
separateness you will seek a vision. Aside from the daily responsibility of the stone pile, you are free to be who you want to be. This

is the time to forget time, to remember what it is you are seeking, and to take it into your heart.

Traditional threshold archetypes and ceremonial actions will be made available to you during the severance phase. Ultimately, what you chose to do or not to do with them is entirely up to you. But the ancient ways are drawn from the interface of humans and nature and are gravid with the wisdom of our collective ancestors. When you genuinely pray, you will pray with the fervor and intent of all those who went before you to the heart of Grandmother Nature to seek a vision. Deep in the night, the dreams you dream will be their dreams. With their eyes you will watch the constellations wheel and the dawn star fall into the rising sun.

Because you have entered the Great Mother's sacred cathedral, and in faith and consecration have formally set yourself apart from all others, almost anything you do will have ceremonial overtones, especially if you do it with awareness and reverence. There is no "right" or "wrong" way to perform a ceremony that comes from the heart. "All men have access to God, but each man has a different access," says Martin Buber. "What sort of God would that be who has only one way in which he can be served!"

Since you are under no constraint to be anyone but who you are, the ceremonies you use will undoubtedly be relevant to your own life situation. You may want to use sound or music in some way, or you may want to use silence. Perhaps you will feel the need to dance, or to be still. You may want to empower yourself or some symbol, or call in unseen spirits or witnesses. You may decide to abstain from certain actions (sleep, movement, easeful postures), or to make meaningful offerings or sacrifices for purposes of amends or expiation. It is important that you realize you are ceremonially free to bury, burn, smash, change your name, bathe, vow, draw blood, cut your hair, heap stones, chant, rattle, dance, sing, tie knots, light a candle, go nude, make gifts, use incense, pray, kneel, meditate, nightwalk, paint yourself, or behave in any other way that is meaningful to yourself.

But you must not load up with a multitude of symbols and things to do as a means of passing time while you are living alone. A ceremony is not the antidote to boredom any more than makeup is the antidote to nakedness. Too many consciously performed ceremonies can mask your essential experience and lead you to ask for so much that later you cannot remember what you asked for.

In the following discussion of traditional threshold symbols, archetypes, and concepts, the echoes of many mythical systems can be heard. This material can be seen as a list of tools or devices that our sacred ancestors invented in order to comprehend the meaning of their experience of the threshold phase. Some of these devices may enhance your own perceptions of the threshold. Each are windows, chinks in your cavern through which the infinite may be perceived, means of focusing your attention, of poising your body/mind in sacred space, of centering your heart in sacred time.

THE SACRED TIME

Now you stand alone at the gates of sacred time. Before you lie the features of eternity. By your own efforts you have become a worthy candidate. Now the cord binding you to your former life must be severed. You will cut the cord by actually entering the passage. This is an auspicious and powerful moment.

An invisible door stands before you. This door opens beyond the former borders of your ego. In a literal sense, your border crossing will be undramatic. You will simply open the door and step through it. You may want to ritualize this crossing by paying formal respects to the spirits and life forms of this sacral region, asking for safe passage and the blessing of vision.

At first, the absence of civilized things within the field of perception creates a huge emptiness, around which the conditioned self flutters like a doomed moth. The mountains mock your flesh and blood. Their incomprehensible age thunders down a symphony of silence and eternity for your ears. You set up little projects, little duties to perform, passing the hours in bits and pieces. Your mind races through all the old ruts you thought you had left behind.

Eventually you are forced to pay attention to eternity. Your heart must begin to seek other forms of nourishment. Small things arrest the eye. You spend more time staring off into space. You hear what the silence is composed of: the varnish of stones, the dark loom of cliffs, the bareness of ridges, the scat of small animals, the mystery of holes in the earth, the flatness of the dust, the sigh of the evening star. The passage of time is marked by the sounds that break the silence: the beating of your heart, the rumble of your stomach, the wind in the trees, the drone of a fly, the distant roar of a jet plane, the flitting of little rat feet in the sand.

You will also be aware of other sounds, but you will not know their source. You will hear voices, but you will not see another living soul. As your mind is the only interpretive instrument you possess, you may wish to alter your sense of what is real by listening more closely to that which you might otherwise regard as unimportant or unreal. In sacred time, events do not follow human rules of linearity. Past, present, and future become Now. And Now is defined as physical (the south), psychological (the west), mental (the north), imaginative (the east), mortal (earthward), and spiritual (skyward). All directions become one in Now.

You are alone in Now. Surely, there can be no end to this ocean of time as you stand at its shore. You launch yourself, a tiny barque, into the vastness, your heart as captain.

THE SACRED PLACE

You may wonder how you go about finding your sacred place on the Earth, your "power place." Edward Abbey *(Slickrock)* gives good advice:

> The only way to get to know this country (any country), the only way, is with your body. On foot. Best of all—after scrambling to a high place—on your rump. Pick out a good spot and sit there, not moving, for a year. Keep your eyeballs peeled and just sit there, through the hours, through the days, through the nights, through the seasons—the freeze of winter, the stunning glare and heat of summer, the grace and glory of the spring and fall—and watch what happens. Pick a place and stay there. You will become a god.

In other words, you can make almost any place holy if you find it yourself, occupy the space there, and truly respect what is happening all around you.

Another way to find your place on the Earth is to realize that the place has known you and awaits your arrival. Perhaps it has its own way of calling you, and that is why you found it. A stone, a plant, an animal, the wind, an image held in the inner mind—all these are signs of the call. The fact is, you may very well be found by the place, instead of vice versa. Listen to your heart. If your heart says yes, then you have arrived. If your heart says no, keep looking. If your heart says maybe, then you might make up your mind by spending more time there. No one is asking you to be a martyr by living in an obviously risky place. Choosing a place of power brings karmic reverberations on the physical plane. You must live with the consequences for three or four days and nights.

In your sacred place you will hold communion with the Great Mother. You will eat her sun and drink her air. You will dwell in her flesh. But you are not a parasite. You will not pollute or damage her. You will seek to know your place, your function, your reason for being on the Earth. The mountains, plants, and stars of your place are "portions of eternity, too great for the eye of man" (Blake, 1966). Dame Nature is an endless mirror in which we see ourselves reflected. Whatever you chose to sow or risk you will reap with intense self-consciousness. Here at your place you will communicate with Nature's creatures, sent to you for reasons you will trust yourself to comprehend. Whatever is given to you, you must give back, via your own value system of reverence. Observe yourself responding to the gifts of Nature. Your ways of responding characterize your own innate gifts.

Converse with the powers of your place. Address them respectfully, one and severally. Invoke the spirits of growing things. Ask for strength and patience to endure. Listen to what the wind and the stars and the dead and decaying things tell you. Do not be afraid to look into the beautiful heart of ugliness. Give a portion of your drinking water to the soil of your place. If you can, remove your shoes and walk barefoot. Caress the hard stones. Go without clothing and without guilt enjoy the sensual dimensions of your sacred place. Allow your place to accept you, to become accustomed to your sweating, panting body. Curl up against the bosom of the Great Mother, until you have warmed her cold earth beneath you. Dream the dreams of coyote, fox, bear, lizard, scorpion, rabbit, rattlesnake, raven. Dream the dreams of the night wind.

THE FAST

Food will not pass your lips for three or four days and nights. You have chosen to follow a "cloud of witnesses," ancient and modern, who have traveled this ceremonial path to spiritual insight. As a ritual tool, fasting is the oldest and finest. The two-thousand-year call of the Essene Jesus rings in our ears:

> For I tell you truly, except you fast, you shall never be freed from the power of Satan and from all diseases that come from Satan. Fast and pray fervently, seeking the power of the living God for your healing. While you fast, eschew the Sons of Men and seek our Earthly Mother's angels, for he that seeks shall find.
>
> Seek the fresh air of the forest and of the fields, and there in the midst of them shall you find the angels of air. Put off your shoes and your clothing and suffer the angel of air to embrace all your body. Then breathe long and deeply, that the angel of air shall cast out of your body all uncleannesses which defiled it without and within.
>
> —The Essene Gospel of John

The fasting process is one of readying the soil for a seed to be planted in it. The seeker empties the body so that the spirit may be cleansed and filled. Abstinence from food encourages death, who wants to fill your emptiness. As you live naked, vulnerable, in alignment (verb: to ally) with death, your life is enhanced, made brilliant and terrifying.

A three- or four-day fast does not endanger most people. You can go only a few days without water. But you can go weeks without food. As long as you drink water, the physical effects of the fast will be mainly psychological. With no meals to organize your day around, you will learn a great deal about your psychological need for structure. You will discover how much of what you think is physical hunger is really social programming.

During a fast, certain psychological states find greater ease of expression. The psyche is open to orchestration by the elements and rhythms of the natural world. The environment rushes in to fill the void in the pit of your stomach. Sunrise is your meat and noon your wine. The dark wind sets a banquet for you. Although your physical strength slowly wanes, another kind of strength builds up in you—the silent, immovable strength of the stone you sit upon. Even as your knees shake your weakness, your "spirit knees" stand firm, treelike.

Without ballast in your belly, you begin to understand what Sun Bear means by "walk in balance on the Earth Mother"—compensating for loss of strength by applying weight of spirit. You walk carefully, economically, in harmony with the terrain. Because you are not under pressure to get anywhere, you begin to notice what lies in your immediate field of vision. You have time to pause, look, examine, and communicate. Anomalies of size, shape, color, function, and species catch your eyes: a piece of white quartz, a freshly dug burrow, a blossoming creosote, a hairy cactus, a smooth stretch of wash sand, a flake of obsidian, a rodent track, an ant hill, a belly flower, a pile of coyote scat, the sudden drone of a hummingbird, the shadow of a stink beetle, a lizard doing push-ups, a bunch of native grass, a kiss from a deer fly, a withered sagebrush root. You walk amid the bounty of earth and measure these things with the myths, values, and perceptions of a fasting mind. The fast teaches you your own pace, your own way of composing your itinerary, your own methods of charting a "map" of your place of power.

When you stop to rest, you have nothing to put into your body but water. You cannot sit down with the evening paper and some munchies and enjoy the view from the terrace. All you get is the view. And because you have nothing else to eat, you eat the view. You hear your empty belly gnawing on the silence. A cool breeze stimulates your taste buds; you salivate shamelessly. You feel your body turning inward upon itself for food, eating up your stores of glycogen and other sources of quick energy. The shadow of death nudges your heartbeat up and engenders a strange mixture of feeling: exhilaration and exhaustion. Your body is reduced to imitating the animal hunger that exists in the life around you.

Your civilized veneer begins to crack. Your sacred ancestors, no strangers to fasts such as these, compel you to look down at your hands, scarred and roughened by repeated embraces from Mother Earth. How beautiful and mortal they are! You watch the way you occupy space, aware of the signs and marks you leave behind: urine stain on a rock, boot marks in the dirt, a blackened stone from your fire. The earth becomes for you a single, whole, living entity, a Goddess.

Frail, intense, vacant, fertile, open, heavy, light, mortal, awkward, exposed, your fasting self searches the distance and senses the subtle rolling of the earth. The motion grips you with the nausea of emptiness and yearning. Now you are ready to find truth in the Arapaho fasting cry: "Great Spirit, have mercy on me. I am starving. I have nothing to eat."

THE STONE PILE

The heaping of stones is an ancient practice, a symbolic act of communication, a mute affirmation: *This is the way. This is the meeting place. Borders touch here. Someone died and is buried here. Peace to all who pass.* In the Mojave and Sonoran deserts, besides faintly discernible foot trails, archeologists find piles or shrines of heaped stones 10,000 years old. Some archeologists call them "spirit quest cairns."

The stone pile will serve as a "post office" between you and your buddy. Each day you will go in the morning to this marker and leave a sign that you are alive and well. Your buddy will do the same in the afternoon. This daily trip will become a ritual by which you celebrate your "response-ability" to another human being. Should either of you fail to leave a daily sign, it is the duty of the one to discover why the other did not come to the stone pile. If you find your buddy sick or injured, there is no one else to provide immediate help but you.

The heaping of stones, then, is symbolic of the fragile, precious link that binds us together in common survival. Unique and alone though we are, our destiny is common and the Earth is shared between us and all living things. We must care for those we are linked with. Without them we would not live another day.

The stone pile is a symbol of love. It is constructed at a common border of human responsibility in a beautiful, prominent place, where it can be found easily.

THE DREAMING

The water-bug is drawing the shadows of evening
toward him across the water.
—Yuma Indian

One of the reasons you came to the Great Mother was to dream. Perhaps you anticipate that she will speak to you in dreams. Perhaps you have been inspired by the great American Indian dreamers (Black Elk, Lame Deer, Wovoka, Crazy Horse, and others). You must remember that your dreams are your own, not theirs, that no matter how mundane your dreams may seem, they are every bit as sacred as the dreams of the "great ones."

Sometimes the dreams of the threshold are singularly clear and powerful. Within them the dreamer finds a name, a story, or a mission. Sometimes the dreams are ambiguous and confusing, like a maze, seemingly involving the dreams of many other dreamers. Sometimes the dreams are personal and emotionally demanding. The dreamer awakens in tears, overcome by sudden feeling. Sometimes the dreams surface only vaguely, disturbingly, in the waking mind. Sometimes the dreams come and go like the tides, wreaking their changes on the shores of consciousness, though the dreamer is totally unaware. Many times the dreams occur when the dreamer's eyes are wide open. Daydreams, wool gatherings, waking fantasies, and so forth are not to be discounted, for they are also drops from Oracle River.

Your collective unconscious, your "dream-oracle," creates the dream for you to remember. The Oracle is very wise and seeks to help you grow into a fuller understanding of your place on Earth. Like the fabled aeolian harp, the dream-oracle is sensitive to the changing winds that pervade your psyche as you change your environment, move your body, and relate to others. The Oracle opens itself to the wind-shadows of change, emotion, thought, memory, imagination—trembling to life like the waterbug draws the shadows of evening into the center of its skittering dance.

Wherever you are, wandering or lying asleep in your bag, attempt to write your dreams down. See them as portents, lessons, messages, riddles from the collective oracle. Notice how your dreams appear in your waking experience weeks, even months, later. The symbols of these dreams can be used to empower your life. But you must own the dream, feel it deep down to be true, and follow its guidance. For dreams are unawakened acts. Our little life, our frail breath, navigates a sea of dreams. There is a very old school of thought that insists all life is but a dream, that there is no reality apart from this dream. Another equally ancient school of thought insists that all life is but the dream of God. A third school agrees with the first two and adds the notion that you are God.

Are you dreaming or are you awake? Open your eyes and look around you. You are surrounded by natural cycles of waking and sleeping. Even as the spring flower wakes from its slumbering seed, it falls into a dream of endings.

THE FIRE

In a very real sense, all things are on fire, rusting rapidly or slowly. Among the by-products of this general oxidation are warmth and light. Necessary for the perpetuation of all life forms, warmth and light are also released from the heart of a human being. Just as the fire of the sun is the heart of our local planetary universe, so the fire of the heart is the center of your local personal universe. As you move through the world with the godlike fire of your heart, you radiate light and warmth. You are felt by all things.

As a symbol, force, element, spirit, or god(dess), fire is an integral symbol in the world's mythologies, and has played a major part in countless traditional ceremonies, including wilderness passage rites. Fire is available to you, but only if you use it with respect and skill.

You must be clear why you want to build a fire. If you just want a nice heater to take the chill off your bones, you will be wasting wood that more appropriately belongs to the environment. If you plan a specific ceremony with fire as a central symbol, then a modest, carefully designed fire will burn brightly and teach you many things. But you must take pains in considering how and where to build this fire. In most national parks and monuments, campfires are not permitted except in certain designated areas. In a national forest, a campfire permit is needed. At any rate, a fire should not be built at all if the fire danger is high.

The building of an ecologically sound ceremonial fire is itself a ceremony. The fire pit should be no more than six inches deep and a foot in diameter. Scoop out the hole with your bare hands in a spacious area of sand or soft dirt free of ignitable vegetation. Roots from nearby trees or bushes should not protrude into the pit. Do not scoop a pit on desert pavement, fragile meadowland, alpine sedge, thick chaparral, pine needle cover, or any other delicate surface. Ring the completed firepit with spark-arresting stones. Gather your fuel from widely scattered locations. It should only be dead and down wood. All you need is one armload of twigs. Logs are far too large for a ceremonial fire. Your fire will last no more than a few hours. When darkness has fallen, ignite the carefully laid tinder with a wooden match. As the flame reaches up you will feed it with the wood that represents the flesh and bones of your life. Twig by twig you will give yourself, the persons, events, and symbols of your past to the warm light of your oxidizing life. With the last twig, the dying begins. Slowly the coals will grow black and cold. When the fire has sunk into complete darkness, consider your former life to have ended.

Erase all signs of your fire. Make sure the coals are cold and cover them with the same dirt you scooped out. Remove the ring stones and scatter them unobtrusively over a wide area. If it is godlike to make a fire, it is godlike to make a fire disappear.

Perhaps the most dramatic fire ceremony in this hemisphere was performed among the Aztecs at the end of their fifty-two-year calendar cycle, in the year Reed 2. On the last night of the festivities, all the fires in the kingdom were extinguished and the people were plunged into total darkness. At midnight the high priest ascended the temple stairs with a sacrificial impersonator of the god of the sun. At the top, the god-man was laid out on the sacrificial stone and his heart was cut out. In the dark, bloody cavity a spark was drilled into tinder. The tinder was added to pitch. The pitch was added to kindling. The kindling was added to brands of wood. Torches were thrust into the burning brands and down the pyramid and out into the darkness the torch fires sped, spreading to every hearth fire in the kingdom. Soon all eyes were aglow with the light that came from the broken heart of the slain hero. The old sun had died. The new sun had risen from the dead. For the next fifty-two years dawn was assured.

THE GIFT OF A NAME
You did not ask for the name that was given to you. That is because you were not aware to name yourself. Now you have the opportunity to exercise the awareness necessary for a self-naming.

As you pass the days and nights of your threshold fast, seek to find a name that identifies, in the most inward shrine of your soul, the life of you. Good places to look are within dreams, waking visions, at the tops of mountains, at the bottoms of dark canyons, along the way to the stone pile, under rocks, in the sky, among the plants and animals, in the dirt under your boots. The whole of animate and inanimate existence surrounds you with potential names. The wind that sings in your ears is laden with the syllables of your name.

The search itself confers the name. You become what you have been seeking. What you become is your name. Your search is both outward, through the physical landscape, and inward, through an inner landscape of thought, emotion, crisis, and dream. But the name does not come until the search is complete. You must not be afraid to travel in realms where language breaks down, where all maps, sign posts, roads, and directions are anonymous. That is why it is so important you become aware of how Grandmother Nature sees you, for she does not communicate in the English language. Her names for you are found in wind and storm, cloud and sky, creature and creation. If you perceive these things with the conditioned eyes of civilization and pigeonhole them into labels or nomenclature, you will never attain the secret-name magic you seek. A hawk will call your name and you will never hear because you think you are looking at a hawk. An ant will tell you your name but you will ignore what it says because you think you are watching an ant. Your inability to recognize a messenger from the Great Mother is a sign you are not ready for your name. Only when you are emptied of conditioned perception will you be able to experience the *connection*, the knowing that has been lost to civilized peoples.

This process of giving oneself a name is potent medicine. The specific object of self-mythology is to transform or energize oneself with a name that signifies a story. This is possible only to the extent to which you are willing to assume ("own") the story given to you. Those who lend little time, thought, or understanding to self-naming invariably derive little benefit from the act. Those who wait before they discover, who strain at the darkness, who grope on their knees among the broken stones, will be rewarded with a mythical destiny that is like a beacon in the night.

THE PURPOSE CIRCLE

God is an intelligent sphere whose center is everywhere
and whose circumference is nowhere.

—Hermetic Axiom

Alone, the aged bushman of the Kalahari Desert waits for death in
a circle of thornbushes. When his food is gone and his body is too
weak to defend, the hyenas break through the circle and the dying
is over.

Keep the bushman in mind as you pass through the threshold.
From the first day, start looking for a place where symbolically you
will wait through your dying to the moment of birth. To this
"dying place" you will go ahead of time to prepare your "grave"
for occupancy through an all-night deathwatch.

You are merely symbolically doing what God does. You are
transforming yourself. You are shedding your skin. You are orienting yourself for your death passage. Like Jesus in the Garden, you
are asking that "God's will be done" with you so that your people
will live. Like Inanna-Ishtar, you are preparing to descend and be
ravished by the underworld so that the corn will arise in the spring.

But first you prepare to die. You build your circle of self, your
"circle of purpose," your "death strategy" against the hyenas of the
dark passage. This circle of purpose may be composed of stones or
sticks, crystals or rubies—the material does not matter. What matters is its spiritual substance. As you construct this circle of your
purpose you ask yourself: "With whom or what do I want to
compose the substance of my purpose circle?"

Usually, stones are readily available for use as the material stuff
of your circle. On a symbolic level, each stone is a loved one (living
or dead), a god or goddess, a teacher, a spirit, a shield, an animal,
or some other entity or concept that comprises the invisible circle
of your life purpose.

You must also pay attention to the matter of properly orienting
yourself to the six directions of your universe, traditionally associated with the six powers of the cosmos. The north and south
points can be aligned to the North Star. The east and west points
can be aligned to the rising and setting places of the sun. The
earthward and skyward directions can be depicted at the center by

the poles of your standing body. Once the cardinal points are set down, the rest of the circle can be filled in.

When complete, your circle will outline the mythical terms of your death passage into birth. It will stand psychically anchored to the six directional powers of the universe. The stones will encircle the center (you) as the body surrounds the heart, as the mother surrounds the egg, as the Self surrounds the self. The circle will form a protective enclosure, a "ring pass-not," a spherical interface of awareness between "inside" and "outside" that is mutually integrative, reciprocal, and healing. When you have completed your timeless, patient work, you may decide to consecrate your circle with prayers, offerings, or songs, remembering to thank the forces represented by your power place for allowing you to make your "last stand" here.

As the light of the last day of the threshold is swallowed up in darkness, you will enter the vulva of your purpose circle, your circle of thornbushes. Through the night, encompassed by the darkness, you wait for death's hyenas to break through.

Within your circle that last night, express yourself as you wish, for it is you who are dying and you are dying alone. You throw the desire of your dying heart into the void of darkness. Everything is still. The womb of the Great Mother embraces you with unknowing. Your eyes are blinded by the absence of light. You are pushed and pulled by barely sensed, irresistible forces. Impatience is of no avail. Darkness lingers, punctuated by the infinite gleam of stars beckoning from the lostness of space. It is so cold! Can it be that Death assumes the mask of longing to be warm? Or is it the longing to be filled?

In the time of an eternity, the Great Mother labors to give birth to you. Imperceptibly, you enter the light.

THE CRY FOR A VISION
It is the last night of your deathwarding. You are crouched in your purpose circle, confined by your version of the bushman's thornbush. Look around at the outline of your grave. It is cold and unmoving. The night wind chills the marrow of your bones. How alone you are, how helpless, how insignificant, out of place and afraid! How inadequate your carefully constructed thornbush, when measured against the vast purposes of the cosmos!

Of what use are your puny hopes, your myths, your gods, your "beliefs," your dreams? How could your prayers matter in the least to the designs of the Great Mother? The silence mocks you with unattainable eloquence. The stars peer down at you with light generated long before Homo sapiens appeared on Earth. What is this game you are playing with your circle of stones? Does the dark wind care? Does the horned owl care? Does the Milky Way care? Do you really believe your cry for a vision will be answered? What right have you to expect it? Aren't there many who are more worthy than you? Isn't this another example of the presumptuousness of a human, to consider himself or herself worthy of a special connection to the powers that be?

But you will cry in spite of yourself. You will cry from an empty belly and a lonely heart. You will cry for a vision because you must, because you have exhausted all other possibilities, because you have nothing else to do. Whether your prayers are silent or spoken aloud, they will be clear and to the point and will come from the core of longing to be answered. The spirits of all those you have made a part of your death journey will be praying too—with your voice and will.

In a noble threshold ceremony described by Black Elk, the Oglalla Sioux "lamenter" staked out a six-direction circle and walked back and forth between the cardinal points and the center, crying, "O Great Spirit, be merciful to me, that my people may live." Why "merciful"? The lamenter cries for *merci* (thanks). Such *merci* (gramercy) can only be granted by the One Who Holds Absolute Power. It is bestowed on you, not for your benefit but for the well-being of your people. If you cry for yourself alone, the heavens will become impenetrable. Your cry will not extend beyond your own mouth. No one lives on this Earth who has the right to cry for divine regard exclusively for self. We are all linked by the gramercy of Love.

Of course, there is no set form as to how or what you should cry. You will conduct yourself within the circle of your purpose as you see fit. No one will be there to criticize or applaud your piety. There are a multitude of spiritual disciplines, prayer forms, and meditative practices at your disposal. Or use no "technique" at all. You do not have to use words. An appropriate prayer for a person feeling deeper than words is a literal cry, unadorned, unformulated, unhindered by any tradition. Cry as long and loud and hard as you need to. No one ever said the spiritual quest was painless or polite. Cry for love and caring; cry for loneliness. Cry for helplessness, fear, and doubt. Cry for a vision for your people. The world you belong to is filled with people who seek power, but it is not the power of vision. As you lie in the dust like any wretch waiting for death, may the cry that goes out from you spring from your deepest longing to complete yourself and your world.

Your cry will be answered. The hyenas of death will break through your circle of thorns and your life will be complete. At that moment, the darkness will pass. The long night will be over. Dawn will complete your passage. Cry for a vision, then. Cry again and again, until the cry is a grain of sand and you are the mother of pearl.

THE VISION

There is benefit to be gained from the act of seeking a vision, by learning the sacred, solitary postures of countless pilgrims who have sought to extend themselves, to know. But you must not allow yourself to be fooled by the grandiose stories of the visions of others. Let them have their pearly gates or angels descending on ladders of light. Their dreams are not yours. Ask the powers, not for what you want but for what you need.

The vision you seek, and need, can be many different things. Vision is wisdom. Vision is insight into the nature of things. Vision is the ability to see the future. Vision is the ability to dream. Vision is the surging upward of personal creative energy. Vision is one's life work. Vision is a marrow-deep feeling, a knowing, a recognition of self, a realization of what you can do. Vision is transcendent, mystical knowledge—cosmic consciousness. Vision is the sight of the sun rising in the east to answer the hope that another day will come. Vision is a series of "ahas!" about what your life has been and could be.

There is another kind of vision that comes on that last, cold night of dying. It is akin to the silence, the waiting, the painfulness of cramped limbs, the emptiness of mind. Time seems to stand still. The stars do not move. The hour is always midnight. Sleep drags at the eyelids and pulls the body back against the earth. There is a desperate desire to rest, to fall out of attention to such matters as vision, to wearily succumb to one's own mortality. Dully, you look up at the stars, for the thousandth time. You wish the long night was over. Isn't this also a vision, a vision of how it must be just before the moment of death?

The fact is, by the time you step out of the open vagina of your purpose circle into the broad daylight, something has happened, whether you know it or not. "Forces will have been set in motion beyond the reckoning of the senses. Sequences of events from the corners of the world will draw gradually together and bring the inevitable to pass" (Campbell, 1970). If you are young, your vision will lead you toward fulfillment in your adult life. If you are an adult, your vision will guide you through the necessary changes ahead in such a way that you will grow and your people will be blessed. If you are very much older, your vision will prepare you for the ultimate transition and give you the power to die victoriously and with dignity, enriching the lives of those you love and leave behind.

EMERGENCE

Be careful at completion as you were at the beginning.
—The Book of Tao, 64

The first light of dawn is often called "false dawn." But even the feeble light of a hidden sun dispells the gloom of night. Objects and natural features fade into color and clarity. But direct sunlight is at least an hour away. Light has arrived, but where is the sun? Through gritty, sleepy eyes, you will look out on an imperceptibly brightening world stirring to life with bird song and insect chorus. You shiver in the gray light and chafe at the bit. The last mile is the hardest. Now you must play the trickster game of false dawn. It says, "I'm going to trick you into thinking that this morning, of all mornings, the sun will not rise unless you do something to bring it up."

The newborn comes into the world singing. You might want to do the same. Or you might find some other way to bring the sun into the world, for if you do not make it rise you will abort your birthing and live the rest of your life in a false dawn. Soon your head will crown the night thighs of Mother Earth; your eyes will open to the direct light of birth. This will not happen if you are not ready to aid your Mother in the extremity of her need to give birth to you so that her people may live. When she pushes, you must come forth, singing in gratitude for the gramercy she has bestowed on you. Then you must cut the cord connecting you to your power place, the placenta in which you have gestated.

Remove the stones of your purpose circle. Scatter them. (If you wish, you may leave the stones representing the four cardinal points. Later, when you return to this place, the stones will mark the physical location of your purpose circle.) Whatever you have to say to your place, say it now. Give some of your precious water back to it. Sterilize the torn ends of the umbilical by cleaning your place of any sign that you stayed there. This is not a time for nostalgia. It is a time for resolution. Of course, your place will always hold a memory of you. Many years from now, though all physical sign may be obliterated, something of you will remain here.

When you have purged the earth of your sign, you must shoulder your pack, recross the threshold, and enter the body of the "profane" world. When you cross the boundary of people and other eyes again view you, you will possess a body, a personality, a set of defenses, self-consciousness, a purpose circle, and a vision. You may find that you are reluctant to return. This reluctance is a form of self-indulgence. You must face the life you have inherited by right of passage. To turn back would be to succumb to the spell of the sacred world: "Having departed from your house, turn not back, or the furies will be your attendants" (Pythagoras).

Soon you will be enveloped in human warmth and laughter. Arms will fling open. Words will fill the air. Love will be reflected in the eyes of those around you who have come back from their own threshold journeys. No matter how sensitive or exposed you may feel in the dawn moments of incorporation, it is a given of your new life that you take your place among your people. Now you must contend with the gravity of the gross body of the world. God has to become mortal. Self must become self. Spirit must descend into ego-body.

Try to give something of yourself to each person you meet on the other side. It is dangerous to receive gramercy from God without channeling its flow to others. You may not feel particularly powerful or holy, only filled with gratitude to be back with the others. It is the *willingness* to be a channel that matters. For some, the power of the vision makes them over into a channel for its expression. For others, the humble effort to be a channel is what creates the vision.

Now it is time to recross the threshold. Your buddy may be waiting for you at the stone pile. As the ancient Polynesian sailor kissed the shore before embarking on a voyage of two thousand miles, so you must embrace the dark earth of your Mother before you push off into the limitlessness of your life quest. Give yourself to loneliness now, one last time, so that you can give yourself to your people.

Incorporation

We returned to our places, these kingdoms,
No longer at ease here, in the old dispensation,
With an alien people clutching their gods.
      —T. S. Eliot, "Journey of the Magi"

Your birth into the secular body of the modern world is the most difficult step you will take in the entire vision quest rite. The joy you may feel upon returning and being with people again must not seduce you away from the reality of your situation. You are coming back to a world you were only too eager to leave behind. In a way, you are like an innocent child who must now start the painful process of growing up. You must be centered and grounded in the physical reality of the life state you have entered.

It is useless to resist the third and final phase of the vision quest. Committing to severance, you also committed to incorporation. Your people, work, and vision await you. You could putter around base camp for a few days, but that would only delay the inevitable. You could kick and scream and cry, "I'm not ready to go back," but the truth is, your threshold experience prepared you. The threshold, however, was only a test. The "real thing" awaits you, the sea of indifference and confusion that you know only too well as "civilization." Will you fall into the same trap as Orpheus, who successfully endured the rigors of his underworld journey only to lose all he had quested for in one tragic moment of doubt? Do not look back to see if your vision is following you. It is.

The first few hours of incorporation can precipitate a crisis. You tense against the impact of social boundedness, the laws of human space, time, and conduct, the claustrophobia of four walls and a roof, even the too-soft embrace of a bed and mattress. The tension produces the same kind of gut-wrenching fear you felt the night before you stepped across the threshold. It is essential that your questing spirit be brought back into your body and your body into the gross body of human life. You must leap like a cat into the very world you have associated with poor footing. It is very important at this time to be *conscious* of being back on the other side—not to wholly submerge in the flow of events but to keep your eyes open and your head out of water. Each action you take, each word you speak, must consciously attune you more closely to the life in which you have chosen to dwell.

Hence, when you return, it is a good idea to deliberately hug and be with people, to eat and share food, to give gifts and be given to, to stoically hike away from base camp and leave the sacred mountains behind, to carefully wash off all the dust of the threshold world from your body, to don clean clothes, to consent to the dangerous, confined, social space of a motor vehicle, to brave traffic, to tolerate towns and cities, to welcome stores and restaurants, to relate to strangers, to cheerfully adopt the noise and confusion and the laws that regulate them—and to bravely accept the consequences of crossing the threshold of your home. After all, you owe your very existence to the goods and services of civilization. You are hardly equipped to live the rest of your life without it.

Familiar symbols line the road home. Dine here, drink there, stop and shop, amuse yourself, fill up with whatever you need. Stops along the way often provide returnees with opportunities to test their balance. How easy it is to overload, to eat too much, to obey the call of old addictions, to buy what is not needed (because everything is offered). A balanced quester tolerates the plenitude, is not seduced by it, and does not fall into deep remorse if he or she makes a "mistake." As you incorporate you will make distinctions between "want" and "need." You can do this with a finer sense of discrimination now that you have endured the solitude and fasting of the threshold.

Once you have reached home, you may experience both elation and alienation. You can still feel the sun in your eyes and the wind in your hair. But when you try to tell loved ones about it, they do not understand, or do not seem to care. Their incredulousness, indifference, or threatened silence may tax the very love you brought back to give them. You must realize that while you were away they were absorbed in their own dragon battles, in their own concerns, living at a pace that hardly gave them time to miss you. Sometimes their own fear or jealousy makes it difficult for them to be enthusiastic or empathetic. Sometimes unfinished business has smoldered in the angry breast of the one who stayed behind. Into the wilderness of your home you will step. Soon you will realize that the only way to communicate the experience is not to talk about the vision but to live it.

With the dew still fresh in your hair, it is easy to live the vision. Who has not seen the unbounded horizon and been, at least for a time, unbounded? At first, you are buoyed up by the vividness of your recent adventure. You feel great love and nostalgia for your place of power. You also feel at home in your body. Your senses are alert and active. Illumination still washes over you in waves of joy. From the realm of the gods you have come to this mortal world like the mythical protagonist. Where are the dragons to slay? Where are the trials now that you have the strength to face them?

This feeling of power and "at homeness" in your body may persist through whatever reunion or incorporation activities your guides have planned for you. In some vision quest traditions, a sweat lodge or sauna ceremony is in order within a few days of your return. Other teachers may hold an "elders' council" wherein you are asked to talk about the meaning of your time alone in the threshold world. Still others may schedule a series of incorporation meetings dealing with the implementation of your vision. The purpose of such activities is not to indulge in regrets about being back in the human world. They are further stepping stones on the path to the realization of your new life story.

In the days following your return, it may be to your advantage to ask yourself questions (and to answer them) regarding the meaning of your experience. The equation behind such questions would be, "As in the vision quest, so you behave and react in your life." The questions might run as follows: Why did you participate in the vision quest? What monsters did you face? How did you deal with them? What ceremonies did you perform? Why? Who or what came to you while you were fasting and alone? What was communicated to you? What happened the night you sat in your purpose circle? What have you brought back for your people? What are the names of the monsters you now face? What are you doing to implement your vision? The answers will clarify your experience and validate your newfound resolve.

The final, official step in incorporation will occur one year later, when you return to your place of power and spend at least a day and a night there, fasting and rekindling your sense of purpose. This concluding ceremony will enable you to measure your progress toward the life objectives you set a year earlier.

The routines of "time by the clock" will gradually draw you away from your fond memories of the wilderness. Necessarily, you will take up the everyday business of survival. Your gizmos await you, their tanks to be filled, their buttons to be pushed. The phone starts asking to be picked up. The well-being of the refrigerator and the contents of the newspaper again become matters of concern. The time must inevitably come when you wake up in the morning and realize that the visionary flame you returned with is barely flickering. You kick yourself for not being awake to see the sun rise. You wonder why you have been so forgetful, so unobservant, so preoccupied with people, problems, and events. You try to remember your threshold experience but much of the detail has slipped away. You wonder if all the important little lessons of the quest have been lost. Will every memory be swept away by time and exigency? Depression sets in. The journal of one incorporating quester (age fifty-nine) speaks for many:

> Why can't I remember the revelation? Why can't I feel the freedom? Why is it lost? In no way did I intend this loss of vision, this doubt, this descent from the mountain top. I *fell!* There must be a kind of spiritual gravity. Such energy it takes to struggle up toward the Vision! Such self-examination. Such effort it takes to break through into the illuminating insights, and with what ease we fall after the Quest is over. Why? Why?

The hero has returned from the realm of the gods with the spark of life that will kindle the spirit of a dying world. The world, however, does not seem to care. Now the magnitude of the task ahead can be clearly seen. The dragons, overawed at first by the shining presence of the protagonist, have shrunk back into the shade. Seeing, after all, that he or she is a mere mortal, they sally forth, their mouths belching fire. Encompassed by the likes of these and seemingly separated from the healing influences of the Great Mother, the hero fears the quest has been in vain.

At this point, you can either let the flame die or you can begin your new life in earnest. If you decide to "go for it," then the first dragon you must face is the universal law of change. As "time and chance happeneth to us all," so you must face the fact of the "fall." What was light must become dark, even as day becomes night. What was clear must become confusing; what was full must become empty; and what was high must be brought low. If the vision is to succeed, it must be tried. If you want to be absolutely certain, you must go the way of doubt.

How many heroes and heroines have refused the call at first, preferring to believe that if God summoned them then He would make it smooth sailing all the way to victory? But turning aside only made it worse. Jonah, for example, wound up in the belly of the whale. It would seem this vision quest business has gotten you into a bind. The closer you come to the "doing" of the vision, the fiercer the opposition appears. But if you refuse the call, you wind up in the stomach of a dragon.

The "fall," then, is a necessary precondition of the gramercy of vision. Illumination must be tested by an ignorance equally as powerful. The greater the doubt, the greater the faith. Pray then that the going will not be easy. Take up the burden of your quest. Accept the conditions of your new life station. Do not be so naive as to think that once you have been illumined, you will always and forever be so. Dan Millman *(The Way of the Peaceful Warrior)* quotes an old story about enlightenment:

Milarepa had searched everywhere for enlightenment, but could find no answer—until one day, he saw an old man walking slowly down a mountain path, carrying a heavy sack. Immediately, Milarepa sensed that this old man knew the secret he had been desperately seeking for many years.

"Old man, please tell me what you know. What is enlightenment?"

The old man smiled at him for a moment, and swung the heavy burden off his shoulders, and stood straight.

"Yes, I see!" cried Milarepa. "My everlasting gratitude. But please, one question more. What is *after* enlightenment?"

Smiling again, the old man picked up the sack once

again, slung it over his shoulders, steadied his burden, and continued on his way.

When you pick up your burden, implementation of the vision truly begins. This is the second dragon. His hot breath scorches your hide and you back away, crying, "How? How do I begin? How do I make my vision a reality?" There are, of course, no simple answers. You pick up and go. Vision, if it is anything, is your life story *in action*.

Errol, a thirty-seven-year-old vision quester, wrote a letter to us two years after he had returned from the threshold. His story contains valuable clues as to how the dragon of implementation might be successfully faced.

> I came home excited, positive, and full of spirit. What I had not prepared for was the impending intensity of the incorporation period—which turned out to be my VISION QUEST. I found myself faced with all the boxes I had created for myself: father, husband, money earner, therapist, home keeper-upper, friend, etc., and it felt like none of them were really me. My spirit was too big to be confined in the narrow realities of my life.
>
> So I resisted. It was hard to be here and hard to work. I resented my life, but I also could see no alternative to escape it. I had, and chose, the responsibility of loving and caring for all that I was connected to. I was in a middle place, trapped between realities for about six weeks, with a fairly heavy depressed feeling. Fortunately, I love life enough that I never considered giving up the struggle. But I felt stuck.
>
> After a long time, I began to experience a deep, inner feeling that my quest was to find a home for the bigness of my desert spirit in the expanses of my everyday life, that my vision quest was not to go away from my life but to come back into it as an adventure. It was as if I had been severed long ago, when I was born, and that life itself was my transition. This life transition is much harder than being alone in the desert. Intuitively, I sensed a future incorporation that was my true coming home—but that

coming home depended upon the quality of my loving here in everyday life.

So I renewed my commitment to my life, let go, merged into what is in each moment of my life but without the feeling of those experiences being in boxes. They were now opportunities to love, to seek, to quest, to be, to support, to connect to the Great Spirit all around me, in others and within me.

This has continued to the present.

Literally, *incorporation* means "taking on the body." Taking on your body means shouldering your burden and climbing down from the mountain of vision into the dread canyons of humanity. The vision itself must also take on a body (yours) and live in your house with your loved ones. The sacred mountain of vision must be internalized. Once the vision has come to dwell in your heart, then you have come to dwell on the mountain of vision.

The returning hero must learn to live in two worlds. One world is visionary, consecrated, and wholly natural, the threshold world of the Great Mother. The other world is the "real" world of people, places, and things, the incorporation world of "taking on the body." The first world is the garden world of the spirit passage. The second world is the "fall world" of your mortal existence as a "civilized" human. You passed through the first world so that you could be born in the second. In the first world, you have intercourse with vision. In the second, you give birth to and nurture the vision. In the first, "Joys impregnate," In the second, "Sorrows bring forth" (Blake, 1966).

The terms of the vision quest of life require that you master the ability to walk in balance between these two worlds without getting caught between them. To a certain extent, it will be necessary to internalize the world of the Great Mother, for her perfect silence and solitude will not always be physically available to you. One way to ensure her constant presence in your heart is to perform a simple daily ceremony. Find a place apart, a retreat (preferably in a natural environment), and spend a few precious moments sitting in your purpose circle. In your imagination put the stones around you again and sit in the darkness of your dying-into-birth, waiting for the hyenas of death to break through your thornbush. Cry for a vision once more, cry for strength, wisdom, and understanding to carry your life purpose through the dragon-infested swamps of the second world.

Times will come when you can physically return to the wilderness and again hold communion with the heart of Grandmother Earth. But never will you go to her because you want to escape. You will go because you seek to return to the human world with the benefits of her teaching and empowerment. She will offer you temporary asylum and will send her messengers to validate and clarify your life purpose. She will give you further insight into the resources available to you. Treat her with reverence and she will reverence you.

There will be many times when you stumble and fall, when you are certain no one in the human world knows or cares. Then you will want to crawl back to your power place and begin all over again. Remember that these are the times of greatest potential, when you are looking your dragons square in the eye. When all is said and done, only you know what you have hidden away, growing steadily and surely with its magical roots in your subsoil. As you grow, the vision grows. There is no other way.

BOOK 4

THE PEOPLE

I implore you . . . to submit to your own myths.
Any postponement in doing so is a lie.
    —*William Carlos Williams,* Paterson

Those vision questers who helped write this book are Americans. Their desire to resolve the crises and transitions of their lives was born in the meaninglessness of a culture that is itself in crisis. Conceived in the fires of the revolutionary passage, America has never reached cultural maturity. Millions of us behave like adolescents stuck in the childhood-to-adulthood passage.

Look around you. How many Americans, regardless of age, are caught in an adolescent holding pattern, waiting for the time when they will magically become adult? In the meantime, they will dream the infantile American Dream of wealth and power, addict themselves to alcohol and (legal and illegal) drugs, become enamored of the glittering surface of the material world, fall into puppy love and get married, readily dream the clever dreams manufactured for them by media and politicians, fight their own kind with rocketships, lasers, and nuclear bombs, worship celluloid and stereophonic personalities, become obsessed with sex, wallow in the depths of narcissistic depression, persist in self-destructive excess, dislike having to be responsible for personal actions, fantasize as a way of facing tomorrow's verities, try to stay forever young, ignore the eventuality of their own death, put off cleaning up their messy room in the house of the Earth, and restlessly cruise the neighborhoods of the world looking for action. These signs of cultural crisis, and many more, point to the inability of the culture itself to provide meaningful rites of passage by which Americans can initiate themselves into expanded stages of growth.

How difficult it is nowadays for so many Americans to evade complacency and anxiety born of their contempt of hardship in order to seek growth events that truly mark their attainment of maturity. In one way or another we are weaned into this culture, dragged along by its irresistible currents. We become adolescent and enter a long holding pattern marked by a myriad of attempts to "prove" our maturity. In homes that half the time are broken, we yearn for completion at the age of twenty-one, when magically we become adults overnight and, unheralded, enter the great mystery of adulthood. We join the ranks of working people or the unemployed, find a niche somewhere or restlessly look for one, fall in and out of love, divert ourselves in a variety of ways so that we can endure bumper-to-bumper traffic, the rising costs of living, the inroads of alcohol, boredom, depression, and the horrors of the newspaper. We marry or cohabitate. Under the threat of thermonuclear annihilation we bear or do not bear children. We make money, or we barely have enough, or we steal to get it, or we go on welfare. We separate or divorce. We grow older. We enter the many anxious transitions and identity crises of middle age, and wake up one morning to the fact that our children are gone and there are wrinkles on our bodies that cannot be erased by another wife, a new fad, a different hairstyle, a new car, a dunk in the hot tub, another hit, or a sensational new pill. We feel lonely and wonder what our life has amounted to. We think about going somewhere else, take a vacation, maybe travel abroad. Maybe we take off, maybe we do not. Money is or is not tight. Our health is not what it used to be. We become grandparents, join the "seniors," are "put out to pasture," or find ourselves in rest homes. Many of us retain our youthful vigor and are wise, but we are largely ignored by the rest of the community. Many of us become senile, others largely forgotten. We do or do not prepare for death. And then it comes: We die.

Those who vision quested with us were a part of the cultural flow of America. They could have suffered through the crises of their lives like many Americans, refusing to encounter the passage leading to real maturity. But they had life stories, myths about themselves that would not allow them to buy the American cultural assumption that passage rites are no longer necessary. Like snakes in the springtime they popped their heads out of the fissures of depression and saw the sunlight. They decided it was a good time to shed their skins.

From the beginning, when we first spoke with people about the enactment of a vision quest rite in the wilderness, there were some who seemed automatically to understand.

> When I first heard the idea I knew it was for me. I can't say why I knew so well. But even when I was a little boy the times of being alone, all by myself, were especially powerful. I got a hidden, deep, sensual thrill from knowing I was alone, and free to be whoever I wanted to be.
>
> —Creosote, age 34

It is probably true that such a response to the challenge of a rite of passage such as the vision quest is due to an ancestral knowing, deeply etched in the collective archetypal memory. Yet there were many who were attracted who could not have put it into such fancy words.

> I thought, a vision quest? All alone, without food, crying my lungs out? Am I crazy? Do I want to do that? My friends said I was insane. . . . It was the *challenge* that made me do it.
>
> —I'd Pick a Daisy, 15

There was no particular class of person or personality that took up the challenge. The juvenile offender, bored and defiant behind the bars of juvenile hall, was as compelled as the lonely woman whose children were grown and husband divorced. The housewife and the burned-out professional responded as eagerly as the artist seeking vision or the old man dreaming dreams. They may have had different reasons for questing for a vision, but they all shared one common attribute: They were willing to put their bodies on the line, to step across the threshold.

The memory of their faces returns to us: sunburned faces smeared with dirt, honest and uncontrived faces stained with healing tears. Nature undid their guises, turning their eyes into silence, their ears into wind, their bodies into animals, and their souls into waterholes. The wilderness had entered them while they were alone and starving with nothing to eat. The force of that entry, irresistibly gentle as the pressure of sunlight, faulted, folded, and uplifted them like the mountains they stood on. The Great Spirit of the Universe had heard their cry and had sent the bellies of their souls something to eat: dawn.

COMPANION OF THE WIND
Companion of the Wind was fourteen when he went with us into the White Mountains to fast for a vision. Though he was young in age, he had been readied by his life. His mother and father were divorced; the mother was crippled by polio. He was holding down a job as a busboy at a restaurant and holding up his family. He saw it as a ritual that would symbolize his attainment of maturity. He went because he felt that he was ready to become a man.

He chose an exposed 12,000 foot ridge overlooking Cottonwood Basin, his only companions the thin, cold wind and an ancient, twisted, mostly dead stump of bristlecone pine. He did not want to hole up like a turtle and wait through the trial. With touching, idealistic courage he said good-bye. He was ready to face the worst of it.

The warm mornings turned cold every afternoon. Clouds gathered and scudded dark and low across the treeless ridges. Rain threatened. Thunder whispered in the southeast. His journal says he spent one night crying. His journal also contains a remarkable dialogue with the wind, a sacred exchange between himself and Nature that was carried on intermittently for two days and nights.

Wind, can you help me on my vision quest?
Yes.
I have so many questions to ask. Who am I? Why am I here on this planet? What is my name? How can I help my family?
You will receive two names, one I will give you and the other you shall give to yourself. The one I shall give you is Companion of the Wind. You may share this with your friends and relatives. The one you give to yourself shall be for your sake alone. As long as you remember this you shall be

able to know the answers to all your questions. As for the other questions you have asked me, I will help you find the answers on the last night.

I thank you, Wind. I also think I love you.

There is one last thing you should remember. I am always listening but not always speaking.

I will remember. Wind, there is one last thing I ask of you.

Yes?

Will you protect me from anything that might ruin my vision quest?

I will protect you until your day has come.

I thank you, Wind.

He learned to put up his tarp so tight it would not luff in the wind. But he was cold, so cold he could never get quite warm. He missed his family and felt sad. Once, when the wind died down, he stuck several dollar bills between the needles of the branches of the bristlecone and took a picture of them, bedecked with a sign: MONEY TREE. But mostly he talked to the wind and thought about what it meant to be an adult: "I feel much better about myself. I think I am beginning to understand more about myself and·everything else. Maybe this is what the Indians thought was adulthood. I must also remember what my friend Allan told me: 'An adult is just a child with responsibilities.' "

The evening of his last night the sky flared up with a most unusual high-altitude sunset, transforming the white limestone of the mountains with fiery orange and red. He built his purpose circle and sat down inside it to keep his vigil and to speak with the wind, which by now was a beloved and trusted friend.

I think it is time to build my circle. How big should I make it? Since I'm not going to sleep in it I'll make it big enough to sit in. What rocks should I use? . . . I'll just pick out the rocks that work best.

There, it looks pretty good. Maybe the Wind will speak to me and answer some of my questions.

Wind, I am here in my circle and wish to speak to you.

I want to ask you some questions that I've been thinking about. Why am I here, Wind? What purpose do I have in this world?

How can I control my emotions, like anger, fear, and all the others, so that they will help me instead of tearing me apart? How can I make my family happier? Teach me to understand them. Please!

Your purpose is to help and make happier the people on Earth.

Who am I, Wind?

Take off your ring. What shape is it?

It is a circle.

What are you sitting in?

A circle.

How many sides does a circle have?

It doesn't have any sides.

Good. Now, where does it end?

It doesn't have an ending.

You are right.

But what does this have to do with the questions I'm asking you?

Have patience and listen. I am like a circle. I have no ending. You are also like a circle. In your cycle you have no ending. But when my cycle ends, your cycle ends.

Why is this?

Because you are a part of me and I am a part of you. Remember this: When our circles end, the world ends. Understand the circle and you will understand yourself. As for your emotions, you do not want to control them but to understand them. Then you will be able to deal with them. This goes the same with people.

Wind, how do you know these questions before I ask them?

Remember, I am a part of you and you are a part of me. Now go and enjoy your surroundings. Tonight I will speak to you again.

Thank you, Wind.

You are welcome, Companion of the Wind.

The wind blew him back to base camp the following day. He bore two new names, one public, one private. He declared that he felt secure in himself, and looked it. He had proved something to himself that no one could take away. Some months later we asked him if he could remember the private name the wind had given him. "Oh yes," he replied, as if we had asked him a very silly question.

For this young man the vision quest was a rite of passage in the traditional sense. Symbolically he left childhood behind and went out alone, facing his fears and his destiny, to find in the spirit of Nature an ally and a name. In the same manner, hundreds of young men and women have come, challenged by the opportunity to enact a rite of passage to formalize their passing from childhood to adulthood.

Each youth carefully prepared for, then entered, the silence. Each was a world unto himself or herself. They would show up for meetings at schools and churches, intense, naive, full of energy. When they talked about the vision quest, we could see them weighing the idea in their minds. (Can I do that? Has my upbringing prepared me to undertake such a challenge?) Many went even though they were not certain they could do it. Many succeeded in staying out three days and nights without food. Some returned early, for a variety of reasons. They kept journals, in most cases fragmentary and episodic, but filled with life and emotion. Their voices return on the wind, in scraps and pieces.

> My buddy and I sat beside our rock pile, our only means of communication, and wept before we departed. I think we're both feeling many anxieties and fears, that ahead of us lies a huge question mark.
>
> —Free Bird, 17

> I'm starving. I'm very weak and I just feel like sleeping. But I can't sleep. My back aches from lying on this hard surface for two days. . . . I find myself daydreaming about food: oranges, hard-boiled eggs, fresh bread, anything. . . .
> Oh please let the sun set. Please, please, *please!* I feel so

goddamned empty. I can't wait until I encounter society again. Isn't that what this is all about?

—I'd Pick a Daisy, 15

The thunder is shaking and I am scared. . . . I sure hope that there are no flash floods. Don't rain, please. I am not ready for rain. I want someone to hold me. I feel lonely, very lonely now that those rain clouds are coming. . . . I hate the fact that all I can do is sit and wait, sit and wait. I can *feel* what loneliness is. . . . I HOPE IT DOESN'T RAIN! I'm not the homesick type, but I would give almost anything to be with my parents.

—Weak Stomach, Strong Heart, 17

It's all so lonely and cold, so long and drawn out, eternity, black, endless tunnels and no time for food or love and I miss my lover very much. My heart is aching and it's all getting so dark I can't see her in front of me anymore. . . . So many empty thoughts floating by—my past, my future, etc. I know I'll live. I know I'll survive. Wind howling now, howling, howling. So cold are my hands. . . .

—Moon Song Crying, 17

Today I made my circle and named myself Lone Stone Among the Rest. . . . Then later this afternoon I sang my name and walked around my circle. Doing this gave my name more depth and meaning. After I had been walking around my circle I had to quit because I was losing my balance. I started singing it again, when I got to my place overlooking the valley. I started to cry, yet I continued. My name symbolizes my cutting the line connecting me to my parents, making me a separate and unique human being.

—Lone Stone Among the Rest, 17

La montana de la visión is high; it took me four hours to conquer. It won't allow just anyone to reach its crown. Sweat, thirst and intense heat try my stamina. Still I climb. My pack is heavy; it burdens my back with pain. Perspiration rolls down my body. I'm going through hell, but soon I will reach the heaven awaiting me. I stand on the top. A cool breeze welcomes me. I feel accepted. I look far below. *La Bahía de la Concepción* rests in the earth like a baby in mother's arms. The Sea of Cortez shines in the East. I feel very close to the heart of the mountain. Its power is inside me. It is strong and spiritual. Never will it cease to be.

—Linda, 16

These are the voices of children becoming strong. They are beginning to see into the life of things. They are beginning to assume the burden of heroism in this world. They are engaged in the sacred task of creating a survival myth for themselves and their world. They must find their own way.

I must even let my own son go to a place somewhere out on the eastern flank of White Mountain Peak. Right now he is battening his tarp down against a hailstorm. For cover he is using a thick stand of mountain mahogany and the good sense to get low if there is lightning. All I can do is trust that he is all right.

Crisp and cold. I awoke with a bloody nose. I'm tired today; my energy is gone. I sit in darkness surrounded by light. My eyes see beauty, but my bones feel death is near. My mind tells me that soon I shall rejoin and rejoice with my people.

I get cold so easily. The silence of the place makes me hear the ringing of my ears. I imagine I see wisps of smoke in the trees—hallucinating, maybe. I think maybe I'm seeing the spirits of long-dead Indians still using this land.

Oh, the wind is cold when it blows across my body; it makes me feel so alien—though why should this be? My ancestors lived with the land for hundreds of thousands of years. But I feel so puny, so exposed, like the spark of life within me is so small.

—Keenan, 16

FIRE STICK

Rich, a burly, clean-cut, handsome young man with a slight Armenian accent, showed up at a vision quest meeting at the local high school. When he also attended the next meeting, we could see that he was hooked. Yet he hardly seemed part of the group, even when at the last meeting before we left for the wilderness, he held hands in a circle with the rest of us. Rich was not easy to get to know. There was something aloof about him, something that seemed to annoy others in the group.

A month after Companion of the Wind had vision quested, we were back in the same White Mountains. It was mid-August. On the floor of the Owens Valley the temperature was in the nineties. At 12,000 feet there was a chill in the air, and menacing clouds appeared in the west. That night around the campfire Rich began to talk more about himself.

He was a "jock." Not only was he the best high hurdler in the league but he was also all-conference fullback and homecoming king. And he was a loner. He spoke of being unable to enjoy the fads and frivolities of his peers. He spoke of high personal ideals, of becoming a lawyer or a doctor someday. He spoke of drive and hustle and challenge. It was easy to see that he placed less value on love and sentimentality than on ambition and competition. He said, "I don't need anybody. I have learned to get along by myself." Looking Through the Eyes of a Hawk (17), who had been on a previous quest, replied: "Tell us that when you come back from being alone." "O.K.," he said, taking up the challenge.

And then, as if to cement his resolve, he requested my permission to leave for his quest one night early. Already he had begun to fast to intensify his experience, and his request seemed to indicate that, like the high hurdler, he wanted to be out in front. We told him he should first check it out with the group. His buddy agreed to accompany him to his power place and set up a stone pile the two of them could check the following morning. The group gave its consent with varying degrees of enthusiasm. We felt it was a bit unfair to the others, but nobody seemed to object.

So Rich went out one night early. That same night, after everyone had gone to bed early to be up and off at the crack of dawn, the heavens fell down. In the midst of clouds so thick you could see no further than a hundred feet, a lightning storm struck. It was a god-awful storm that would not let go. The flashes of lightning bolts glowed eerily in the thick gloom. Thunder cracked and howled and leaped from the fog, and there seemed no end of it. Finally hail and sleet fell until our tarps were laden to the bursting point, and fell some more. Out there in the gloom we could hear a couple from the group singing the Beatles' "Here Comes the Sun." We were all cold and wet and miserable, but something deep inside us was excited. We called out to each other in the dark: "Are you guys all right?"

Just before morning the storm subsided. We awoke to a clear cold dawn. Whiteness lay all around. Somebody said, "I wonder how Rich is doing?" Rich was writing in his journal.

Last night I experienced what our leaders had warned us all to be prepared for—severe thundershowers, hail and the whole bit. I was blessed by the fact that I had discovered a natural shelter. I'm quite proud of myself and how I reacted to the situation. I didn't panic. . . . I can't believe I survived the night. I started thinking about the group, how they were probably scared, especially Steven. I know he hates lightning. I wonder if they're thinking about me? Anyway I'm real happy. . . . I thought about everybody last night. I felt emotional. No—that isn't true. I am emotional, but I'm afraid to express myself. . . . I seem to be adjusting O.K. I feel very close to all of the other vision questers. But somehow I'm not allowing myself to become too compatible. Friendships and relationships are hard for me. . . . I'd love to return from the vision quest filled with such joy and love and compassion and just let down my guard and love people and accept them.

Day Two
One thing I've learned: The day sure is long. I dozed off yesterday evening, and when I awoke I couldn't figure out whether it was morning or evening. The sun was still shining. Last night I was overcome with loneliness, fatigue, and hunger. I wept. It hailed again last night. I thank god for providing such superb shelter. I miss the

family. I can't seem to get my mind off them. I can't wait to get back and see Gail, Dad, Jr., and everybody. The mountains seem to be staring at me. They must realize that I'm an oddity. I can't help feeling I've invaded their territory, that I have no right being here. They said they understand what I'm going through. They accept me.

God, am I ever tired. Sometimes I dread having to go to the stone pile. The trek involves climbing precipitous rocks, ledges, and crevices. My hands are all scraped. I fear that at the height of my fatigue I may fall to my death. Last night while lying in my shelter I observed the rock formation that encompassed me. I noticed that one gigantic rock was set on three points of smaller rocks. I imagined how death would feel if the gigantic rock were to fall on me in the night. I imagined that it would be a real warm experience, very painless, and that the rock would choke my last living breath out of me and I would fly away. I would take the form of an eagle and fly away.

I can't overcome this intense feeling of loneliness. I keep thinking I won't make it. But I know I just have to. The day is so long. The sun never seems to set. I'm very hungry. I just can't go to sleep. I cried tonight. I cried because I'm real lonely. I've never experienced anything so awful. I'm not scared and I can overcome hunger, but the loneliness is too intense. It haunts me. I can't wait to get home. I just can't wait. I'm trying to think of ways to cope with my loneliness, but there aren't any. The time goes by so slow. I never leave my area unless I go to the rock pile. I just sit and wait for the day to end, but it never does. I wonder if anyone else is feeling this lonely. I will never do anything like this again in my whole life. Please God, help me make it through the night. . . .

DAY THREE

Last night, before I built my fire, I was in a desperate state. I couldn't stop thinking lonely thoughts. More than once I thought of turning back. . . . During the night I had a lot of dreams. These dreams were very much the same as the dreams I've had every night since I've been here. They involve teachers and students I knew at my other school before I moved. . . . I've decided to keep busy today to keep my mind clear. Today I will construct my circle. I will die in the presence of Mother Nature! She will witness the rebirth of a new soul.

I have realized during my vision quest that I am a very lucky person. I live with people that love me and I love the people I'm living with. Only this experience could have brought this realization out of me. The test will be when I return.

Fire flashes through my mind. How comfortable I feel when I sit next to my fire. I feel strong again. It is very rejuvenating. I've decided to name myself Fire Stick. Perhaps it is an indication of my fate. Will I die in fire? Will I burn in hell? Or has a burdened, weather-beaten flame been rekindled to warm and comfort my life forever?

The next morning when he returned there was no question that he was part of the group. He was a like a big, happy puppy, wagging his tail and hugging everybody. Love, pure and strong, came through him and suffused us with happiness.

I have returned. All feelings of loneliness and hunger have perished. The joy of returning to base camp was overwhelming. Such a feeling of happiness and warmth. Somehow my feelings of loneliness are gone. It's over and I'm glad. Tomorrow I continue my life. I will never forget my vision quest. I still miss my family. It's too bad that they will never really understand what I have been through. It can't be expressed through words. It's a feeling experience. I feel sad for some reason, perhaps because at my camp I was really in tune with myself. I felt empty and pure. Will the vision quest alter my life?

At the reunion three weeks later he brought his journal to share with us. He had added a postscript.

The ultra-high I experienced on my vision quest is one I have not been able to duplicate since. Although I feel as though I have failed the expectations I promised to fulfill on the last night . . . (the height of my emotionalism), these I have learned: I have shared two conditions that unfortunately exist widely in this world—hunger and loneliness. I have shed the mask that shielded me from being my true person. I have realized that in the past I elevated myself to false heights of virtuousness and morality, and that I am no better than my peers, beneath them in many respects. I have also shared the most profound experience of all my life with a group of people that I respect and love tremendously. These feelings will remain with me always.

Among the young, the vision quest is a ritual to formalize the transition from childhood to adulthood. Among adults, it formalizes other life transitions. The older people who come with us recognize how growth requires little deaths and rebirths. They are willing to confront what they fear. They step onto the path with courage, having arrived at a place in their lives where three days and nights in the desert without eating, symbolically seeking a vision of self-transformation, appeals to them.

GIFT BEARER I
Virginia, a former professor of social and cultural anthropology, came to us two years after her beautiful husband, to whom she had committed herself as though to God, had died of cancer. He had died a happy, brave death, with his loved ones gathered around him. In the intervening years she had also sought to die, to join him, not by committing suicide but by rationally seeking with her whole being to die, as did the aborigine or the Eskimo. She relinquished her possessions to her children and loved ones, set a date for her death, and concentrated all her energy and the energy of those who loved and understood her on the moment of her death.

The moment came, and passed. As she had secretly feared, she did not die, but fell instead into a deep sleep. During her sleep she dreamed that a dark figure in a black hooded cloak appeared before her and forcibly pushed her back into life. For a long time she would not accept the verdict of her dream and fell into a deep depression.

82

She came to the vision quest with a complex and unhappy heart, yet conducted herself with the understanding and deliberation of a first-rate anthropologist in the field. The power and direction of her quest drew her to the most barren place, destitute of any growing thing, in the blood-colored hills of the volcanic, waterless Saline Range in southeastern California.

For two days a violent sandstorm smothered the face of the desert. In this place of power, deliberately chosen because it closely resembled what she was feeling inside, she sought ritually to reach across the void of death to contact her dead husband. A foreigner to the deserts of the southwest and a long-time resident of Florida, she disappeared into the wind with her buddy, wearing a T-shirt saying, "It's Better in the Bahamas."

> I came to my place and put down my pack. Without thinking, I took one of the sticks I had brought—my "snake stick"—from the mesquite spring on the way here. It was in my left hand. I knew I had to make an Invocation to my place. I stood in the center of the ancient stone circle, faced east, then west, then north, then south. This is what I called out, as nearly as I can remember:
>
> Hear me, Place. I have come to spend three days and three nights in You and be with You.
>
> As I face the east, I ask that you grant me light—let the Light of Love be shed upon me.
>
> As I face the west, I ask you to teach me to die gracefully so that the richly colored sunset beams may bless the hearts of those I love.
>
> As I face the north, I ask that you give me your strength—the strength of your barren mountains, your rocky ridges. Send me a lodestone vision that will last me the rest of my life.
>
> As I face the south, I ask that you grant me your blessings of gentleness. Stark and sere as you look, I know you can confer the sweetness and softness I have known so well in the warm seas, in the gentle surges over coral reefs. Grant me the gift of your gentleness.
>
> When I was finished I wept, standing in the circle. Then I put the water jugs in the shade. I spoke to the

spaces in the rock pile where I intended to build my shelter. I said:

"Snake, I have come to spend three days and three nights in this spot. If you are in there, please do not harm me and I will not harm you. If you are here, speak now."

Then I poked in all the holes with my stick. There was no rattle. (A tiny insect just landed on my hand as I wrote. I realize I must not kill any living thing while I am here. Not an insect, nor any creature. Ask them to leave me, yes. Swat them, no.)

Now I will build my shelter.

But the wind-whipped sand seethed through her shelter and forced her to find another place, a fissure, deep enough for her body and out of the full force of the wind.

I took the cup of water and made my invocation telling why I was here, what I wanted to learn and experience, and asking the permission of the fissure spirits and the snake people, if such there be in that place, to stretch my tarp for shade over the depression. Then I drank three swallows of my water, spilled three swallows onto the ground at the center of the depression, and drank the rest. I asked for a sign if I was not welcome there. Now I will begin the work. If I am not welcome, the sign will come as I try to erect the tarp.

The wind is powerful again tonight. On the lee side of the huge rock pile, it is only eddies. When they drop off for a moment I can hear the sound of the wind in the wide, barren valley. It is a hissing sound, very like the sound of a distant rushing river. I could swear there are cataracts rushing through the empty canyons between my perch and the far ridge to the west.

As I hear the wind blowing across the darkening mountains I am reminded of yesterday's lesson—and gift—the desiccation and defleshing of attachments to the past that would prevent my clean dying. Again the burning sensation under the breastbone. Though I am not so mercilessly exposed to the defleshing wind, it reminds me of its surgery of yesterday. This is different from "letting go." One's umbilical cords must be defleshed and withered. There are some you cannot just let go of. Yesterday the cords were burnt, dried up, preparing for freedom from the past. Today it was: "Sit. Wait." Tomorrow? I have prepared my prayer. I have spoken it to the circles.

As the bleak desert wind dried up her attachments to the sorrow and bereavement of her recent past, her love for her husband held and grew in the soilless rock that edges the chasm of Death. But how could she reach her husband? It seemed some transformation was necessary, some kind of rebirth that would bring her wholly to death.

The silence is deafening! This is a day of utter motionlessness. Yesterday the terrible desiccating wind and grit. Today the absolute stillness, the incredible motionlessness. What is Mother Nature's message today? Don't move? Be still? Do not act? My head aches. Two very fat black flies with striped shoulders buzz my shelter. They buzz but do not bite, and when they land on my bedpad they are utterly motionless for minutes. It seems I have waited so long. How can the Great Spirit require yet more stillness, more utter motionlessness?

I check my watch—and realize how ridiculous that is. I am bored, wanting this trial and these discomforts to be over—and embarrassed because I am bored. I feel inadequate, dull; I despair of a vision. I despair of the change I so desire. I am not to be transformed—any more than these mountains. I will go on forever, the gray half-life stretching to eternity. Even those words of despair I have written a hundred times over in the last three years. There is nothing new, neither a new pain nor a new joy. Even the brief joys . . . I know to be ephemeral even as I feel them. My head aches with my boring sameness. I am bored with being me. *Then be someone else.* But how? *The variations of life are infinite.* I know, but how does that help me be someone else? *Come back into me and let me put you out again in a new form.* How can I do that except die physically? *Sit. Wait.* Hoping for the change? *Stop hoping. Just sit. Wait.*

For three days and nights she sat and waited through the wind storm, settling into the earth like a stone. As her umbilicals to the past were "defleshed," she began to see that part of herself which remained fresh and intact, and that part which was dying.

> I do not feel alone. I am surrounded by spirits. They are neither friendly nor unfriendly. They exert their power over me at the behest of the Great Spirit. They are incisive. They clean my soul. They cut the restraining cord, drawing all the pulsing blood energy from it, drying it, withering it, releasing the energy that has been stored there.
>
> The life energy from the wellspring of my past is being drawn out, released. My past life—love—is becoming desiccated, preserved, like a corpse found in hot desert sands, still with incredibly legible detail—or like a dried flower, still with color and shape and beauty but without the need for food or water, with no drawing upon the energies of love which know no past or present or future and spend themselves as easily upon memories as upon present relationships.
>
> Perhaps with this ancient psychic surgery I will be able to love Aldie [husband who has recently died] now as he is coming to love me, free of the yearning for the shape and color of our past love. I can love Aldie in and through the loves of the present, whatever they are or will become. Nothing of the old love, the dead love, the dying self is lost; the body is preserved in all its beauty forever unchanging, its spirit free to create further bodies—to the glory of the Spirit of the WE, the glue of the new, the microcosm of the macrocosmic social structure birthing itself.

With the realization that she could love her dead husband through the loves of her present life, she awoke to the morning of the third day.

One of my prayers has been answered! So now my cry, my prayer is: "Teach me how to become the Gift, that I may take it to my People in death."

It is exciting to realize that we come into this physical and social dimension in order to fashion a gift, an enrichment, an addition. It has always seemed so one-way before. This awareness strengthens my belief that my gift will have to do with the *way* of dying.

I feel at peace, content. My questions have been answered. I can accept my alone-life, knowing its purpose. Interaction, *love,* is the purpose and the core. Now I see the possibility of a different kind of interaction—and it is something I can start to learn as soon as I get home, beginning with my little place/house and my plants. How to interact with people this way I do not yet know.

She returned from her quest with a name, Gift Bearer. She joined us in our work and asked not to be paid. She bore love to us, and a strange kind of joy.

SOLO

Natalie, a psychotherapist, became interested in the vision quest when she conducted in-staff training at the old Rites of Passage, when it was still a drug abuse outfit. She had all eight of us get down on our knees in front of a big piece of butcher paper, gave us crayons, and said, "Draw your life myth." We did. I looked at the incredible mural we had created and understood none of it, except for my own picture. Then she said, "Connect your life myth with all the other life myths." That was a bit more difficult. Eventually, we did that too. And by connecting our myths to each other we formalized and came to understand a common purpose.

Several years before, Natalie had chosen to uproot herself, leave her marriage and Boston home of twenty years, and hit the road for California. She started a new life there, designing her own work, making new friends, and shedding a great deal of her material past. For a woman brought up within the "woman's place is in the home" tradition, her solitary move to California represented a great leap into the unknown. What she desired above all was the right to be herself.

As an artist, a dancer, a student of consciousness, and an emotional adventurer, she brought all of herself to her work. When she heard about the vision quest, she was hooked. She gracefully bore herself through a series of meetings with an oversized, rambunctious bunch of kids at an alternative high school; she took notes, absorbed in her own careful preparation.

It was Eastertime in the Funeral Mountains, and the wind was full of cold fury. A storm had come down from Alaska. The snows caught on the teeth of the Sierra Nevada, but the wind came on unchecked, across the Inyos and the Saline Valley, up over the Panamints and down into the great wind catcher of Death Valley. The temperature went down to freezing at night, making ice in our plastic water jugs.

The night before the threshold time, as the group sat and talked, I went into an uncontrollable fit of shivering and shuddering. I could not unclench myself from a vague, overpowering dread. Natalie heaped her sleeping bag upon me and lay down upon my shuddering body with her weight and warmth, until I lay calm. The next morning she went into the wind.

> To grasp it, the reality-unreality of it, I need to write. I am fortunate that I am out of the cold wind, in a spot not far from our base camp. There are no trees or large bushes on the whole horizon. What faces me is a bare mountain, stone, sagebrush, and craggy rocks jutting upward. My god! What *am* I doing here, alone for three days to come, with only water? . . . I've never slept outside alone anywhere and here I am in the middle of the most barren of places for three days alone without food. It is a challenge! . . .
>
> This is sobering, very sobering. As I walked away from my warm, cave-like shelter, I was stepping lightly, feeling carefree. Suddenly I froze stiff as I saw before me a coiled snake, black tail upward, body rigid, waiting to strike. It was about sixteen inches long, sandy colored, exactly the hue of the pink-brown earth. It had dark stripes and a small, triangular head. . . . It looked more like what I remember as a copperhead than a rattlesnake. Its black tail did not appear to have rattles on it, but I was paralyzed

with fright and not sure what I saw. I stared: It was powerful, poised, ready to strike. Apparently it heard me coming. Damn lucky I was looking where I was going. I moved uphill and it slid sideways, slinking down the slope.

Cold and scared, she entered the first night alone to find that she was living in a temple of great beauty.

How can I possibly sleep? It is so beautiful and exciting here. I'm snuggled in against the cliff in my high-up perch. I watched the mountains in the far distance turn soft-edged gray-pink. Dusk was soothing. I wondered if I'd be frightened, but instead am awestruck. The stars appeared so slowly, and I was trying to recognize the constellations when I realized that behind me was a very bright light. I turned to see the full moon appear over the deep black evening mountain.

During the night, the spirit of fear visited Natalie.

Last night I dreamed that I was in the middle of Death Valley, and I was in a phone booth. The phone rang and when I answered it, I said, "Hello, this is the wilderness."
Then I suddenly awoke knowing that something was moving on my head and hat. My hands started to jump toward my head to find out what it was, but fortunately the sleeping bag was constricting my movement, and I was awakened enough to *think*. "Be quiet, hold still, listen!" My heart was pounding. Adrenaline shot through my system. (This is one way to get warm, I said to myself.) As I stayed motionless I felt the movement on my head again. It seemed like scratching. My fear was that it was my friend the snake trying to join me in my sleeping bag to get warm.
After about ten minutes of wondering, listening, and moving slightly now and then, my panic subsided. I decided to move the top of my head out of the drawstring hole at the top of my bag. I could see clearly, in the

moonlight, but did not see any animal. I pulled myself to a sitting position, still in the bag, to take a look around, being careful to move slowly. I saw nothing. By then I had figured it was a rodent; the scratching on my cap was so definitely a paw. It was obviously not a large creature or it would have made more noise moving. Figuring a rat wasn't going to do much damage to me if I let it be curious about my hat (thank god for the hat), I went to sleep.

Gradually she began to adjust to her surroundings and to sense the quality of the solitude to which she had come.

Listening to the silence is one of the most powerful and profound experiences I am having. At first I avoided listening. The lack of sound is so totally foreign, it is frightening to allow myself to become more aware of it. I can sit quietly awaiting the sunrise and—now that the wind is quiet—hear total nothingness except for my own breathing and the rustle of my movements, however slight. I will try to soak in that silence more completely later. It seems that I fear the letting go of myself into that total quiet, yet that's what I want to do.

What am I learning out here anyway? That I have tremendous inner strength and resources if left to myself and if I have a little luck and support. I don't get lonely when I'm alone. I am discovering that if I have a pen and drawing materials with me I don't need much more. I'm learning that I care enough to care for myself. That seems foolishly simple.

I am learning, somehow, about death. Although I have tremendous energy and excitement about living, the idea of dying—for me to become at one with the cosmos—does not frighten me. I find myself self-protective, but not out of death-fear as much as life-wish.

Nature was also giving her a name to match the strength and independence of her quest: Solo.

I saw three hawks soaring as I cried out to the sky, and watched the two pair off and leave together. The third (me) went on and on alone, higher and higher, and finally out of sight beyond the mountains. I cried as I saw that as the metaphor of me—yet I liked it.

On the evening of the third day she performed a ritual based on Black Elk's account of the *hanblecheyapi*, or "crying for a vision" ritual of the Oglala Sioux.

As I walked from the center position to each point on the compass, I moved slowly, with my eyes down, not focusing on anything. I concentrated on my breathing, being aware to breathe deeply with each slow step. When I reached the pole with the power object, I stood with my head raised to the sky and sang out my chant, loud and clear. It felt good inside to give full strength to my voice. It brought to the surface a lot of strong, indescribable emotions. I thought of my family. I appreciate them fully, without reservations, lovingly. When I stood in front of the objects on the south pole, I wept for love of my daughters. Being a mother of such fine persons is a great joy, forever, for me.

I thought of many other people I love. And I didn't think of anything. I lay down within my circle, for a time, I don't know how long. I was calm. Then I started moving around the ritual path again. When I got very cold, I left the circle quietly.

The next morning she returned to the others.

I remember warm feelings of reunion. . . . Finally the sun gave us a break and warmed our bodies for our last afternoon united. We found ourselves sitting close together, talking rapidly of all our experiences, good and bad. After a while it was time to go. We packed up. The hike out was light and easy. I was in better physical shape than when we had arrived. My feet seemed to move across the rocky ground in the dusk with ease. . . .

The moon was out again as we drove north on the eastern side of the Sierras. White, snow-capped mountains illuminated by the moon accompanied our pathway home. We turned off the road at a hot springs around midnight. The scene was like a Chinese scroll. Below us was a wide, quickly flowing hot stream. We took the winding path down the hill, hearing the gurgling and bubbling as we walked. The backdrop was high mountains in the distance with the moon watching over us. An arched bridge crossed the stream. Slowly, one by one, we undressed and slipped into the delicious water . . . our first in a week. So many beautiful people bathing in the warmth, the moonlight, the friendship. The steam from the river cast an unearthly air around us. Laughing and playing, quietly rejuvenating, I declared it was the most lovely Easter morning I'd ever seen.

MARK

The stories of vision questers do not always conclude with beatitude. It is not rare for an individual to return early, before the three days and nights are over. Those who do return early tend to feel that they have failed. This feeling of failure may persist if the person is not helped to look clearly at the reasons for returning. There are many good reasons. People sometimes go on a vision quest when they might better employ their time facing some problem at home. It might be difficult for a person to realize this until he or she is alone with a chance to reflect on the world left behind.

Mark, a popular and respected young high school teacher and counselor, returned on the second night of the threshold from high on a ridge in the Panamint Mountains. He appeared at the edge of the campfire late at night, looking as if he had been wrestling with the devil. His first words were, "I feel like a failure." Subsequent scrutiny of his journal revealed that after an initial surge of happy feelings on the first day, he began to go back over recent events in his mind: the death of a close friend and the imminent deaths of his mother and father.

EVENING OF THE FIRST DAY
After having my cup of tea, I thought, "What's next?" It

didn't take long to figure that out. I thought of my friend Karl, who died on December 22, and I cried for at least half an hour. Then I cried for my dad, who is slowly dying in the liver and lungs, and my mother, who went into the hospital for cancer the night before I left on the trip. I didn't know if I was going to quit or not. I was scared. I was all alone, and that was more frightening than death.

I prayed to Karl for forgiveness in not seeing him in his final days. Would you believe I was scared to see him because I didn't want to cry in front of him? Just like dad. . . . After crying it out, I had another cup of tea, then prayed and meditated. I found myself with a lot of inner strength. I also did a small ritual with the fire. I gave and said small prayers to all the people on this trip with me, each and every member of my family, and my really close friends. Then I placed a solid piece of wood for all those friends and acquaintances I have known and worked with, partied with, had confrontations with. Then I stepped over to a high ridge and yelled out, HAPPY NEW YEAR, WORLD! and went to my sleeping bag, to sleep through the New Year, stone cold sober on that night for the first time in my life since age fifteen.

MORNING OF THE SECOND DAY
God, how I am weak. I had to go down that friggin' mountain to build a few rocks for my partner, and I simply didn't want to. When I was halfway down, thoughts crossed my mind to give up, to say fuck it to the whole thing. Then came the thought that last night I was weak right before I started crying, and that after my cry I actually had a lot of strength. So I sat on a rock and cried for about a minute and pleaded with myself and the Lord not to give up. . . . I just need to continue opening up with my heart and soon I will find strength.

AFTERNOON OF THE SECOND DAY
I'm beginning to feel nauseous again. I'm also crying right now. I don't want to give up! My gut tells me to go

back to base camp, but my *macho* tells me to stick with it. I don't know which one to give three cheers to. I just don't think I failed anything and yet I feel like a failure for just thinking about it. . . .

I have given my present situation some serious consideration. If I feel nauseous during the night or extremely weak in the morning, I'm going back to base camp, where I'm hoping to get hugs, because I sure need them.

He returned that night, hiking two miles back to base camp. We talked at length, until the moon was almost across the sky. We tried to help him see that the threshold trial is not a matter of duration but of intensity, and that his feelings during the quest were an inner motion picture of his life in general. He began to talk with great affection of his mother and father. He also began to see why he had come back.

Why did I return? Fear of death and dying was the issue. I have been avoiding any mention of dying with my parents, and I have discovered that that has nearly brought my own demise.

My present quest is the need to discuss this issue openly with my father and my mother. There is no doubt in my mind that I love them both dearly. I need them as much as they need me.

I need to focus on death and rebirth, to find out what it is that's so frightening. I find it easy to tell people that I fear death. It was something else, though, when I looked at death right in front of me. I confronted it internally for the first time in my life.

THE TWO SISTERS

Two Dominican sisters went with us into the Panamint Mountains to seek a vision. Teachers both, they were drawn to the idea by their love for the desert and the Biblical stories of Mt. Sinai and the prophets of old. In the two of them the traditional and modern, the flesh and spirit, were blended in a special way. Listens With the Heart chose an alluvial terrace above Lost Springs Canyon, and the other, Ruth, went up Anvil Spring Canyon.

As their journals reveal, each went about the quest in a different manner. Ruth, more traditional in her outlook, prayed for that which would bind her closer to God. ("Lord Jesus, I would like to be more ascetic . . . to be disciplined and to fast . . . to become closer to You in prayer.") The record of her three days and nights is filled with affirmations of faith and prayer and quotations from scripture. When she arrived at her place she climbed a mountain.

> I feel the need to see beyond my valley. . . . I am content and have no desire to check out other mountains, partly because of the realization that I have no food for further climbing. I thank God for such beauty and ask for His protection during my stay. I feel very secure with the gentleness of all the elements. I am not worried and know I have lots of time.

On the other hand, Listens With the Heart approached her quest with passionate, sensitive, self-critical energy.

> I washed and wrote up dreams and drew and felt yukky. Why did I come here? Yes, it's beautiful and quiet, but life is to be lived with people. People come into my thoughts and dreams. It seems meaningless right now to live without people and relationships. I am thinking of the quote, "It would be better for you to meditate in your own room. You are not ready to go out into the desert. You are still too attached to the world." I guess I had to come to find that out. . . . I find it hard to articulate why I wanted to come. Why have I come? To know God. I feel His presence, and it's so unemotional.

With her feelings of loneliness and doubt came also the cold winds of the night, to further test her.

> Cold—not wanting to be cold. Now the chills go through my body and I watch them and don't tense up. And warmth follows. Can I let the chills from people go through me the same way and not tense up and allow the warmth—trust it—to follow? Will I?

For Ruth, the experience was one of innocent delight in little things. Having given her life over to God, she felt free to enjoy herself without doubts or critical self-attention.

> My problems and worries have become as insignificant as sand shifting in the wind. Yes, I wish to seek a vision—a vision of Love. A Love that will free me to be really sensitive and caring. A Love for my God, greater than all loves. . . . To cry for Him with a desire yearning for nothing else. For with His Love all else is possible.

She went for a walk on her second day.

> As I turned toward the west I was surprised by a little rainbow. A rainbow in the evening sky in the desert—no clouds except where the sun was setting. I knelt down in gratitude. A rainbow is a special sign of hope and new life and joy. I decided to follow it.

As the sun set, she walked up the gradually opening canyon and was greeted by a bat and a jack rabbit. She picked a tiny branchlet of purplemat to leave for her buddy at the stone pile.

> My thoughts were going back to the others, hoping they also caught a glimpse of the rainbow. . . . I continued walking a little further, then stood still to see the sun slip down behind the hills. In my own way I gestured a prayer of thanks and then returned.

Listens With the Heart also saw the rainbow, but she followed it to her dreams, which were laden with archetypes illustrating inner conflict.

> An old Indian woman's face and a man came to me. There was a child in the cradle board. I took the child, to care for it alone. There was a stigma attached to it.
> A red, yellow, and white light appeared at the end of a black tunnel. There was a heavy silver chain suspended

from a black iron fastening on the way [through the tunnel].
I gave birth squatting. To twins, a boy first, then a girl. My love went more to the girl. The afterbirth came and . . . I put [the children] in warm water after holding them against [my] skin.

Remarkably connected with her dreams, she was disturbed and fascinated. Her experience of the final night also shows strong intuitive and instinctive feelings regarding her life, her destiny, and her deepest, innermost spiritual vitality.

When my circles were complete and I had brought in a sitting stone, I sat and waited for the moon to rise as she had the night before over the Mystical Mountain. She was slow in coming. I sat and waited until she was full over the peak. . . . She came forward like a host: "This is my body, given for your freedom."
My circles were ready. I was ready. But what to do? I did not know what to do. I, the prayer-teacher!
I began to walk around my circle and talk to the Lord. Did the Lord know I was there? In the vastness? Would He take time and be with me tonight? Now? Would He love me?
I wept in self-pity or from the pain of the cost of celibacy. And then I remembered all who have loved me in my lifetime. So many. I recalled them, place by place, where I had lived and gave thanks for them and prayed for them now—wherever they are—and my family, member by member.
I remembered an exercise about carrying a heavy rock as a reminder of the karma we carry. I chose a large one from the inner circle and held it in my arms and walked. It was heavy. I remembered my anger in my back and put the rock in my day pack and on my back and prayed for release of that anger.
Not only I carry karma. I prayed for the sick and lonely and disabled and divorced and alienated and mentally ill.

And the moon was halfway.

I sat in silence surrounded by my circle and by the ridges on both sides forming an earth womb with the mystical mountain at the opening to the northeast.

The giant mountain—the rock.

I wanted to take it into me.

The rock—a symbol of rebirth according to Jung. I do not understand.

I take it in and sleep takes me.

A friendly fly buzzes by to awaken me.

No dream. . . .

Then I hold the planet in my heart and wrap it in light and it is encircled by two gold rings moving around it. I remember my first dream: a warm, brown earth house in the desert. Out front, a sign: "Everybody welcome. Water and maps available." Maps to where? Inner journeying. Maps of consciousness.

The moon is three-fourths across the sky. I sit and wrap up in my sleeping bag. I build a fire. I bury it and sit on it and then sleep.

"Yaweh, I know you are near."

Two blue eyes look at me. Feminine eyes, teenage eyes. Loving, detached, inward, childlike.

I open my eyes. Morning has broken. A flash of lightning pierces a grave. Easter. Resurrection.

Alleluia, Alleluia, let the holy anthem rise.

And the chorus of heaven chant it in the temple of the skies. . . .

Ruth reported her last night more simply. She did not feel the conflicting emotions felt by Listens With the Heart. She did not have to wrestle with the devil, or at least such a struggle with doubt and disillusionment is not recorded.

My last night at my place of vision was long. I prayed, thought of all those people I touched in some way. I prayed for them and our world today. As the night wore on I dozed off some. The moon stayed up all night.

I saw the sun rise. Beautiful red, reflecting off the

mountains across the valley. It quietly swept the sky with colors like the Grand Canyon. . . .

The birds are beginning to wake up and sing their morning song. I too will sing before my God.

Sing a new song unto the Lord!
Let your song be sung from mountains high.
Sing a new song unto the Lord,
Singing Alleluia!

On the last morning Listens With the Heart left her circle and her place with some difficulty. Although she had been very lonely, now that the time had come to be with the others she did not feel the pangs of separation from them as keenly. Her place had held her, taught her. Here she had become deeply connected to the Earth.

Time to get up and leave. I look at my circles and love my "home," the only home I ever built for myself. My tomb, my womb. I have to go. Reluctantly I pack up.

I walk three times around my home. Father, Son, Spirit. I rededicate myself. I water the Earth seven times as my gift and in thanksgiving. I linger. Perhaps I should wait for the orb of the sun to show? Procrastinating. Time to go. I put on my pack and deliberately step out. I survey my home with love and walk to meet my buddy. One more look. I wish I had a camera.

Down at base camp I open Barbara's Tao book: "The longest journey begins with the first step."

Later, she reviewed her experience, applying the same rigorous, critical standards of self-appraisal she had used during her time of aloneness.

The beginning of what? I had asked as I walked in circles. Trust. It will be good. No answers. No specifics.

I was a bit resentful that it was only a first step, after so long. Later I rejoiced. A first step to whatever I have come for. I know it was a time of rebirth after so much death. Yes, it had happened.

What?

Nothing had happened.

I didn't even stay awake all night.

No dream. No vision.

Had I wasted the time? The opportunity?

Maybe. Vacillating between acceptance and disappointment?

Maybe if I'd known what I wanted? Had a clearer purpose?

Hours later in the car a flash came over me. I had reviewed the first one-half of my life. I was awed at what I had done. What had I done?

Hours later. Maybe I did too much? Did I listen? Was I passive enough? Did I allow space for the Other? No. Typical me, I talk, walk, do, and then fall asleep. . . .

The next night, tonight, my room is a mess—camping gear, Christmas, clothes, mail. Feeling closed in and like I have to hurry. So much to do. I'm almost shaking.

I have to meditate.

I sit on my bed, close my eyes, and I am on my hill in my circle once again. Peace comes and expansion and light and letting go of muscular holding.

So this is why I went.

So I could be this now. Could I be this big under pressure? At school? Do I have to close my eyes and be alone?

Centered and expanded—both.

Ruth later described her fasting quest in the same pure, simple terms that premise her life.

My experience of Nature is like a mother folding herself protectively and lovingly around her child.

Every rock, plant, cloud, sound, and smell was kind to me. I felt safe, warm, and peaceful. I tried to be very attentive to everything, listening with all my senses.

My visions were simple: the rib of a bird, shining, silvery rocks, the dancing bat, the rainbow around the sun, the frightened rabbit, burro prints, little flowering

plants, quiet peace, the gentle wind, and a strong awareness of friends, loving and caring.

O God, what more do I need than I have been led
deeply into the very center of your love? Amen.

But Listen With the Heart was aware of something else. Her
desert quest for a vision had troubled a deep well within her, the
well of emptiness.

Since I returned I have wanted to eat and eat and eat—
and I have eaten a lot. But what do I want? It is not
food/stomach hunger, really, although I attempt to alleviate it that way. What am I hungry for? What do I want?

Indeed, what *do* we want? How will we fill our hunger? The
journal of every vision quester, in one way or another, has phrased
this question.

CREOSOTE AND LOOKING INTO THE FIRE

A brother and his sister vision quested with us at different times
over a five-year period. Each enacted the vision quest twice, on
separate occasions. Each had an unsatisfactory first experience.

Creosote, a college teacher and divorced father of two, expressed
interest in the quest at an early date, when the idea first began to
take tentative form. Trained in intellectual and academic pursuits,
he found the School of Nature to be in stark contrast to the ivory-
towered life he led.

He went to Death Valley with a group of people from an alternative school and spent much of his time alone thinking about his
children and his unhappy love affairs. He experienced no vision
and had few insights that seemed notable to him. He did, however,
have a near-fatal experience with the unfamiliar desert.

This morning I decided to take a hike from where I was
on the northwest topmost cliff above the canyon to the
valley floor, which seemed a short stroll. I was thinking
about my girlfriend and the fact that she was seeing another man, and I did not think about what I was doing.
I thought a hike would lull my raging jealousy.

When I finally reached the valley I realized that I had come too far, that I had overstepped my ability. Although I had drunk water before I started out, I did not have any with me. The day was hot. I lay down in the shadow of a rock and went to sleep. When I awoke I was in full sun, and two ravens were circling over me. My throat was parched and dry. I felt dizzy and sick. I looked up to where I had come from. It seemed impossibly far away.

For a long time I just sat there and cried and felt panic. But the heat drove me to my feet, and I decided to try going back anyway. It was then I spied a shack, a half-mile away. It was an old miner's shack, seemingly abandoned some time ago, but the door was fastened tight. In my desperation I broke in. Inside, on a rough-hewn table, were two gallon water bottles. One was empty, the other was full. Beside them was a note: "This is good water. Please don't drink it all."

I don't have to emphasize how sweet that stale old water was. I might have died that day. I didn't, thanks to another human being with forethought.

I drank half a gallon of water and rested in the shade of the shack. Then I fastened the door as it was when I found it and walked back up to the top of the mountain.

Despite his experience, he was eager to try again, though he did not do so for nearly a year. In the meantime, he began to plug up some of the holes in his bucket. He began to see his children, whom he had not seen in some time, and settled down into a relationship with a woman who later became his wife.

His second fasting quest, in the Last Chance Mountains in early April, was marked by terrible cold winds from the north, winds that took the legs out from under people, winds without mercy. Hoping to expand his awareness of the infinite, he was instead forced to come up with concrete, immediate answers to the question of survival. He found a place behind a low ridge to the leeward side of the wind and hung on, making brief forays to stretch his legs. In spite of the wind he wrote a great deal in his journal. At first, he was pleased with his situation. He enjoyed the opportunity to live in the third person of self-consciousness.

I adjust, make compromises, wait patiently, am impatient, examine my myths about myself, discover beauty in barrenness of rock and rude, red soil, in cactus thorns and the hissing, yellow blossoms of creosote, in blood from cuts in my hands, in the droppings of animals, the stainings of mineral, the precise artlessness of the way nature is arranged. I thrill to the morning sun breaking chill and clear on the wings of the North Wind. I find a belly flower in the bones of a dry wash. I feel my body in motion—it's hot and fluid, even in the cold. What a strange creature I am. I go to the edge of a cliff and gaze into the distance. Whatever, whoever I am, I'm alive.

Being with humans creates "time." Being alone in the wilderness creates a dimension other than time, a rhythm that is not in time. Time is a myth invented by people to mark their position in space relative to each other. But the other dimension, the rhythm that goes on and on, that is contacted only through the act of being *alone*, without the need to mark relative position—that is *eternity*.

On the second day he began to see things with a ritual eye.

I had been thinking about what it is that obscures my ability to take proper stock of my life situation. I was getting nowhere. Then I noticed an ant crawling up the side of my coffee cup. Absentmindedly, I watched. I had nothing better to do.

The ant climbed to the rim of the cup and looked around, groping aimlessly with its antenna. Then it proceeded to crawl around the rim of the cup in a perfect circle, stopping where it had begun, where a tiny bead of moisture clung to the rim. As if by magic, three other ants appeared, attracted by the moisture and the gyrations of the other ant. Suddenly I was off, off on a flight of feeling and thought.

I can't say what it was all about. But I looked around at the dry, wind-swept desert and thought about water, the absolute importance of it, and how these ants knew that there was a little drop of water on my coffee cup. I spoke to them, told them I was pleased that they had found water, and promised that I would leave some water in my cup for their enjoyment.

The episode passed. I became aware again of the passage of time. But the rest of the day I found myself thinking about perfect circles.

On the third day depression took hold of Creosote. The insidious wind and the bleak landscape evoked a similar inner geography.

The wind blew all day, always from the north, with a steady, rending force that I could not resist. I screamed at it, cursed it, and finally accepted it. The chill fingers of the wind penetrated the micropores of my sleeping bag and the stones of my shelter wall. I spent the night in the grip of a strong, foreboding quasi dream of disaster, of being consumed by the wind and cold. Toward morning something relented, said O.K. to the cold and the screeching of creosote in my ears. I went to sleep, only to awaken to another day of even higher winds.

I crouch against the shelter, my back to the wind. I can see across a ridge and down to the bleached bones of the valley. The terrain is bleak and uninviting. It is a metaphor for the way I feel about my life back there. Yes, there are a few cases, but generally things look pretty grim. I'm reminded of Antonioni's film, *The Red Desert,* and Eliot's poem, "The Wasteland."

Is that what I came out here to do? To contemplate the wastelands of Nature and to think black thoughts about what I'm going back to? What is my place in this wilderness world? What's it all about? Why am I here?

The prophet went into the wilderness and came back to the people crying, "Repent." I am no prophet. I am no saviour-god. I *am* one of those who need to repent. I confess. The abilities I possess have been used to gratify my own ego. Love? I have not learned how to love. Three wives later I am still trying to love people without hurting them, or manipulating them.

Why am I so bleak, so cold? Life seems absurd. "All life

death does end, and each day dies with sleep" (G. M. Hopkins). I am afraid of death. I am more afraid of dying. I am sick of myself. I'll die like a coward. I'll live without love. Nobody will care. . . .

The wind continues to hiss in the creosote and thunders in my ears, and I hunch deeper into myself, into my misery of loneliness and self-pity. Everything around me, so ageless and enduring. What possible use my tears shed on this stony ground? Why, dear god, this stony ground?

I don't understand why I am so lonely. I didn't think I would miss people so much. The wind keening in my ears, the unresolved questions of my life lumped upon these rocks, in a sackful of flesh and bone. . . .

In a few more hours the sun will set on my last day here. The darkness will come on and I will wait for the morning light. . . . I must see the people among whom I live as those who have come to watch me die, even as I imagine them grouped around me now. I must walk among them as if I were a condemned man. But not as a stranger, or an outsider—as a fellow condemned human being. There is a kind of comfort in knowing that we all share this destiny. But what remains after we have given it all away? Whatever is left must be the way to live, to seek life.

I know I can grow and change and procreate and be astonished at myself and other people. I know that I can seek to live, somehow, in others, after my death. I can love individuals: my children, my ex-wife, my mother and father and sister and brothers and others of my family for being who they are, and, if I fiercely desire, I will love them beyond the grave.

I don't know what I can do about the rest of the world—the starving millions, the oppressed, the suffering innocents, and all those who seem to care for nothing but themselves. But I guess I can love as well as anybody and have faith that I can rise again like the wind and seek the branches of the creosote.

I'll try to stay alive and healthy and yearning to love, to put on new green leaves. And when I die my body can be used as fuel to keep somebody else warm—for a while.

The wind that carries the deadly snow is the wind that carries the seed. So my love shall thrive, even in the barren desert.

The stars are out tonight.
Looking up at them I experience the nausea of vertigo.
My body is getting older.
Slowly I am dying.
How terrible and how sweet:
The stars are out tonight.

Looking Into the Fire, Creosote's sister, also enacted the vision quest twice. Linked to her brother by blood and the shaping influences of a common family history, her experience points out similarities in the sheer persistence of their efforts to realize their vision. There are also differences between the two that contrast the cultural roles of male and female. Whereas Creosote more actively and aggressively pursued his vision, pinned down by the wind and fiercely desiring to find love, Looking Into the Fire sought vision by opening up, by becoming sensitive to the power and healing of Nature.

Looking Into the Fire had been living in Canada for three years on a lovely island in the British Columbian sea. But some part of her could not be happy. She became aware that she would have to leave her husband and the home she had helped build, and reenter the mainstream of civilization. At the suggestion of her brother, she appeared at our door looking for what she knew not. She volunteered to work with us for a while and became absorbed in the ongoing crises of our small, nonprofit corporation. Before long she found herself on a spur of Hunter Mountain (Panamint Range) surrounded by great slabs of granite and a forest of pinyon. It was hot and dry. Alone and fasting she went into a sharp depression reminiscent of her brother's experience in the Last Chance Range. She remembered her beloved island, the cries of the cormorants, the lapping of the waves. She cried for the memory of her home.

All I can think about are the mistakes I've made in my life;
all the bad choices, or at least what feels like bad choices;
all the manipulating I've done; all my big know-it-all-ness.

I don't love myself. What a terrible thing to realize. All I can think of are times when I've spoken without thinking, times I've said things to impress others with my vast knowledge. Now I'm starting to cry, and it's self-pity. Poor me. I haven't learned how to take care of myself yet, nor do I know how to love. What a mess.

Great Spirit have mercy on me. I need to learn how to be silent. I need to learn how to love. I'm dirty, I'm tired, I'm hungry. I'm unhappy and I know nothing. Please show me how to live.

Later in the morning . . . I finally got up, started my fire, and sat at the end of my sleeping bag to carve on a piece of sage—mainly cutting out the dead wood and exposing the new under the gray, weathered surface. I thought about myself and maybe this trip is symbolic of what I was doing to the piece of wood—cleaning out the dead and useless to see what kind of shape and texture is really underneath, which is me without all the trimmings I think I have needed all these years.

Wait, wait. I get so impatient. What is my name? I want a name so badly that big sobs form in my throat. Everything looks rare. Everything is in focus. The colors and brightness of objects jump out at me. I see faces, mouths especially, in all the rocks around me. Each one is heavy in deep repose. I search for beds, beds to sleep in, make love in, beds to die in. I would die by lying in the sun and have the sun slowly bake away my flesh to expose my bones. Then I would lie for years while the sun slowly bleached my bones to white and they were buried in the sand.

She stayed with us for six months and then declared herself eager to try again. This time the knot of despair inside her was ready to come undone. She tested herself with questions. "Am I just hanging on to the past? Am I scared of the future? Can I really trust in my fate, in my karma, to see me through? Do I have good karma? These are words that don't say much. It's all in the *doing*, and I am afraid sometimes."

She found a huge, gnarled, half-dead yellow fir beside a small stream high in the South Warner Wilderness and on the first night dreamed a dream.

I am standing at the edge of a huge chasm. There is a house at one end of the chasm—it is my house. I *have* to get to the other side. I could walk around, but for some reason this is not an option. Instead I take a long ladder and lower it over the cliff so that the top of the ladder reaches the other cliff—barely. I then start across the ladder on hands and knees, one rung at a time. I am afraid. I am trembling. I cannot see what is at the bottom, probably a stream, rushing fast over rocks. I cannot fall or I will die. As I am almost to the other side I slip and just in time grab a rung of the ladder. I am left dangling from the ladder, not knowing if I have enough strength to reach the other side.

The ladder was the link between her first quest and her second. Sleeping quietly through the night, she came to a new day and recorded heights of feeling and awareness that are the antithesis of her first quest.

I'm home! The stream sings in my body, flowing, flowing down through.

I am alone. I'm happy I'm alone. Maybe I can find in Nature some of the closeness, the unions my body craves. It is very dark now. The sky is immense and filled with stars. Please accept me, universe. I am just a tiny speck here, crouched over the fire by this stream flowing from this mountain I sit and lie on. The mountain is only a tiny speck. The Big Dipper has moved along the horizon. Oh, the stars! I'm thinking of those I love so dearly at home. I am grateful for those who have loved me and love me still. I love. I *can* love. I *do* love. If I can love then I must be a good person. I am a good person. Tomorrow I'm going to tell my tree friend who doesn't mind soaking up my tears in his dry hard skin.

I love this silence. The speaking is done by the wind in the trees, the birds who occasionally chatter, the buzzing of flies. We *need* the silence. It is in the silence that nature can speak to us.

Before she left her place, she had reached certain conclusions that were to affect her deeply and bring her back to us, balanced and certain within herself that she was ready to commit this time of her life to the work of Rites of Passage.

> Bonded to the earth. Bonded. What good fortune led me to this place?
>
> I asked the stream to give me a name as it seemed to be trying to say something. It said, "Looking Into the Fire." So I've been sitting here trying to figure it out. Maybe I'd better listen some more. . . . Now the stream says, "Vision, vision, vision. . . ."

Companion of the Wind, Fire Stick, Gift Bearer, Listens With the Heart, Sister Ruth, Creosote, Looking Into the Fire, Solo, and Mark reach out to you who read this book. They have allowed you into the heart of their faith and despair. They are trying to Give-away. What they, and we, are trying to say is that we have experienced an ancient way of knowing, that we have endured, that we have listened to the silence, and that our loneliness makes us want to give.

Each of us, in our separate ways, faced an experience that was undeniably real. The events of the vision quest did happen. We watched the sun rise and set. We heaped stones. We found a place to exist, a place that knew us. The earth gave us signs, spoke to us with wisdom we could never quite fathom.

We were miserable, ecstatic, bored, anxious, afraid, brave, at peace. We believed in ourselves, found myths for ourselves. We doubted ourselves. We pitied ourselves, respected ourselves. We looked within and began to see. We saw ourselves within the cosmic scheme. Sometimes we felt insignificant. Sometimes we felt the universe within us. Sometimes we remembered death. Sometimes we sought to be reborn.

We climbed mountains and hugged trees. We sat in the sun and thought no thoughts. We tried to sleep, to still our racing minds, only to fall into dreams of ancient times. We poked our noses into holes and caves, unraveled the mystery of canyons and alluvial fans. Animals came to us and spoke. Wildflowers pushed up through the dry wash of our eyes. In the shriveled, thirsty deserts we found springs.

Each in his or her own way learned how to endure loneliness, isolation, deprivation, fear, and the silence. Each of us learned a secret something, a way to hold out through the darkness and the cold and the hunger of life. Each performed his or her own solitary ritual to prepare for, and to accept, the oncoming night. Some experienced "visions." Others did not. Regardless, we waited for the path to stand clear.

And then we were together again. We want to emphasize that because we were alone and starving we began to learn something about how to love. We are trying to say that it is not easy to love if you do not have the opportunity to be alone, cut off in the silence with your own cries ringing in your ears.

We returned to civilization, to routines, crises, schools, work, families, the clang and clutter of our suburban lives. Under the onslaught of the clock, we have all lost much of the memory of those vivid moments we spent alone with our creaking bones as the wind swept through our roofless, wall-less mansions of solitude. But what we remember is sacred beyond the telling. It was given to us by our Great Mother and will be ours until she takes us back into herself. What we will become is her secret. For now, she has given us back to life so that we can Giveaway. That is her part of the exchange, the gift of life.

And what is our gift to her, other than our bodies? What is our part in the sacred exchange? Are we worth nothing? Surely not. We make the earth fruitful with our consciousness.

> So conscious of the play, the battles of the sun and wind. The sun's eternal pounding, warm and soothing, bringing death and life. The wind, sensual as it curves and flickers, sweeping down to mingle in the brittle dryness of this stone and the sturdy elasticity of the desert shrubs. My body changes in the desert dance of the elements. I become brown and lean. Then my weakness overwhelms me and I am ash in the sun's path. The earth will retrieve

me. I become mulch craved for a single creosote. We are born wet, fresh, and die bones.

I feel that nothing can blow away but the core of me. Nothing can be lost but my life. I feel solid and smooth and precariously balanced. A speck of polen in the wind.

—Lonely Heart Outreaching

BOOK 5

THE MYTH

*To this mountain you shall go in a certain night
(when it comes) most long and most dark, and see
that you prepare yourselves by prayer. Insist upon
the way that leads to the mountain, but ask not of
any man where the way lies: Only follow your
Guide, who shall offer himself to you, and will
meet you in the way. . . . This Guide will bring
you to the mountain at midnight, when all things
are silent and dark. It is necessary that you arm
yourselves with a resolute heroic courage, lest you
fear those things that will happen, and so fall
back. . . .*
> —*Eugenius Philalethes,* Lumen de
> Lumine, *1651*

The vision quest takes life, concentrates it into a brief/eternal span
of symbolic/real time, composes a story with a real/symbolic
meaning whose mortal/immortal protagonist (you) undergoes a
trial or ordeal in a bounded/limitless environment where ordinary/
nonordinary exist simultaneously. The story is both the stuff of
action (rite) and the stuff of contemplation (myth). As the protagonist moves through the plot of the story, he finds himself in a
"double-meaninged" universe. An animal is both animal and spirit.
A mountain is both a mountain and a quest. A star is both a star
and an angel. A direction walked is both a trail and the Way. A

dream is both a dream and a divine visitation. A mosquito is both a mosquito and a messenger.

The story is always different, depending on the life that is telling it. But no matter how the episodes differ, there is a basic, underlying similarity among them, a kind of archetypal plot or dynamic. This dynamic energizes countless heroic myths, ancient and modern, and stands at the head of Christianity, Buddhism, Islam, and many other religions. Joseph Campbell (1970) identifies it as the "mono-myth."

The mono-myth itself is a kind of story: And then the hero left everything behind and went alone to a sacred place on the body of the Great Mother. There the hero was tried by the monsters of his life (or karma) and visited by a spirit guide, an angel, God, the Great Spirit. Through a long, dark night of the soul, the seeker was rewarded with wisdom, strength, and understanding. He was revived, reborn, inner eyes were opened, a vision was granted. But the main condition of the gift received was that the protagonist had to return to the mortal world with the vision of healing or regeneration.

Such is the basic mythical foundation of the vision quest. Likewise, the modern hero leaves everything behind and goes off to a wild place on Mother Earth. There he is tried through a long, hard time, seeking a glimpse of the visionary treasure. He returns with gifts to give away, seeds to sow.

In this correspondence between mono-myth and vision quest lies the essence of the therapeutic formula that underlies all passage rites: "As in the rite of passage, so in life." The mono-myth is not only the basic myth of the vision quest; it is also the basic myth of life. The vision quest merely provides the chance for modern individuals (heroes and heroines) to live this basic plot in a formal ceremony and setting, matching their sense of who they are against the archetypal motifs of the mono-myth.

> It occurred to me as I awoke and crept out of the warmth of my sleeping bag that all of life is like a vision quest solo. That is why I have always held to the secret knowledge of the beauty and desirability of death—why I yearn, now that my task is nearing completion, for the end of it and the return Home, to comfort and peace. We came into

this life as we went out on vision quest—not to have fun or be happy. We even anticipated dangers, discomforts, challenges, unpleasant sensations. Yet we came for the vision and to learn, to grow, to change, to evolve. Surely, there are joys in life and there are moments of insight and delight in the desert we have chosen for our quest; but the experience here is only embroidered with joys; the basic material on which the delightful designs are worked is Trial that borders on sheer survival. So it is with a life.

I will be glad to return to camp and have something to eat after my fast. I will be glad to return home to take a bath, get the grime out of my hair. So it is with death. The return Home. To rest. Then to use what we have learned in this life for the purposes beyond our present imagination at levels of consciousness we can only dream of. Thus to die well so that the maximum learning can be taken Home to our people.

—Gift Bearer, 59

It has often been said that our modern world lacks mythical meaning, that people no longer see themselves as heroes and heroines. Certainly there are reasons why people might feel powerless or incapable of influencing the directions of their lives. But how many of us have been infected by the rabies of cynicism? If you take an ordinary citizen of the modern world and plunk him or her down, alone and without food, in the middle of a vast desert, the heroic is often there, with hardly a need to scratch beneath the surface.

The Latin word *mythos* (from which we obtain the word *myth*) is derived from the Greek term *muthos* or "ethos of the mouth." As we read the journal accounts of those who fast for a vision, we observe people engaged in the making of myth. They are formulating a language that is their own unique expression of the urge to be. As this urge is ultimately inexpressible, myth is the only tool by which it can be measured.

I'm hungry. I'm bored. I'm lonely. But oh, this desert-stark, lunar landscape that goes straight to the soul! A place so aboriginal that the only way to respond to it is to recognize it as oneself. Its hugeness too, especially from up here, is literally beyond the point of measurement. It's so big that it becomes the size of me. Or maybe bigness like that is incomprehensible unless you turn it on yourself where there is space enough for anything.

—Martha, 27

The myth of Self is big enough to contain the universe. This myth, finally, is the only way by which an individual can meaningfully understand his or her relationship to the world.

The following accounts are to be read as modern variations on the ancient mono-mythic theme. Some of the accounts are written in the first person; others are written in the third person. All are illustrative of the way in which people of the contemporary world are able to render their world spiritually significant, through their actions, their *muthos,* via their archetypal participation in the vision quest. All are illustrative of the need in modern culture to involve people in forms of behavior that catalyze the full potential of the collective *muthos* within them. Only then can we altogether transform ourselves and our environment.

You Must Leave
Everything Behind

> *Little lamb, who made thee?*
> *Dost thou know who made thee?*
> —*William Blake, "Songs of Innocence"*

Having ventured forth across the threshold of birth, the child is cut from the mother. This necessary physical act of severing the umbilical cord, of separating the child from the oneness that was before, is merely the first step toward preparing the hero for the time when he or she must again be severed from the mother world. This mother world, from which the hero must be severed for a second time, is, or is like, the peacefulness and security of childhood. It is attached to the protagonist through a variety of umbilicals or life-support systems. The heroic journey of the life quester does not begin until the individual is strong enough and ready to cut the umbilicals voluntarily.

The mother herself plays a leading role in preparing her child for the heroic journey. This role is complex and demanding, and requires that the mother love the child, knowing that the child must leave her. The mother must also trust the inherent destiny of the child, for ultimately that trust will be tested by the reality of separation.

In a variant of the mono-myth, the mother is killed by her offspring, so that the heroic journey may begin. That is to say, the maternal ties that bind the hero to the mortal world are removed. The hero must stand alone at the threshold of birth. This birth is like a death and is, in fact, a symbolic enactment of the ultimate act of physical death.

From this paradox of symbolic birth and death comes the following account. My wife, vision questing with our nursing, eight-month-old daughter, describes the nature of the maternal influence and the richness of its impartation. The child, Selene, became sick with the croup. The weather turned bad. Mother and sick child lived for three days together in the eastern Inyos, far from the support systems of civilization, in an archetypal relationship that recalls the experiences of mothers throughout human history. Within the account of this experience are found the seeds of the child's eventual severance from the mother and the mother world, perhaps most clearly expressed in the mother's wish that Selene, for the moment, did not exist, and in her trust that our child was strong enough to survive the crisis.

There are two archetypal tales of severance contained in this account. One is told by the mother, who, like the Great Mother, nurtures, teaches, and protects her young, living to enrich and strengthen them to survive the ordeal of life. The other story is told by Selene, who, having been born, must now begin to prepare for eventual separation from the mother and for the heroic journey.

MEREDITH AND SELENE

JANUARY 8. EVENING

The hills are quiet, eternal rock. The sun slowly laps across the valley, flaming pale orange on the hills. And only this vastness calls comfort, striated in color. The peeling dust of the mountains erodes my feet; the taste is dry. All I want is for Selene to sleep, and for me to have time to think. I want the night to pass.

I'm scared that she'll wake up choking. Right now I wish there were no such being as Selene, that I never knew the slightest taste of the devastating love she has awakened in me. I wish it were Steven and I, no third, no worry but ourselves, no tentative breathing that even now cracks as she breathes. But there she lies, asleep, beside the fire.

I'm restless, can't possibly imagine sleeping. I look to the mountains and they are too stern, too eternal . . . never having felt the split of heart over a small child who is sick.

Oh Steven, I long for you. Pray god that she sleeps the night through.

Great Spirit, have mercy on me, For I am alone and ache for my child.

January 9. Morning

Because I had imagined a long, hard night, each breath she drew seemed strained, hinted in rasps next to my ear, and my adrenaline shot sharp flashes through my body, rotting my stomach, banishing the tiredness. But slowly the tiredness soothed my fears, her breathing calmed, and I slept, knowing I'd all too thoroughly thought of the worst possibilities and considered what I would do in each case. Throughout the night we shifted in the dark, pressed tight, and though her ragged breathing grew worse, it never reached choking, but only became a hoarseness that calmed at my quiet words to her. My milk flowed, no doubt from maternal urgency.

The sun rose splendid. The clouds eternally sweep across the sky. What will today and tonight bring? Was that a whistle far up the canyon?

Are those rain clouds? They seem to be moving to the higher mountains, to be broken into snow. I'll keep the fire stoked, wait, keep Selene quiet, though she's anxious to roam. Her throat rasps at each breath, but she eats well and seems to be as full of smiles as ever. If she'll sleep once more I'll let her loose.

Walked up Paiute Canyon with Selene on my back, drawn toward Steven. It was the only way Selene would sleep, finally. Now she lies in the sleeping bag, coughing every so often, roughly. I feel confident and strong when I walk.

How I love the quiet. I confused the rush of atoms in my ears with the hope of footfalls. Time has no relevance for me today . . . only the watching of signs in Selene, and the threads of sound and movement. . . .

Now we have returned from Willow Creek spring, a mile or so away. On leaving she cried, feeling sick and restless. She had awakened from her nap feeling worse, rasping. She ate a little, drank a little, and wanted to be held quietly a lot. So as she began to cry in the backpack I took her out and held her again for a while, and she fell asleep. I enjoyed the walk, keeping a strong, steady pace

121

and watching the small movements of silence. Bird, sage-brush flicker, dust, sky-clouds, a burro, a willow branch, track shadows on the parched wash. For the first time I *see* how mountains erode. . . .

I see the sun break through the clouds above where others in the group must be. Down here the mountains shade the sun, passing only shafts of light. I miss the group, watching them discover. To be sitting, listening by the fire, with my man at my side.

JANUARY 10. MORNING

Up again before the chill dawn. Selene hacks more than ever, but still she is good-natured. After I bundle her in the sleeping bag, build a fire, and feed her orange pieces for her dry throat, her ragged breath quiets.

Dust, the matting of dust everywhere—in every crack, seam, hair, pore.

The clouds thicken up the canyon. The peaks are shrouded in foggy cloud. More seems on its way. Snow? Perhaps. I'll keep a fire going. Must get more wood. I continue to have a difficult time eating.

My milk is intermittent, like the stream winding its way down Paiute Canyon.

Just went and got two more gallons of water from Willow Spring and collected screwbeans (mesquite). Now drops of rain are falling.

AFTERNOON

Selene is asleep, but restless. Very overcast. My eyes keep wandering to the sky. I walk up to the top of this gulch searching for the direction or intent of the dark clouds. The valley is beautiful. The sun's rays slant down to the salt lake.

I feel at one with all the mothers through the past ages who had no doctors and were exposed to earth's elements. My concerns are trying to keep Selene quiet or sleeping; gathering more wood (we must stay warm); looking up, around, always to the sky, trying to see where the storm moves; feeling my breasts (do I have enough milk?—the only thing that can provide her antibodies now). The weather is deteriorating. I must keep drinking water. So hard to eat. Feel sick at trying—though overall I feel healthy, dirty, dusty, and strong.

Sometimes, maternal preparation for severance is incomplete. The heroic act of setting forth alone and freed from the mother ends prematurely. An individual may match her or his ability against the terms of the mono-myth only to discover that he or she has aimed too high, at least for the time being. The first step often proves to be the most difficult. Failure to take the first step into the threshold of the heroic passage does not indicate a lack of heroism. For many who have been ill-equipped by the maternal world, even spending a few brief hours away from that world is a heroic act.

Lucy, a sixteen-year-old girl, with an overprotective mother who nevertheless was anxious that her child become self-reliant, went with us into the desert to vision quest. There had been some question about Lucy's ability to live alone in the harsh land of cactus and stone. But she was resolved, though a bit naively, to go through with it and had obtained permission also from her doctor, who noted that she was subject to *petit mal* seizures.

Accompanying a group into the mountains east of the Saline Valley, she encountered severe winds and a bleak landscape utterly foreign to her. The night before the morning of the threshold, she exhibited obvious signs of fear. Obviously, her fear was genuine, deeply felt, as only a heroine might feel. The next morning I left her at her place. She said an apprehensive goodbye. For the next three days I would be her buddy. The following is from my journal.

LUCY

Some time during the first night I was awakened. Someone was shining a light in my eyes. Then I realized I was lying on my back and the full moon was in my face. The fire was out. The wind whipped through the ashes. I tried to take a drink from the water bottle. It was frozen. I threw more creosote on the ashes and relit the fire. Everywhere the quicksilver of the moon. For an hour or so I sat by the fire.

The wind sat up with me, passing through the upper air like an invisible horde, scattering the silence into crystals of raw sound, pounding my body into gusts. Day was breaking on the teeth of the wind.

I placed my bottle near the fire, to thaw it out. I wished I had mittens and a warmer coat. It was Good Friday.

I had awakened because I had been dreaming about Lucy. Now a premonition that all was not well permeated my cold, cramped world.

Reluctantly I said good bye to the tiny solace of my fire and its cave of attention. I bundled up and went into the kingdom of the wind, looking for a girl named Lucy.

Half an hour later I found her pack. Its contents were scattered and blown in the wind. Kleenex and clothing plastered the mesquite. I picked up a comic book that was caught on a claw of desert holly: *Horror Comics.*

For a long time I just stood there, looking into the maze of the mountains. I called her name into the wind. There was no answer.

Up the wash was a tiny hot water spring that had been used for thousands of years by people migrating west into the Inyo Mountains, looking for rabbits and pinyon nuts. Before crossing the great valley to the upper slopes of the mountains, they had lingered here.

As the girl had expressed fears about being alone for seventy-two hours, we agreed that she would keep her vigil here, near the spring, where I would stop by each day. I said the spring was a friendly place, that many people had camped here with gratitude and happiness. She seemed to accept the positive side.

But something had obviously gone wrong. For some reason she had left this place of security. I wondered if I should contact the others and organize a search party or if I should continue on my own for a while. I decided to look for her, reasoning that if I increased my altitude I might see her.

Imagine a human being as seen from the unblinking yellow eyes of a raven riding motionlessly on the wind. From a thousand feet high there is not much to be seen. A dark speck changes direction, climbs out of a canyon, and takes to the ridge. From this height the motions of the speck seem aimless, random. There is no emotion, only pure motion: distance covered and time taken to cover it. From the raven's point of view, hanging on its invisible strings of air, nothing is amiss, except that now there are two specks, one that is moving and one that it has been watching for some time and might have a hankering to eat after a while.

The moving speck winds along a south-tending ridge. It stops and looks down. It sees her, somewhat below and to the west. It was a long time before she was able to recognize my presence. When finally she calmed, she said she wanted to go home to her mother. The raven circled above the two human forms crouched in their world of fear and love.

Lucy had listened too intently to the night wind and had heard the voices of dead Indian souls who hovered around the spring. And then she saw them, fierce, proud, alien people, and she cried for her mother to help her but her mother was 500 miles away. Panicked, she went into the night in search of her buddy. Failing to find him, she succumbed to terror as the sun rose.

The wind howled out of the north, like death, ever present, colder than the gaunt, black bird that hung upon it. And the Earth turned on her axis and the sun dawned in a cloudless desert sky. On the cold, red-rock deserts of Mars the thin wind seethed, and the sun, a small, dully glowing ball, drifted across the whistling sky. In the ammonia-methane wastes of Jupiter the wind congealed into the ultramarine clouds of liquid, poisonous atmosphere, as the sun, a large star, drifted across the skies of purple and yellow. On the frozen inertness of Pluto the wind did not blow and the sun did not shine and the heavens were eternal night.

And into the wind Lucy cried, "I want my mother." The wind muttered and moaned at the gravel beneath her feet. Lucy called again, "I want my mother!" and again the wind replied, only this time its language could be understood. The wind said, "Here I am."

You Must Go to a Natural Place That Is Sacred and Apart

The eyes of fire, the nostrils of air, the mouth of water, the beard of earth.
—*William Blake,* Proverbs of Hell

The hero severs the ties to the maternal world and steps alone across the threshold into the sacred world of Nature. In this world, the wind and the stars, the stones and weeds, the sun and waters are symbols of regeneration. In this world the terms of life and death are clearly defined: The Great Mother gives and the Great Mother takes away. Hers is the testing ground, the arena, upon which the quest is staged. Symbolically, the wilderness is a grave, or a womb, wherein the hero dies and is reborn.

In this sacred place there is a mutual exchange between the body and the environment, occasioned by the solitude and emptiness of fasting. The object of hunger, the food desired, is the body of the Great Mother herself, which is given sacramentally. Those things desired by the Great Mother and given by the quester are flesh, urine, dung, spit, sweat, semen, secretions, breath, and words. This stuff given to Nature is the same stuff that, in archaic myth, God infuses with divine life.

In the following account, a young man from California, with no formal training in the self-generation of ritual, celebrates his union with the Mother Earth. Her stuff is arranged by his consciousness into a meaningful, dynamic configuration of death and rebirth. The location is *La Bahia de la Concepción,* Baja California Sur.

BROKEN HEART LAUGHING

> After waking and preparing this morning, I was given a sign: A prairie falcon flew south along the water and dove in that direction. It was the way I had decided to go last

night. On the shore I lifted up a piece of driftwood. Underneath was a mouse who told me this was the land of innocence and understanding. A butterfly said: Walk lightly, not heavily.

I sang prayers of thanks as I walked along. When I came to a large tree by the edge of the road I stopped, sat down, and put my hands over my eyes and stared into the darkness. Soon a red light appeared, then it took on more shape and seemed like a heart artery. The shape was round and had little threads on it. The middle would change shapes and colors. Then it changed to bright blue and white and changed shapes, growing large, then shrinking. In the core I seemed to see shapes of the desert, big cardone cactus, and the mountains. Suddenly I heard a noise that sounded like a car coming down the road. I opened my eyes quickly and still saw the blue-white light. It was so strong that the cactus and the road surrounding me were hard to see. I walked down the road staring at the ground and the white light which veiled its detail. After a minute the light disappeared and things returned to normal. . . .

Found the right spot for the circle. A butterfly showed me where to build it so I started building it four stones at a time—to represent the four corners of the Earth. The circle is almost completed. I only left a space through which to enter it. I think I will also put sand on the bottom of it. One thing I didn't notice until it was almost done was that it is right next to a red ant hill. A voice told me it would be O.K. anyway. I imagined the circle being my womb and tomb.

A butterfly told me I already have much of the power I ask the Great Spirit for. Raven said so, too, when I thought of it again. What I really seek is understanding. . . .

Walked into the circle through the opening I had left for that purpose. Placed my sleeping bag and pad in the middle and went through everything in the bag and my possessions to make sure everything needed was there. It was.

Next, the five remaining stones needed to close the circle came out of the bag and took their positions. The circle was complete. Prayers and songs symbolizing this completion came forth.

Next, the four directions represented by a black lava rock (west), a white oyster shell (north), a yellow clam shell (east), and a red rock (south) were positioned. I sang to each of the directions as they appeared within the circle.

A sacred herb found a resting spot on each of the directions, and I asked it for its healing power so that my people may live. Then I sang a prayer to the One who is all the directions for strength and wisdom and understanding that my people may live. I cried loud and long, then sat down and wrote a little.

Soon, it seemed right to put my pen down and watch the last brightness of the day be engulfed by the night. I sang more and prayed more. Loud was my cry in the desert wilderness. For three days I had lived in it alone, spending most of my time under a bush home, and now, enclosed by a universal circle, it was culminating.

I listened to the voices of the night and the rustling of creatures close by. Thoughts of loved ones, work, and destiny filled my head.

Later, the night found me upon my back. It was time for lamentation. Personal and world events doused in sorrow and pain welled up from my stomach. Each one was released by a mournful cry toward the starry heavens. Cries arose from my plexus and were uttered forth with a loud wail. This continued for about one-half hour. Then I was finished and felt the surging power of life pulse within my middle.

The stars moved above me. Coyotes sang to me and reminded me to stay awake. Flute pranced out of its green house and was offered as a gift to the great one. Many of the notes reverberated in secret places inside of me. A few birds added their own melodies to the gift song. Cardone cactus stood still and tall on the perimeters of my circle, silhouetted by the starry sky.

The vigil was growing longer. I stared at the seal skull and thought of my body's eventual death. Will the part of me that cries and listens also die? Or does it remain a conscious pulse in the universal life? Only death holds the answer to these questions for me. But in the night I imagined the seal skull disintegrating and becoming soil for new life. And the green seed pod—it must turn brown and die before the life within it can spring forth.

More singing of prayers; one asking for strength to heal, another for understanding. The night, by this point, seems endless. Star companions moved all the way from the eastern horizon toward the western one, then they turned and traveled north. I long for the sunrise and search the east for the slightest sign. The blue-black sky framing the red eastern mountains has turned half a shade lighter. I wonder if it is just the moon. But the shade stays and not even a sliver of moon appears. The light-dark spot grows larger; it seems certain now that it is the sun. I make prayer and song to it as the giver of life to all living things. Behold, the warmer of the earth!

The light shade grows lighter and creeps further along the eastern horizon, both to the north and to the south. Rising to my feet I absorb it. I feel wide awake and very alive. My heart pounds in my chest, soft muscle sends hot blood coursing through my veins. Orion fades as the red sky races north and south over the mountains, then jumps over my head and caresses the western range beyond the bay. Many birds have joined my salutation. I see them dart through the brush on their first flight of the day.

All my gear is placed outside the circle. I shed my cotton skin and stand in the circle which represents both my womb and tomb. Skull and seed pod are nestled at my feet.

The eastern peaks glow red and soon the sun warms my chilled body. Loudly I sing my last prayers for strength, understanding, and peace. I feel as if I already have many of the gifts I ask for. The day has come. The earth has once again been reborn in the greenness of life.

Skull points east from the center of the circle. I form

a cross in the sand stretching to the four directions. Seed pod clutched in hand I am ready to go. The boundary is crossed.

Seed pod finds a new home in the bank of the wash and is encouraged with voice to continue. I sing to the mountains and my fellow questers as I travel north across the salt flat toward base camp. A joyous vision appears at the edge of the salt flat: My buddy Anthony is walking toward me. My heart soars, and soon we embrace. We leave our rock pile standing and walk toward camp together.

In the threshold place of the vision quest, symbolic death and rebirth take the form of actual entry into the body of the Great Mother, being reborn through a kind of regenerative incest with the things of the earth. Shorn of the past, the hero descends into the abyss, into the sea, the pit, the belly of the whale, the dark cave, seeking the spark of identity, regeneration, and vision.

Wandering in a wash at the foot of the Dry Mountains, a vision faster found a natural equivalent to the heroic passageway in the body of the Mother Earth. Entering, he reenacted the mythical womb death and came forth with new insight.

ROCK

Last night while exploring just before dark I discovered a power hole, where I am sitting right now. The power hole is a natural hole in the top of a rather hard, volcanic-like, glass rock. The hole drops straight down about four and a half feet. The opening is egg-shaped and just large enough for a person's shoulders to slip through. I am now sitting in and absorbing the power generated by this hole. . . . There is a faint trickle of water that I use as a mantra. Of course it is completely dry in here, so there must be an underground stream within ten feet of the inner walls.

The walls of this small and magical place are ornate and detailed. There are thousands of small holes and caverns that form patterns of color and texture, each one with a history and story of its own. It's interesting to think how these little holes took hundreds of years in their development and yet find themselves all collected together in the same place at the same time—like people surprised to find themselves alive in the same era as their friends and lovers.

Had I been hiking around trying to reach some destination on the horizon I would never have bothered to spend several hours in this damn hole. I shall return tomorrow for more of the hole's wisdom. . . .

I must create my own myth with me as the center. Whenever I notice myself giving people the right to judge me or watching myself through their eyes, I must tell myself that I need to depend on only me to derive security. The more I seek the approval of others, the less secure I will ultimately be. I see myself as a beautiful rock in the desert among thousands of other rocks. While the actions of certain rocks will affect the position of nearby rocks, no one rock is seeking the approval or guidance of any other. Rocks don't really need other rocks. It just happens that they usually are together, like in this wash.

My mission is to be me and to attain this by exerting as much effort and worry about who I am as these rocks do. My myth is a rock. All the rocks around me are as beautiful as I am. How could a rock ever wonder if he is a rock? Well, I asked all the rocks around the creosote tree how they got so confident.

"Rocks, how come you're so confident?"

"Because I'm a rock, just a beautiful rock."

"Rocks, tell me what it is all about, please."

"Because I'm a rock, just a beautiful rock."

"Rocks, how come you don't fight and quarrel and try to impress each other?"

"Because I'm a rock, just a beautiful rock."

"Rocks, you must make love a lot because there are so many of you."

"Because I'm a rock, just a beautiful rock."

"Rocks, I want to be a rock too."

"You are a rock, just a beautiful rock."

The sun is long gone and I am keeping watch over the fire. Yes I am hungry, but not very. I will tend the fire as long as my eyes stay open.

I've taken LSD.

I've taken EST.

I've taken Mind Dynamics.

I've tried Jesus Christ.

I've read Perls, Rogers, Jung, Maharishi, Meher Baba.

I've driven fast.

I've been to bed with beautiful women.

I've come close to death.

I've been in jail.

I've been stoned years at a time.

I've met criminals, millionaires, geniuses, musicians.

I've been loved and I've loved.

I've traveled a little.

I've had quasi-mystical experiences and fantastic psychological insights.

I've been a hero.

I've been a bum.

And none of these things has ever changed me drastically.

And all of these things have changed me a little.

I am a rock.

I don't need to change.

I only need to experience whatever comes up.

The search is over.

I AM, and I'll probably forget that I AM.

But I know now that seeking change is the best way to avoid being beautiful.

I AM.

I AM a rock, just a beautiful rock.

Here You Must Be Tried.
You Must Face the Dragon.

Tyger! Tyger! burning bright
In the forests of the night,
What immortal hand or eye
Could frame thy fearful symmetry?
　　　　　—William Blake, "Songs of Experience"

The heroic passage is a road of trials. Separated, alone, given over to the Great Mother, the hero enters the fearful darkness and confronts the naked self, the apparitions and shadows of the mortal state of being. Here the solitary battles against the inevitable monsters must be fought.

The hero does not court fear; but fear must be faced. The treasure of the quest cannot be found without enduring the despair of ever finding it. The trials of the heroic passage exist because strength and courage exist, but these traits are found only in combination with vulnerability and fear.

In the following account a young woman, alone in the vicinity of Starvation Canyon, Death Valley, succumbs to fear, only to encounter an even more fearful situation brought about by her own decision to retreat. Her response is heroic in the mythical sense and demonstrates that the ability to be heroic has not been lost.

TRISHA

The plan was that after we found and established our power places, we'd meet back at the stone pile and from there we would all go to everyone's spot to get a good idea of where they were. As it turned out, we were damned lucky to be so efficient in our plans.

When I first found my place, before returning to the stone pile, I was filled with apprehension and wondered what the hell I was doing in the middle of the desert by myself. I was so upset I actually started crying. Bill, who was on his way back down to the stone pile, found me, and I told him my fears. He was so nice, he offered me the choice of going to his camp with him. I told him no, because I didn't want to ruin his vision quest. Then he suggested that I try to stay out one night, and he would be in to check on me in the morning. That really made me feel better and I was determined to give it a try. Then we went back to the stone pile where Laura [a third buddy] was waiting.

After returning from the stone pile and my other buddies' places, I figured I better set up my tarp in order to keep out of the sun. I did and got myself situated underneath the tarp with my journal. I proceeded to spend the whole day there—almost.

As the hours passed I was getting more and more fearful of the thought of spending three days and nights alone. People who aren't in that position can't fully understand what I mean. Even now, trying to recall those feelings is really difficult. I don't feel I can describe them.

Anyway, this big, dark cloud almost covering the whole valley was overhead. The next thing I knew I was involved in the biggest, loudest, longest clap of thunder I've ever heard in my life. That's when I decided I needed to go to base camp. The simple truth (but it's not simple at all) was that I needed people, even one person. There was another clap of thunder and that set me to shaking, trembling.

I packed up as quick as I could, not even stopping to untie the string on the tarp—I cut it with my knife. . . . As I was walking toward Laura's place I remember thinking just an insignificant thought: "Oh, I'll go see how Laura's doing."

When I reached her she was sitting (or trying to sit) near a creosote, on her jacket, without a tarp for shade. It was literally impossible for her to lift her head by herself, and mucus was pouring out of her nose onto her shoulder and it filled her mouth. I tried to calm her, although I was not feeling well. Actually I think seeing her in that state made me grab hold of myself and realize that her safety was my responsibility. I tried real hard to do anything to help her, but everything I suggested to her brought the replies, "In a minute," "This is an emergency, help me sit up," "Help me lift my head," or "I want to lie down."

After talking to her for what seemed like forever, I finally got her to realize that I had to leave to go get help, that we needed help. I promised her I'd be back in fifteen minutes with Bill and that he would help us (she didn't even know who Bill was). . . . By this time I was really feeling ill, while at the same time feeling that I had to run to get Bill. I was afflicted with the dry heaves a couple of times. Finally I started puking water and yellow liquid. I had to lay down twice to clear my head, saying, "Everything is going to be O.K. You're doing fine. No more barfing, O.K.?" I reached my spot and realized that Bill was not too far away. I commenced yelling his name as loud as I could. While I waited for him, I figured out a cry and started saying it over and over again: "Great Spirit, I am in fear for my friend's life and mine. Please help us."

When Bill and I reached Laura she was still incoherent. She asked us where she was and what she was doing here. We answered her, and it seemed she realized what was happening, because she said, "Oh yeah, solo." Bill then left for base camp. He said he would return in about an hour. We waited. It began to get dark, and I started to get worried, even though in the back of my mind I knew that they would find us. I made a fire pit and was on my way to gather wood when I heard voices. I thanked the Great Spirit.

The dragons of the threshold are real. The dragons of life are real too. In the end, the fears are faced alone. The hero recognizes this and, for the sake of future fulfillment, in the name of humanity, endures the dark night. The trials of the vision quest are the everyday trials of life, battles with loneliness, depression, self-doubt, anger. Engagement with such dragons is absolutely necessary if the hero is to attain "Death of the self in a long, tearless night/ All natural shapes blazing unnatural light" (Theodore Roethke, *In a Dark Time*").

But a distinction between symbolic death and real death must be made if the quester is to return alive. In some haunted lives, the distinction blurs. "Death of the self" comes perilously close to real death. Thus the candidate may unconsciously, but somehow deliberately, become irretrievably lost, dare a slope that is too dangerous to negotiate, refuse to drink water, or otherwise court death. In the following description of Eric's vision quest ideations of suicide almost prevail. This man had to brush up close to death before he was ready to allow himself to be helped.

ERIC

Eric was raised in a Nazi family. He was twelve years old and a member of Hitler's Youth Corps when World War II ended. Like many young Germans of that generation, he suffered pangs of guilt over his former Nazi affiliations. An idealistic adolescent, he turned to religious studies as a life occupation. He became a Presbyterian minister, got married, and had three children.

By the time we met him he was a gray-haired, tall, distinguished-looking man of fifty-five with a haunted look in his eyes. He came to us because he was "stuck in the birthing passage." As he characterized his plight: "I think I am in a very dark place. Wherever I look I see dying and death—the trees, the mountains, the little animals squashed on the road. I think the Earth is coming to an end."

Five years before, he had resigned from the ministry and had joined the Green Party, wanting to become more actively involved in the politics of ecology. He worked hard for the Greens, as an activist and protester. He moved his home from place to place, depending on party needs, and became a stranger to his wife and family. Despite his unswerving dedication to the cause, he began to doubt his effectiveness. As he put it, "I never did enough."

Gradually, his life began to fall apart. His oldest daughter began to behave differently, assuming a punk style and falling in love with a man twice her age. His only son began experimenting with drugs and a fast life. One traumatic day the son confronted his father with

136

hard, emotional evidence of neglect, coldness, and lack of love. He had since been unable to reconcile himself to his son. His wife, patient and long-suffering, became stronger in his absence. This threatened him. Their love life faltered.

In his extremity, Eric quit the Greens and embarked on a journey of self-discovery. He went to a "birthing clinic" near Munich where he sought to deal with his fears of personal unfulfillment and inability to feel or express love. Insights gained at the clinic did not heal him. They merely peeled off the first layer of the onion. He went into a deeper depression regarding the future direction of his life. Though he could clearly see many ways in which his life had been a failure ("Everything I have done wrong!"), he could not see how to alleviate his guilt.

Alone, unfeeling, he flew to San Francisco, where, under the expert guidance of Ralph Metzner, he began a regimen with empathenogenic drugs. The therapist took a good look at Eric's condition and told him to call us.

From the moment of his arrival, Eric openly discussed the possibility of committing suicide. He entertained the notion he could plunge a knife into his belly and twist it—in the *hara-kiri* tradition. At first we thought it was histrionics. But his ideations persisted. We decided to "buddy" him from base camp during the four days and nights he would be alone and fasting.

When his preparations were complete, Eric and four others crossed the threshold and went alone into the Last Chance Mountains. It was early October, but the temperature was in the nineties. The fall sun roared unshielded through the barren canyons. A forecast storm brought nothing but wispy clouds and hot southern winds. The next four days would not be a piece of cake, especially for Eric, who was not accustomed to desiccating heat.

On the second day, he left a note at the stone pile, with directions on how to get to his new place of power. Apparently, he had decided to move his place up the canyon from where he had originally established it. Although the map was unclear, it seemed to indicate that Eric had experienced some difficulty finding a home. Part of the note ran:

Me: not so well.
   I live with the karma of my place being a long way off.

Last night and now: temperature and headache because of too much sun-heat yesterday. WEAK.

Bad dream. But I take care of myself (shadows).

Need your *spiritual* help.

We replied with our own note:

The best spiritual help we can give is to tell you to monitor your own health. Stay out of the sun. Drink plenty of water. Return to base camp if your fever gets worse.

The fourth morning, Meredith went up to the stone pile to check on him. He had left another note the previous afternoon:

Fever still present (last night more) but I can deal with it. Has its function in life just now.

I'll go to base camp if it gets much worse (for a few hours of *good* sleep!).

Please honor my wish and will:

I decided *not to come down to the stone pile anymore.* The way back is *too* long, *too* hot, and *too* hard in my present weakness and it brings *stress* to me because I need so much time for it.

Please agree! Give to me the permission by spirit! I need a longer *uninterrupted* time in silence!

Thanks only for care of emergency if I'm not in base camp the morning we come in.

His note did not allay Meredith's fears about his condition. She decided to contact him briefly, for safety's sake. Was he calling for help? His words were filled with dark clues she knew well from her Suicide Prevention days.

With the aid of Eric's map, she started up the canyon toward his new place. Deeper into the mountains his bootprints led her. An hour later, walking at a good clip, she still had not reached him. By then the canyon had narrowed into sheer cliffs and precipitous falls. She halted at the foot of an almost impassable dry waterfall. Why had he gone this far in search of a place of power? She had seen scores of ideal places on her way up the canyon. What was going on in Eric's mind?

Carefully, she inched her way up the water-slick, quartzite fall. Above, his footprints continued. She followed them for a half hour more. Finally, she rounded a corner and there he was, sitting beneath his tarp, in the midst of a great jumble of boulders. He was looking her way. He must have heard her coming.

He jumped up in apologetic consternation. "No! Why do you come?" he exclaimed. "I do not want you to come this far!"

"I decided I had better see how you were," answered Meredith, irked at his attempt to make himself inaccessible.

Profoundly sorry for inconveniencing her, he invited her under his tarp. "Maybe just as well," he muttered. "I need to talk."

She felt his forehead. Dry and feverish. "Have you been drinking your water?"

"Not much water. I do not like the taste." He had drunk less than two quarts a day. He was obviously dehydrated. Gray stubble accentuated the palor of his sunken cheeks. His blue eyes were rimmed with red.

At first, he talked about his failed attempts to burn certain ceremonial objects in a sacred fire. He was feeling guilty because they had not burned. He was also feeling guilty because he had tried to burn them in the first place. Obviously, he had worked himself into a snit over the subject of "how I do bad things to myself."

But there were more layers on the onion. Head buried in his hands, he admitted that he was very depressed because he could not feel emotion. He had attempted a "death lodge" ceremony (see Book 3) but nobody had come to say good-bye. "No one cares— and I do not care either. Not even the gods care. I have no gods!"

"Don't you have friends who care?"

"No. Not anymore do they care."

It became clear why Eric had chosen such an inaccessible power place. Because nobody cared, he would put himself beyond the reach of help.

"What about your children? They need you, Eric."

Long pause. "No they do not need me." Suddenly, he began to sob, silently, painfully.

"I am like an insect encased in stone, a fossil. Walls all around me. I cannot break out. I am dead. I have no feeling."

"Eric, do you want to live or die?"

Another long pause, punctuated by small, choked sobs. "I do not know," he finally answered quietly.

After he had cried for a while he began to talk about an incident that had occurred between himself and another member of the group, a young man named Jimmy, who had accused him of being insensitive and unfeeling.

"Were you angry with Jimmy?"

"Yes. I was *very* angry."

"*How* angry?"

Naturally, spontaneously, Eric began to express his anger. He clenched his fists and jaw and talked about the things and people that angered him, including himself. Recklessly, he was going to express his anger regardless of the usual consequences of guilt.

At that point, Meredith broke in to ask if he would like to move his place further down the canyon, closer to base camp, as a sign that he was willing to put himself within the reach of care. "Yes, dammit!" he thundered, not done with his anger. He sprang up and started to throw his stuff into his pack with hasty, violent motions. He scattered the stones anchoring his tarp. He kicked the slabs ringing his firepit, flinging them indiscriminately against the cliffs. He picked up his cup, blackened by the fire, and hurled it at a boulder. It clanged in protest. He brandished an object perched carefully beside the firepit. It was his suicide knife—a long, thin, sharp-edged shard of quartzite. He smashed the thing in two against his knee, savagely dug a hole with bleeding fingers, and buried the two halves, swearing all the while in German. "There!" he said. "You did not work either!"

Awed at the great violence in him, Meredith could only stand aside and wait until the anger ran its course. It was incoherent rage that lay beneath the onion peels. And it was rage that was stirring the fossil to life. The insect was shuddering its wings. The walls were beginning to crack. Guilt, pride, self-pity, defenses—they all gave way to the flash flood of his anger. It tore at the canyon walls and roared down the dry wash with the power of a baby being born. Now the anger that he had turned in on himself was flowing outward from him, out into the vast silence of the desert.

When his rage had run its course, he shouldered his pack and together they hiked out of his black hole of despair. It had served its purpose. He had buried his knife in the tear-stained dirt. As he walked back down the canyon, his steps shaky but lively, his talk turned outward toward the beauty of the unnamed canyon he had chosen as his "dying place."

He seemed to want Meredith to find his new place for him. She refused. "It's up to you, Eric," she told him. "You find the new place that symbolizes your willingness to ask for help."

He chose a shady cliff face at the mouth of the canyon, a graceful place that opened to a panoramic view of the Eureka Valley. It was less than a mile to base camp. He insisted that he be allowed to remain there for the rest of his threshold time, claiming that his fever had subsided. In fact, he did look better.

Meredith left him there with a gallon of water and a small wooden flute he had asked for. As she hiked back over the ridge to base camp, she stopped for a moment to look down at his place. Faint, sweet flute notes drifted up from the tiny, dark form sitting in the soft sand of the wash.

In all little deaths the ultimate death is reflected. Above all, the hero respects this ultimate death and so lives with reverence and tenacity in the company of dragons who symbolize this death. Those who endure are not necessarily the strongest or the best prepared. Those who endure will be those who have learned to live with their weakness. Thus the hero allows himself or herself to *be*, to be weak, to be strong, and to face the dragons whose mother is death.

The story of Liz illustrates the kind of monsters that the heroes of the vision quest must often face. They are alone, without help, too proud to retreat, in despair of going on. The situation is one for which their secure childhood never prepared them. What is it that makes the hero continue, in the cold, without a fire, to the warmth of a new day? What follows is from my journal.

LIZ

Liz said she knew how to start a fire. "With wet wood?" I asked. "No, show me." So I showed her how to use the inside bark of sagebrush and peelings from juniper. "O.K.," she said, "now I know."

Then she went off on a vision quest for four nights and three days. The first day the skies became dark, and the air turned cold.

141

It began to snow. The flurries thickened into a blizzard, cutting visibility to six feet.

Overwhelmed by the change, she nevertheless managed to set up her shelter and to get inside her sleeping bag, where she dozed through the oncoming night.

By morning the snow had abated somewhat, but everything was cloaked in white unfamiliarity. She could not make out her surroundings. She thought briefly about building a fire, but discovered she had thoughtlessly left half of her pack where the snow could get to it. Her matches were soaked. She was alone without heat for three days and nights in the wilderness of the headwaters of the Reese River, Nevada.

What did she do? She wept. She wept until the little valley echoed with the lost and lonely sound of her birdlike sobbing. I heard everything from my perch across the meadow where I had set up my shelter. Oh, it was cold. So cold that the sting of my fire could not dispel its embrace.

She wept intermittently for a day and a night. The next day she moved around a little. The weather improved. Snow turned to rain. Rain turned into partly cloudy spring skies. She managed finally to get her fire started, though it was mostly smoke.

Others had experienced difficulties, too. Ted, a young man from Novato, had fallen into the river upstream. Soaked to the bone, he walked several miles through the snow to get to the van, which he broke into, living there in misery for the remaining while.

Times were hard. We clung to our loneliness like bugs to an icy stone, insignificant, at the whim of the weather, which might squash us at any moment. Panic and loneliness rushed into our throats. But in the heart of the deepest pang, flowers pushed up through the snow and opened their petals to the freezing wind.

When the three days and nights were over, Liz came out, with five others who had persevered. She was not the same person. Her fingers were scarred and dirty. Her face was smeared with soot; stains of woodsmoke tears rimmed her eyes, which stared at me like two agates.

"How was it?" I asked.

She wiped the back of a black hand across her nose and a sly smile appeared. "All right," she said.

You Must Wait for Wisdom, Your Guide.

Ask the blind worm the secrets of the grave, and why her spires
Love to curl around the bones of death; and ask the ravenous snake
Where she gets poison, and the winged eagle why he loves the sun.
And then tell me the thoughts of man, that have been hid of old.
    —*William Blake,* The Visions of the Daughters of
    Albion

The entire body of the Great Mother is clothed in symbols, rhythms, and signs that are like solar collectors of human consciousness. The hero of the vision quest moves among the motions of day and night, wind and silence, water and rock, air and fire, and seeks to gather wisdom from the things he or she has empowered with wisdom. If the hero can but listen, the stones of the earth speak.

To obtain this wisdom, the past must be forgotten, the thought process must be stilled, clocks must stop. The hero must enter the crack between the worlds, the universe that exists between illusion and reality. The hero must be able to stop the internal dialogue in order to be receptive, for the treasure is not found by being distracted or fooled.

The attainment of wisdom, vision, or insight is accomplished by persistence. The transformational teachings of Mother Nature are not won without a committed desire to learn and to apply what is learned. The hero may wait and pray through the threshold with great resoluteness only to wring the smallest amount of comfort from the whirlwind. Yet the smallest insight may lead to the greatest victory after the hero has recrossed the threshold and has reentered the mortal world to do battle with mortal dragons. More often than not, God spoke to the prophets of old in a "still, small voice." Such voices can be easily ignored or go unheard unless the hero perseveres in the desire to hear. The story of Carey illustrates how wisdom patiently won during the vision quest was persistently applied to a successful end.

CAREY

Carey fell in love with a man who was twenty-eight. She was sixteen. Her parents knew nothing about it. She slept with him, loved him, and went to great lengths to be discreet. Meanwhile she attended high school and lived at home with her mother, with whom she felt some empathy, and her father, with whom she felt none.

An intelligent, attractive young woman, Carey tended to keep to herself, growing up just a little faster than her peers. Their incessant preoccupation with fashion and fast cars, their drunken parties and boasting exploits, were of little interest to her. "I'm not attracted to guys my age," she said. She was drawn to the mysterious world of an older man, learning aptly the lessons of a lover's attention.

But after a time the romance began to die. The older man turned out to be selfish and fatuous. He was threatened by her intensity, jealous of her world outside him. He was not able to set her free so that she could freely make a commitment to him. Stubbornly, she resisted his ways of dominating her, of trying to dictate her thinking as her father had done. Gradually she began to see that she had fallen into a cycle of dependence, hoping her lover would fill the void created by the abdication of her father.

She realized that she wanted to tell the older man that it was time to call it off, but she found herself unable to do so. He also had fallen into a cycle of dependence. He told her he loved her. She realized that a part of her loved him and cared about how he felt.

Caught up then in a dilemma that her young, fresh life magnified into despair, she heard about the vision quest. The idea of it began to take hold of her. She would be able to get away from it all, the anxieties of concealment, discretion, stolen love, the gnawing guilt, and live alone for three days and nights in some place where she could think clearly. She would have a chance to ponder the questions of who she was and where she was going, away from the measuring eyes of others.

She called to get information. She called again for more. She was persistent. She needed and wanted it. She could not wait. Two weeks before a quest was scheduled to leave for the desert, she was introduced to a group of strangers and took a crash course in first aid, fire making (she had never built one), and desert survival. The group, composed of students from another school, took her in, and she found a quiet place.

Shortly thereafter, she found herself in the Black Mountains of Death Valley, perched alone and exposed on a ledge beneath the ugly beautiful, tortured, steep, western face of Smith Mountain, with two gallons of water, a lumpy old down bag, several boxes of wooden strike-anywhere matches, a journal, and a pen. She was not particularly well prepared for this. She had never camped out anywhere before.

Of the three days and nights that followed, only she can tell. The weather was a little on the cold side. On the first day of the new year and the last day of her lonely vigil, the wind snarled and blew cold.

But we who waited at base camp saw and heard nothing of her. The days strolled by. The velvet-cold desert night illumined by a crescent moon came and went. We gazed into the twisted, alien massif of the Black Mountains and wondered, with an inner ache, how everybody was doing. The mountains answered our questioning with impassive menace. We exist, they said, whether you do or not.

Yet we knew that here and there, deposited in the folds and scales of the mountains, twelve tiny flames of human consciousness flickered.

Carey was out there. And on the morning of the fourth day she returned with her buddy, scratched and worn, but alive and well. As the others checked in, two by two, and the mountain silence was reclaimed by human laughter, the stories unfolded, intermingled, and burst into the windy sky.

Only Carey seemed quiet. There was an inwardness about her, a solemnness that indicated she had been through a struggle. Like others, her story was one of courage and frustration. Her shelter against the wind had not been adequate. Her sleeping bag, second-hand and lumpy, had not kept out the cold. No, she had not been able to get a fire going, despite her previous instruction. Yes, she had plenty of matches. But she went through the box of them, one by one. The wind blew them all out.

What did she do? Well, she looked at the mountains. She slept whenever she could. She thought a lot about her relationship with her lover. She went over and over it, worrying it down, as a dog does a bone. No, she had not seen any living thing but one small mouse. She had pulled her wool cap down over her ears, crouched on a ledge of Precambrian rock, and for three days and nights existed on the growing realization that she must leave her lover.

Several weeks after she came home, she got up the courage to show him the contents of the journal she had kept during her vision quest. It was all there: the perilous descent into self-affirmation, the fear of loss, the doubt, the pain, the loneliness, the self-examination. The desert was also there, in her words, paring down her meanings to the bare clarity of human self-preservation. Even as she had to leave her father, so she had to leave him.

Her lover read the journal, but he read with the eyes of a man who did not want to see. He read what he told himself were the words of a sixteen-year-old girl. "You're just being emotional about this," he said. He yawned, rolled over, and went to sleep.

But she persisted, gradually, fearfully, and in great pain. As she had gone through her box of matches, one by one, so she spent her resolve to be free of the man who might have taken the place of her father.

Within another month her lover had fallen in love with another woman. He transferred his attention to someone more comfortable, and Carey was finally free. But he kept her journal. He never gave it back.

The Great Mother bestows her gramercy on all, regardless of sex or sexual preference. The wisdom of her teachings includes examples of homosexuality among some species. What truly matters to her is the trueness and the persistence of the human heart that comes to her. Her kind of "morality" and "judgment" have to do with the ability of the individual to survive her rhythms and moods and to serve her as a steward or lover. She did not reject Turtle Dreamer because she had two-tone hair cropped close as a boy's and fingernails painted cobalt blue.

TURTLE DREAMER

She called us long distance from San Francisco to say that she was desperate and needed to go on a vision quest right away. When we asked her why she was in such a hurry, she hemmed and hawed and said something about losing her printing job. We told her it would be difficult to fit her into our already full schedule. Then she said the real reason why she wanted to vision quest was because she was afraid of going insane. When we asked her what she meant by that, she said she was a lesbian, in love with another woman, and seriously contemplating living in a "bonded relationship" with her. We asked, "But why should that cause you to think you are going crazy?" She answered, "I'm afraid. I've never committed my life to anyone before. The other day my lover kissed another woman and I went crazy from jealousy. We got in a big fight. I swear I almost killed her. We made up afterward but I haven't been able to sleep since then. I feel so ugly. Why can't I trust her?"

She wanted to go into the desert, to get away from the hectic life she led, to leave her lover and seek a vision of their ultimate togetherness. She wanted to be alone and empty so that she could make an honest decision to be full: "Only a drastic step like the vision quest will work for me." And it *was* a drastic step for her. She had never slept on the ground, never "camped out," and never fasted for more than a few hours. She was entirely unaccustomed to being alone. She was, without doubt, the classic neophyte from the big city. Above all, she was brave. Though her knees shook and scary fantasies about "going crazy out there" whirled through her mind, she drove 350 miles to our school and showed up in dramatic style—being absolutely who she was in our little redneck town. She parked her beat-up old VW bug in front of our house. Proudly it bore a bumper sticker: "Give a Man a Gun/He'll Confuse It with His Other One." We could not help laughing. The prevalent bumper sticker in our town was: "We're Rednecks and We'll Keep Our Guns."

With scant time to prepare, we had to concentrate on the essentials. She had to be ready to fast alone for four days and nights in the Last Chance Mountains. But her body was young, supple, and strong. She was quick to adapt and learn. She found a fine power place, high in a saddle between two prominent, swelling hills, with a grand view to the west, the "looks-within-place," the direction of death and change.

The four days and nights of her threshold trial passed. It was fall. A rare thunderstorm appeared the second evening and drove her under her tarp. Otherwise, the weather was perfect. The desert sun rained down a pure, mellow light. One day she left a picture at the stone pile. She had crayoned in the two peaks flanking her power place. Beneath the picture ran the caption: "Grandmother! What nice tits you have!" She returned, sunburned and ecstatic, with a new feeling of self-reliance and a love for the earth.

What about her relationship to her lover, Janine? She had decided to give it a go. She knew it was going to be hard, that for a hundred different reasons it might not work out. She knew there would be quarrels, scenes, jealous rages, pain. "Sooner or later," she said, "I'll face the fear of losing her to that sneaky, fainting violet, Porcelain Polly." We asked her what she would do if that occurred. "Hey," she answered, "I'm an artist, a poet, and a singer. It would get a lot worse if the Muse deserted me." As she got back in her car and headed toward San Francisco we thought again how brave she was, embarking on her vision quest of love in the "Ruby-Fruit Jungle."

Turtle Dreamer lived with Janine for six months. There were many ups and downs, but they worked at it. Finally, the feared event occurred. Janine left her for Porcelain Polly. T. D. went into her private hell of jealousy and rage. But she did not go insane. She held on through hard times. She got another job. Then she lost it because she excoriated a fellow employee who made her the butt of his sexist jokes. She was living by her guts, biting the bullet hard, drifting.

But her Muse never left her. Just about a year after her first quest, she called us and declared she was going out to Death Valley to fast and be alone. She wanted to let us know she would be there in case she did not come back. It was "do something drastic time" again. We tried to dissuade her from going without a buddy, but she was adamant. She said she could take care of herself now. She gave us the dates of her fast and promised to let us know when she was safely out of the desert. She said "It's time I finished mourning the demise of Janine. I'm ready to seek my destiny as a poet and singer." "Stay low," we advised her. "The first snows are coming any day now." She promised to inform a park ranger of her where-abouts.

Several nights later we were just turning out the lights to go to bed when there came a timid knock on the door. We opened it on Turtle Dreamer, all dusty and sunburned, the whites of her eyes gleaming animal-like in the darkness. "No, no! Don't invite me in," she whispered. "I just wanted you to know that I'm back from Death Valley." We rubbed our weary eyes and wondered where she was going to find a place to sleep. "No way I can sleep," she growled. "I'm driving back." "You're what?" "I'm driving back to San Francisco—tonight!" "Why?" "Because that's where the vi-sion is!"

A week or so after that, we got a letter from her.

> After I got back Janine called one day to attend to a friend of ours who took too many downers. Janine was sick with food poisoning and so I went to the friend's house. When I walked into the room it was darkly lit with three candles and the theme song from "Tommy" was playing on the stereo: "See me, feel me, touch me, heal me."
>
> She was on the bed sharpening a 12″ bayonet with all the might of an angry soldier. So I sat down on the side of the bed and said a few words. We stared at each other a long time. What I "saw" was so sad. Then she put her knife away and extended her hand. . . . We talked on and off all day, till she finally slept that evening. What a day. She's doing good now. . . . I like this work, this life.

In the following account, a young hero of the modern world crosses and recrosses the threshold, accumulating vitally needed power to effect changes within his life and the world around him. As Nature draws him into her secret heart, he begins to unfold himself and grow true.

LITTLE WARRIOR
Little Warrior was referred to us by Juvenile Probation. Actually, his referral was more like an ultimatum. In effect, the judge said, "vision quest or juvenile hall."

Little Warrior, whose given name was Steve, was from a traditional Italian family. His grandfather was one of the moving forces behind banking interests in San Francisco. His father was personnel director of a large corporation. Both his mother and father cared what happened to him and were distressed that he had taken to drinking.

Steve was willing to talk freely and honestly about his personal problems. He described himself as a "pre-alcoholic." "If I take a drink I have to have another one. The trouble is, when I drink I do crazy things." Steve was well known to the local police. He swore me to silence on a variety of capers that might have landed him in California Youth Authority. But he was not a "bad" boy.

There was something about Steve that made you like him no matter what he did. The father had the same gift, an irrepressible spirit, a knack for self-laughter. It was easy to want to root for Steve or go to bat when he was in trouble.

He had lots of problems with school. He did not like school, not even a little bit. He suffered from dyslexia, a learning disability. He fought his teachers tooth and nail and played the clown with his fellow students. The vice-principal finally sent him to a Continuation School. That is when his probation officer called us up and brought him over.

We sat and talked about his going on a vision quest. You could see he was ready for something drastic. "Three days and nights alone, eh? Without eating?" He smiled slyly. "I'll kill a rabbit with a rock and sauté him in wild mushroom sauce." You could see he'd already figured it out. That is the way he was.

He came to all the pre-trip meetings, and when the big day arrived he showed up with his pack, a thirty-pound inflatable rubber life raft, and a T-shirt with skull and crossbones across it and the legend: Black Death Lager.

Up, up, the trail wound, four miles to the spine of the South Warner Mountains. Steve, who had never backpacked before or slept out under the stars, carried his load of seventy pounds without complaint. It was hard work, but he did it.

I was his buddy. The two of us shared a ridge above Emerson Lake. His place was in a nest of boulders looking out over the

Surprise Valley. Our stone pile was on a slope covered with chalcedony and agate. The first day I went to check the stone pile, I found a note from him.

> Good morning Steven
> I feel good. I am moving to the rocks for better shelter in case of rain. Last night I had fried grasshoppers. Not bad with garlic salt and oil. I leave with you on the rock pile my favorite throwing stones. I got a sunburn where the sun don't shine!
> Take care
Little Warrior
> P.S. I did hear coyotes.

The second day I visited the rock pile, I found that he had left me another note.

> Good afternoon or morning
> I have a hard time sleeping. I keep thinking of my favorite pizza. I have stopped eating and I am joining the crowd. Tonite I am going to be on the ridge. Like my spot. Did you hear the sonic boom today? Scared the hell out of me. I was in the cave; it shook the whole joint.
> Little Warrior
Little Fierce One

For a month after his vision quest Little Warrior did not drink at all. But then he began to drink and soon he was entangled with the law. His probation officer called again and two months later he was off with us, this time to the stark, sun-scoured canyons of Indian Pass in Death Valley. This trip he did not vision quest. He stayed in base camp and waited with me for the others to return. Most of the time he was alone, out on the desert pavement of the Amargosa, looking for arrowpoints and ancient stone alignments. Before the week was over he had found a large chert knife, several points (one of them Folsom-type), a sleeping circle (perhaps five thousand years old), a whole pocketful of obsidian and chert flakes, a chunk of lazulite, several fine examples of pre-1900 tin cans, and a large piece of purple glass. He had participated three times in the tedious process of ferrying eight gallons of water from the bus to base camp, three miles away. When we returned, he gave the chert knife to me.

A month later he was back again, in the Black Mountains of Death Valley, where he vision quested for a second time, returning strong and proud. We began to hear comments like, "Steve has really changed." His behavior in school took a new turn. He organized the Madrone High School Mafia, a group that collected money for pizza, which was brought back and shared at lunch time with all.

He started showing up for things like benefit dinners, as part of the cooking crew. He dropped in one night to talk to a group of guys on probation who were contemplating a vision quest. "The vision quest isn't any trip for 'pussies,' " he told them. When we took a group of learning disabled people to the beach, he showed up and was overheard saying: "I've got a learning disability too—dyslexia. I have trouble going from left to right."

I have lost count of the number of trips Little Warrior has taken. All I know is I like this young man. I would trust him with my baby daughter. I've stopped asking him about his drinking. Somehow the question does not fit the man he has become.

Last month we took a group, including Little Warrior, to Indian Pass. It was not a vision quest group; it was a group of adults from the local community college. We were following an ancient Indian route through the Funeral Mountains, migrating from east to west. Finding the road into the mouth of the pass had been washed out, we stopped the bus ten miles short and unloaded our packs.

The plan was for me to let everybody else off and then to drive the bus back down into Death Valley, around the Funerals and south to a point where the group, descending through the pass, would come upon it at the end of the trek. I would leave the bus there and hike the opposite way, up through the pass, and rejoin the group camped at the eastern mouth.

But we had a problem. The washout had caused us to stop short of our goal. The hike to the mouth of the pass would be much longer. From our position it was impossible to see the destination, a low point on the horizon amid a jumble of crags and peaks. Two of us had a sense of how to get there, having been there before: Little Warrior and me. But I had to drive the bus back. That left Little Warrior.

He and I climbed to the top of the bus and looked westward to the swell of the horizon, trying to pinpoint the location of the pass. A couple of hills, six or seven miles out to the right, seemed vaguely familiar. We agreed it would be best to walk in a westerly direction keeping to the left of these hills. When darkness came, the group would have to stop and camp. He and Meredith would be the leaders of the group. He would take over my place while I was away. Meredith, who was unfamiliar with the area, would back up Steve's decisions regarding the proper way to proceed.

I left them then, backing the bus away from the brink of the washout, and pointed my nose away from the little band of modern immigrants moving toward a small canyon entrance among a maze of canyons lost in the immensity of the Amargosa Desert. As I left, a rain squall hit.

Several hours later, as the sun was going down, I left the bus west of the canyon mouth along the main road to Furnace Creek. With a pack and two gallons of water I headed toward the western mouth of the pass, four miles away. By the time it was completely dark, I was at the western entrance to Indian Pass. Sleeping there for the night, I continued in the morning, pacing myself with hard, fast hiking rhythms, testing my body. The canyon narrowed, became steeper. As I ascended I kept hearing voices in the cool, gloomy recesses of the canyon.

I was driven ahead by a kind of anxiety, fearing that somehow all was not well with the party out on the desert coming toward the pass. By mid-afternoon I had reached Poison Spring and began to seek a way to ascend a ridge, to get high, to look out across the vast bowl of the Amargosa to see if I could spy the party. Finding a ridge, I climbed it, with the help of a bighorn sheep trail along the upper slopes. When I reached the top, the sun was low in the west. The Amargosa lay before me to the east, bright and warm in the rays of the setting sun. I looked for a long time, but saw no one.

Then I heard a shout. I was unable to ascertain its direction, but the hearing of it spurred me on. Two hours later at sundown, I found the group camped exactly where Steve said he would bring them. Facing disagreement from other members in a group that included two medical doctors and the quality control director of a large corporation, he had insisted that he knew the way. As it turned out, he did.

Then Your Eyes Will Be Opened. You Will See What You Can Do.

He whose face gives no light, shall never become a star.

—*William Blake,* Proverbs of Hell

The gift to give, the trail to follow, is revealed to the hero when the eyes are opened and the quester sees with the eyes of eternity. The name of the gift is no secret: the gift of love. But it is one thing to know about love; it is another to see with the eyes of eternity. The modern hero, living in a mythically impoverished culture, is nevertheless capable of experiencing mystical insight, of seeing with opened eyes what it is that binds the self and all things together in oneness.

The following account clearly indicates the mythical potential of the vision quest. Not everyone, however, is necessarily gifted with the ability to experience mystical insight. For reasons known only by the Great Mother, this seventeen-year-old heroine was given one of life's greatest prizes.

GLOWING MOUNTAIN IN THE DAWN

DECEMBER 31
I find myself constantly thinking about friends and family, but I feel good about not being with them right now. I miss mom. I really want her to be here so she can see how beautiful this desert is. I've learned so much about colors and shadows and shapes from her. The mountain range across from me is silhouetted by the last glint of light from the sun. There is just a sliver of a moon suspended above it. A faint twinkle from a few stars and violet-hued clouds decorate the sky. Mom, it's really here; it's gorgeous. I give it to you in spirit, and a lot of love along with it.

I miss you, dad. I think a lot about how you would take to fasting. I don't know how I will either. I'm so glad you introduced the kids to Mother Nature at such an early age.

I feel that . . . part of my whole family is with me on this quest. Each member makes up a little of who I am.

JANUARY 1

Last night. Well, I say now that I was horribly afraid. Of what? After I got in my bag and snuggled in tight, I heard footsteps. I could have sworn someone was coming toward my camp. I stuck my head out, not even breathing for fear he'd hear me. Nothing. Nobody. Stuck my head back in. Then I came to the conclusion that these "footsteps" were the pace of my heart. I remember mom telling me once that I should think of the rhythms of my heart as something peaceful. I'm alive!

I feel wonderfully at peace—with myself, with Nature. Today as I was exploring I kept talking to the mountains. They are so majestic and seem to know life. I asked them questions. A deafening silence was their answer. They couldn't tell me what to do, but they let me decide for myself. . . .

As I was coming back up the mountain, I began to gather wood for the evening. All of a sudden a huge, gusty wind came up from the north. I made it as far as the peak below the one I'm on, and then had to throw the wood down and huddle against part of the cliff. The mountain underneath me began to shake. I began to shake. That wind was powerful. I really could have lost my balance and died trying to scale that cliff in the gust.

JANUARY 2

Night came on. I built no fire. I placed my rocks into a circle starting at north, then south, to east, then west. Each time I set a rock in its place, I gave my cry: "Dear Father, We need!"

I let my mind drift, with no preconceptions of what I would see. Little happy memories came to me. It seemed that my childhood was suddenly unfolded before me. I saw my growth through the sadness and joy experienced in that past. I felt at peace, content with the spirit I had become. I no longer felt that parts of my past should have been different. Then came the little images. I got so tired that I dozed off: two, fifteen, thirty minutes at a time.

In one image, I saw a candle burning. It slowly transformed itself into an old-fashioned kerosene lamp, then into a light bulb. History, eternal ideas, the promise of the progress of Love—I felt them all.

I saw a bright, fiery ball. There was a black hole in the middle of it. I felt my whole being rushing, as if vacuumed, toward that hole. I entered it. Blackness all around me. So peaceful. The feeling of being received, accepted. I opened my eyes. I was *here,* on Earth! I realized that that image symbolized my Passage. I was born to this exciting, beautiful, ugly, dangerous, receiving Earth.

But why have I denied this feeling of becoming one with the world? I have been so afraid of feeling naked, stripped of my status, my security from home, my pride, my old confidence, my feeling I controlled the world around me. . . . Those things were my supposedly indestructible foundation. But as I am learning from the mountains, eventually what seems to look like a secure, sturdy rock will crumble under too much force. Someday it will succumb.

I looked at the moon—a glowing crescent. I actually saw a pure, shining dove rise out of it and descend to Earth! I had my eyes wide open. I saw that beautiful bird flying down toward the planet. I closed my eyes and screamed: "Dear Father, We need!" I thought that the image was a hallucination. I was afraid to believe in such a powerful sight.

Then it clicked. I was sitting there in my bag in the blackness. My head was tilted up toward the sky and stars, and my eyes were closed. I began to feel raindrops on my closed eyelids. Then, still with my eyes shut, I saw triangular, no, pyramid-shaped figures of light traveling from every direction, heading for my eyes, going through my eyes into my soul. I felt a surge of power, of awareness.

I opened my eyes. Those brilliant stars were still sending down pyramids of energy to me—I saw it all clearly. Like a river, there was a constant flow of that warmth, power, and light coming directly from the stars into my being, through my eyes.

Everything just seemed to click. The Spirit (I call it God) sent me that mystical message: Love. He gave me that reason why I'm here on Earth. This wonderful planet gives us the place to not only exist as a life form but to grow together. I'm here to participate in that potential fellowship. I'm here to Love and accept. Through those images—the stars, the sun, all this energy in the world—I can collect it within me, and direct it to humanity.

The hero enters the threshold incomplete. Via the solitary heroic journey through the body of the Great Mother, the seeker is healed, made complete. The gift cannot be given to others until the self is whole and well. Love cannot be imparted until the self is loved.

Sometimes the dragon to be encountered is lack of self-love, that is, self-destructiveness. Ultimate victory over certain kinds of self-destructive behavior, particularly those that are addicting, is not won in a single fracas. The dragon appears and reappears to claim its victims, and the only way to fight it is with the rage of love and self-respect. Words and high intentions are not sufficient.

The hero engages the dragon of self-destruction in a battle. By learning how to win, the seeker learns how to fight. Learning how to fight, the seeker learns how to live. Learning how to live, the seeker learns how to die.

Graham, the hero of the following story, is living today in Marin County. He engaged the dragon of self-destruction during a vision quest to Nevada several years ago. He may never be entirely free of his dragon, but he crossed the threshold and was given the gift of wellness, of completeness. He saw what he had to do. Then, fearful as any hero, knowing all too well the gigantic proportions of his own personal dragon, he stepped back across the threshold to do battle.

GRAHAM

He was a nice guy—and he was a heroin addict. He was in a therapeutic community of ex-junkies when he first heard about the vision quest. From the beginning he was the most enthusiastic about stretching his muscles and living alone with the forces of Nature. All his counselors said it would do him good.

Socially he was a star, a vital, magnetic man who spoke candidly and with intelligence. But nobody knew what he would do when he left the support system and friends of the therapeutic community and went back alone to the streets of San Rafael, where his old junkie friends were still lurking for a fix, anxious to prove he was no better than they.

So he went to the headwaters of the Reese River in Nevada's Toiyabe Mountains with a bunch of other friends from the therapeutic community, with his counselor, Al, and a nurse, Angela (to dispense methadone to those who required it). While he was there he took to the mountains like a snake to a warm rock. He caught his limit of Rainbows and Eastern Brooks with worms he scavenged from the banks of Upper Sawmill Creek. He slept in the hollow of a willow tree. He hiked up the ravines and came back with arrowpoints in his hands. He ate like a horse and slept like a lamb. "This is the life for me," he declared, and talked about becoming a cowboy. If he was a star in his therapeutic community, he was a blossom in the high desert.

When he came back from his vision quest, he seemed bigger than life. It had been a good time for him, a time of self-testing and self-analysis. The late summer sun was strong and pure. It burned the impurities from his body. The fasting cleansed him from within. He had picked wild rosehips from the bushes growing near the river and made strong, sweet tea. His eyes were clear and alert, like an animal's; his body was lean and brown. He looked damn good.

That night, after the giving away and the numerous stories, he announced that he was not going back. The city held no more interest for him. He would stay here, maybe hire on at one of the ranches down in the valley.

We talked about going back then, for a long time, as the fire exhaled sweet juniper and the stars danced their slow ballet across the sands of forgetful night. The real monster, we decided, was fear of going back to face the monster.

The next morning we hiked out. It was a sad time. As we ascended the canyonside, the river glistened like a green snake shedding a skin of willows. "I'll always remember what I learned here," vowed Graham.

A month later he graduated from the therapeutic community and went to live in San Rafael, working up in Petaluma cleaning out chicken coops. He rode the bus to and from work, came home exhausted every night. He took up with his old girlfriend, the same one who had first introduced him to heroin. He told us he was staying clean.

I went over to his place a couple of times. It was a depressing apartment with no windows and a TV set at one end. At the other end was a shrine: a little picture-altar with a deer skull, a pair of antlers, obsidian flakes, and photos and mementos of his vision quest. He talked vaguely about getting out to Point Reyes or up to Yosemite, but he seemed full of inertia and sodden with self-disgust at the grind he found himself in. He smoked a lot.

A couple of months later, I read about him in the newspaper. He and his old lady had been caught with stolen goods and an "undisclosed quantity of heroin." He was back in jail, back where he had started.

For a long time I heard nothing of him. Then three years later he passed me on the freeway. He was driving an old but respectable pickup truck with a tool box in the back. "Hey," he yelled excitedly. "Hey!" I yelled back at him, "how're you doing?"

He hung his head out the window with a big grin on his face and hollered, "I'm clean!"

You Must Return with Vision for Your People.

Eternity is in love with the productions of time.
—William Blake, Proverbs of Hell

The return from the threshold is no less heroic than the act of severance. The hero must return to the same mother world, but no longer attached to it in the same way. The problem becomes the maintaining of the visionary standpoint in the face of immediate earthly pain or joy. The taste of the fruits of the temporal draws the attention away from the threshold and fixes it on the peripheral crisis of the moment. The balance of perfection is lost. To complete the heroic journey, the returning hero must survive the impact of the world.

There is a gift to give away, a vision to perform, a path to follow, a dragon to slay, a light to bear. The reincorporation of the hero requires that he or she demonstrate the power and effectiveness of the vision:

> I think I have told you, but if I have not, you must have understood, that a man who has a vision is not able to use the power of it until after he has performed the vision on Earth for the people to see.
>
> —Black Elk

At the return threshold the transcendental power must be left behind. The gift that is given is the self, an active, mortal force applied among human beings of flesh and blood. The miraculous is manifested, not by divine intervention but by taking one human step at a time. If the hero must return to a world of death, then the gift given is love, love that transcends death.

SILENCE

On the top of South Caribou Mountain there is a small clearing of sand. A crooked tree with a low branch becomes a shelter from wind and unexpected rain. Red ants live in a large lava rock.

From 7,761 feet, according to the U.S. Geological Survey map of 1934, you can see a hundred miles in every direction, including Mt. Shasta, Mt. Lassen, and the far lights of civilization in the southwestern distance. In the morning, first to see the sun. At the end of the day, last to breathe in darkness.

I stayed three days alone, fasting on the peak, spending my time writing in my journal, meditating, walking down the ridge to make sculptures at the rock pile, praying for living things, including the Earth, and just sitting around thinking and looking into my heart and out at the world.

The first evening I built a fire even before the sun had set. I wrote then, "The fire is a blessing. The smoke reminds me of our camp-fires earlier in the week and of good people." I went to sleep early, knowing my shelter was a good shield from the wind that would rush over the mountain. Whether it would do much good if it rained, I didn't know. That night it did rain for an hour or so, and by scrunching my body under the very low branch I stayed dry and slept well considering my somewhat contorted position.

I had a dream that night. . . . I saw an old friend and he called me into his office, and I told him I had to hurry to be at work at St. Vincent's (a residential treatment center for emotionally disturbed boys). He read me a letter in the *Examiner* from someone named Gustave Cesoni. There was a guy named John Cesoni when we went to school in Illinois. Seems Gustave or John had asked for my help. He had been injured somehow. A car accident? He was hurt either near Indian Valley (Novato, CA) or Santa Barbara. I think I said it wasn't that close to me and I had to go to work.

Coming back to civilization I was naturally high, happy, and filled with a sense of power and strength. I walked into my parent's house, eyes wide, a week's growth of beard bristling, telling tales of fire and mountain.

The next day I had to go back to work at St. Vincent's School. After a week in the woods, I was not particularly looking forward to working once again and voiced this feeling to my mother and brother. My mother looked at me and said, "I'm afraid there's some bad news at St. Vincent's. One of the kids died at camp."

"One of *my* kids?" I asked, as I began to pace around the house, my mind a whirl, my body moving, not wanting to fully hear the news or hear which kid was gone. In my mind I began to picture each kid, thinking about my life and their lives and my quest for a vision, going around the house, going crazy, trying to collect myself.

"Who?" I asked the inevitable question.

"Sinetti."

I didn't know what to do. Sinetti. Sinetti Melson. He had drowned in the swimming pool. Sinetti, a beautiful, troubled, ten-year-old black kid, wiry, muscular, smiling, hating, wanting to be a major league baseball player, and with his cannon arm, great speed and bat, he actually could have been, if he could have controlled his anger, if he had only lived long enough. Sinetti was the best athlete (and dancer) in the house. How could a kid who could turn one and a halfs off the diving board with ease drown in a swimming pool?

At this point I felt I had two choices. I could either go crazy, meaning everything I believed in, the vision quest, myself, and so forth, would now be false, or else I could stay strong and deal with this. I knew I had to walk up the hill behind my house, which I had named Lew Welch Mountain. I had spent a lot of time on the hill, praying, singing, talking to the earth and sky, but I had never spent a night up there. Now I knew that I must do so. I couldn't return to civilization quite yet. . . .

My mind reeled on the top of Lew Welch Mountain. . . . I talked to Sinetti, recalling good times (playing catch, going to his baseball games, bringing him up to the house so he could get all duded up to dance in front of the whole school) and hard times like the last night I worked before the trip, when Sinetti and another boy were causing trouble after bedtime. I put him in bed. He jumped up and picked up a chair, losing his temper, starting on one of his rages. Finally he did settle down, and the next day we could be friends again.

I began to discover power on that hill. Sinetti was dead. I was making peace with him, expressing my sorrow that his life was so short. I knew I would not go crazy, and that here was my vision—death—and that I must draw strength from Sinetti's life and death.

In the morning I walked down the hill and went to St. Vincent's where I met two other counselors and waited for the kids to return from summer camp. We would have to deal with our own emotions and those of the kids. Many of the kids had an idea he was gone already. When we told them, one blurted out, "Hooray," not understanding what he was saying. Others cried, including his roommate. We tried to find out as much information as possible about what happened, who saw what, trying to make sure no one felt responsible for the death. Quiet talk lasted into the evening. We looked at a few pictures of Sinetti. One close friend said, "I've never had a best friend die before." It was a trying day of return into this world.

Looking back on my dream of "Cesoni" getting hurt, it struck me clearly that on some level I was in touch with what was happening or would happen to one of my people. There is death in this world, and it must touch near me often and one day touch me directly.

I will draw strength from those people I come in contact with; even when they are gone their spirit is with me.

I will draw strength from the places of my vision quest, even when I am far away.

I will work, pray, and sing for my people.

I will love, let go, and continue loving.

I will work, pray, and sing that my people, and the Earth, may fully live.

Who can say what lies ahead when the threshold is recrossed? Further ahead (who can say how far?) lurks the ultimate dragon of the hero's death. He or she returns as he or she went out, courageously entering, mastering the art of walking in balance between what was and what will be, preparing to face what surely will be, death and the ultimate transformation.

PETE
He must have weighed 300 pounds. He had moved to the West Coast recently with his mother and brothers and did not get along

well at the regular high school. He cut classes, smoked dope, and bummed around the streets of San Rafael, his hands in his pockets. Rarely did he spend time at home. His mother, who worked late at night, saw him occasionally on the weekends.

What he did on his lonely jaunts is anybody's guess. He never got in trouble with the police. But he did get in trouble with the school authorities, who were forced to deal with his prolonged absences. Bound by law, the authorities sent him to a "Continuation School."

It was at Continuation School that we met him. We had gone there to introduce the idea of a vision quest course. A group gradually formed, including Pete.

You could see he was struggling to keep his feet among his peers. They laughed at him behind his back and made snide, cutting jokes about his weight. But somehow he was holding on, tenaciously, having finally found, among a school of rummies, burn outs, hustlers, low riders, and dissatisfied, disillusioned, frightened, intelligent students, a place to learn.

He turned out to be a bright young man, gifted with the ability to adapt, to assert himself, to make his way, to make friends, to be a fixture. He rolled with the punches. He was always ready with a story to match the one you told. Somehow you doubted his veracity, but not his sincerity. He was a good person, with a warm heart, who gave gifts and made contacts. He became Vice-President In Charge of Making Sure Everybody Knew What Was Going On. He began to drop by the house regularly, uninvited, only to fall asleep in the rocking chair in front of the fire.

When the time came he declared himself ready and went into the Inyo Mountains with two other buddies, seeking the upper reaches of a canyon, where he would separate and live alone for two days and nights. Nobody's expectations were particularly high. It was a difficult canyon they had chosen, and neither Pete nor his buddies, Scott and Dave, were in the best of shape. We said goodbye to them and took off, leaving them to look up at the eastern flank of the Inyos.

A day later we heard the news, via a note left along the roadway in a bottle, that they had spent the night elsewhere and were anxious to get back to civilization. It was alleged that Pete had encountered a wild-eyed specter in an old cabin they stumbled across. "It's not time yet!" the spectre reportedly screamed at him. We decided to let them alone, to see what would happen, and heard nothing more from them until the two days and nights were up.

Their stories were tall and their faces were brown. Pete looked great. He was twenty pounds lighter and his pants were ripped up the crotch. They had decided to go up the canyon after all, where, stopped by "immense, impassable walls," they camped. Apparently, they spent the last day and night apart, for Pete spoke glowing of his "vision quest," which he might have embroidered a bit with stories of face to face meetings with a bobcat, an eagle, several tarantulas, a rattlesnake seven feet long, and a wicked clump of devil's head cactus.

Two weeks later we got a call. It was Pete. Yes, everything was O.K. at home. He and Mike would be up for a visit in a couple of hours. We were working and not much interested in seeing anyone, so we hardly missed them when they did not show. A day later we found out why they did not.

Thumbing a ride north to our house on Highway 101, they were picked up by a man in a late model pickup truck. Pete seemed to know him, but once they were well away it became evident that the man was dangerously drunk. The drunk accelerated his truck to ninety miles an hour and began weaving uncontrollably.

They pleaded with him to pull over and let them out, but he was too far gone. Braking, swerving to avoid a rear-end collision, he lost control and the truck hurtled end over end, like a tin can kicked across the highway.

Miraculously, Mike was unhurt; the driver was critically injured; Pete was instantly killed.

Few know *how* they will die. But there are ways of *preparing* for death that somehow obviate the need to know how. Life itself is like the severance phase of the vision quest. One prepares to leave it all behind. Perhaps the deepest and purest value of vision questing lies in its teachings about preparation for death. The candidate elects to accept, rather than reject, the inevitable challenge. With incorporation, he or she must now begin the journey through the "underworld" of life that will carry him or her to the threshold of the spirit.

Perhaps the finest gift we can give to our people is a good death.

This does not mean dying the way they want us to die. Rather, a good death has to do with our willingness to face it when the time comes. It has to do with the quality of our preparations, with the quality of our love for those we leave behind. Among traditional peoples, one tended to know when it was time to die. This knowing made it easier for the dying one to take beneficial steps toward "going home." He or she was also honored in rites of dying that confirmed the merit of the steps taken.

Nowadays we have no counterpart for the Bushman's circle of thornbushes. Too often the dying patient's life is prolonged and the pain protracted beyond the limits of dignity. The dying one may be ready to go, but the laws of the culture or the fear of our loved ones will not permit it. He or she cannot say one last farewell and then willingly rendezvous with the hyenas of death. That would be suicide.

Nevertheless, there have been and always will be "dying pioneers," individuals who chose to go, not with the despair of a suicide but with the joy and composure of personal fulfillment. Mythically, such individuals have been saviors, surrogate gods and goddesses, heroes, and saints who died to enhance the lives of their people. On the mortal plane, such people have been mothers and fathers, husbands and wives, loved ones, teachers, and people dying from terminal illnesses. From a purely human standpoint, Gift Bearer was such an individual. She was a wife, mother, and teacher who, when her life was complete, chose to die—and in dying enriched the lives of the people.

GIFT BEARER II

When Virginia returned from her first vision quest she had a secret that she did not immediately communicate. She knew that her remaining years would amount to exactly four, that she would compress the "aging period" into these four years. For a while, this understanding grew in her like an unborn child. She was determined to love her dead husband through the loves of her life—and she did. But beneath her daily duties and relationships ran a deeper motivation. She would consciously choose the time, place, manner, and *means* of her death. Finally set free, her spirit would run to her husband's spirit and they would be one in the love they had called God. This motivation did not come from feelings of loneliness or despair. It came from a positive joy of knowing she was ready to take the final step.

The four years she spent preparing for her death serve to illumine the dying process and may be of help to others who, as she put it, might seek "a chosen death from full health." The following preparational phases, designed by her, were an outgrowth of the vision she brought back from her first fast in the desert: "Teach me how to become the Gift, that I may take it to my people in death."

The first year she called "Decision Road." By this she meant that she began to accept and live with her decision. It was a year of great doubt, for she never ceased questioning whether she was on the right road. Opposition to her decision was intense and came from all quarters. She fasted again, in the South Warner Wilderness, her sole purpose being to question her decision. She returned with greater resolve: "It came to me that the Bond would no longer exist at my death. A bond exists between two *separate* beings, bending them into a whole. At my death we will be drawn into a single unit that the closeness of Earth was but a foretaste of." At this point she took a vow of celibacy and let her intentions be widely known. She started along Decision Road, like a little mouse, her nose up to the ground.

She called the second year the "Death Lodge." By this she meant that she was withdrawing from public life, cutting down on her professional involvements, and spending large amounts of time with her children, loved ones, and friends. Vehement opposition to her stated plans continued. Very few understood. Nevertheless, she persisted in meeting with people and overcoming their resistance with eloquence, clarity, and humor. She said goodbye to some people for the last time. She asked their forgiveness and gave her love (whether they gave it back or not) and went on to the next person on her list. All the while she continued to entertain doubts. Sometimes she overcame them only through great inner struggle.

She called the third year the "Giveaway." By this she meant that it was time for her to dispose of her worldly possessions and divest herself of most relationships. She composed her last will and testament. She arranged for the continuance of investment earnings to benefit her children after her death. In an inner sense she also "gave away." She began writing an autobiographical account of why she had chosen to die in this fashion. Concluding her professional career, she continued to teach on an informal basis. This year saw the full flowering of her elderhood. Many came to learn from her, for she was articulate, joyful, and supportive, enjoying the fruits of old age. She continued to say her final goodbyes to an ever-shrinking circle of loved ones and acquaintances. Their opposition persisted, but with less intensity.

She called her fourth and final year her "Purpose Circle," referring to the vigil circles of her vision quests. By this she meant that she had now moved beyond the reach of almost everyone and was entering the final phase of her preparations. She moved her residence to a state where "suicide" was not illegal. This effectively severed her from her former habitat and circle of friends, intensified her expectations, and solidified her purpose. Living in a small, rented house, she began to perform self-designed ceremonies of preparation (morning and evening) wherein she prayed and asked for clarity of direction. She wrote or phoned her final goodbyes to a host of people and finished her autobiography, *The Pearl of Great Price*.

Deliberately, she prepared the scenario of her final days. She gathered her several children and their families around her, spending precious days enjoying their company and discussing their futures. By that time, most of her immediate family had assented to her plan, although each had endured moments of great anger and resistance. Six months before her death, she went on a prolonged fast, drinking only water and juices for a month. During the fast doubts continued to arise about the rightness of her course. But her daily meditations tended to confirm her preparations. She resumed a semiregular vegetarian diet interrupted by three- or four-day periods of fasting.

One month before her death, she filled a chalice with thirty smooth, black, beach stones from her beloved Bahamas. Each stone represented a day in her countdown to death. Each day, in a sacred place in her garden, she buried a stone. As she buried it, she prayed for guidance, always ending with: "Not my will but thine be done." Most of her family stayed with her, even those who could not give their permission. They say that in the last week she was radiant, like a little girl, and that on the last day she finished knitting a sweater for one of her unborn grandchildren.

The coroner, investigating her death, found the final draft of a "Credo for My Dying" on the table next to her bed. A three-page document, the credo contained her reasons for dying. Portions of it read as follows:

> I believe . . . that death can be the ultimate act of love—the supreme union of parts in a Whole. The time for such a surrender of oneself is when one feels complete.
>
> I believe that completions are as beautiful as births, and that death is as much a gift from God as is life. He gives it, after all, to every living creature.
>
> At some point in every life a completion occurs. It may be heralded by fatal accident or termination disease. It may also be signaled by an inner knowledge for those who dare to listen. . . .
>
> I now realize that it is possible to pick up the signals of completion intuitively and move toward death from full health by conscious choice. This choice, for me, has been the result of a confluence of human purpose and God's guidance through many months of prayer and meditation. . . .
>
> I believe that death from health, after months of spiritual tuning, will become an accepted alternative to the prolonged kind of dying so many people fear today. In the future, a reverently chosen and sacramentally performed death may be increasingly practical, natural, and in accordance with God's purpose for his ever-evolving creation.
>
> The core of my life was a bonded love from which flowed a heightened capacity to love others and the creativity for such contributions as I have been able to make through my work. There are loves that do not last just until "death do us part" but continue in a different form across the chasm between the living and the dead. The love in this form continues to provide a wellspring of energy to love, work, and finish up the unfinished business of the relationship in this dimension. But there comes a time when that phase of love-across-the-chasm also fulfills itself and the relationship presses toward a yet further

transformation. I go now toward that transformation, drawn by the knowledge that each love, like each life, spirals round to a point where it is complete and strains toward new birth.

At birth I took my life. At death I give it back, shaped, colored, and textured by joys and agonies, adequacies and inadequacies, triumphs and inglorious defeats. With gratitude I bear it Home, my gift to the Giver.

The coroner's report read: "Suicide."

BOOK 6

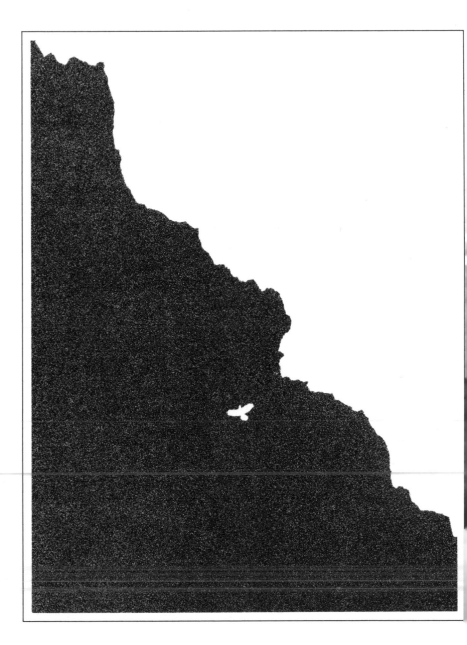

THE VISION

When you have discovered the mountain, the first miracle that will appear is this. A most vehement and very great wind, that will shake the mountain and shatter the rocks to pieces. You shall be encountered also by lions and dragons and other terrible beasts, but fear not any of these things. Be resolute and take heed that you return not, for . . . after all these things and near the daybreak there shall be a great calm, and you shall see the Day-Star arise and the dawning will appear, and you shall perceive a great treasure. The chiefest thing in it, and the most perfect, is a certain exalted tincture, with which the world . . . might be tinged and turned into most pure gold.
—*Eugenius Philalethes,* Lumen de Lumine, *1651*

The time had come. He knew it. Deep down to the quick he knew he *had* to go. All the signs were there: loss of purpose, desperation arising from an inability to live up to his own ideals, lack of faith, numbness, vague and sourceless anxiety, thoughts of suicide, disappointment in love, a sense of failure, not only in the world's eyes but in his own. Was it that his life lacked risk? He was disturbed by the thought. But how could he risk anything amid the responsibilities he had assumed?

This man had enjoyed worldly success. He had lived off the fat of the land, unthinking as a tick. Striving for prizes, he had succeeded in a way, only to find boredom and self-mockery. His sleep was disturbed by dreams of people he had never seen and places he had never been. His waking days were spent hoping for some unattainable fulfillment just around the corner.

Then he began to break away, to think about risking his life. What was the goal? To be someone more than who he was. To be someone more in his own eyes.

So he surrendered his work, settled his accounts with others, set his house in order, said farewell to his wife, children, and friends. He put a few necessary things in a knapsack and prepared to leave the town he lived in, to leave his life of tomorrows and yesterdays and go off into the wilderness, the land of todays, to seek a vision.

The trail began at the front door of his home, through which he walked. His loved ones held him in an embrace that was loving and dangerous. He loved them but he could not remain there. He had already begun to climb the mountain. There was no turning back.

Pathetically his children called to him, "Have mercy on us. We are starving and have nothing to eat." He cursed himself and kept walking. He had nothing to feed them.

His wife turned in her sleep and felt for his familiar body. He was not there. She awoke and called his name. He heard her, but he would not reverse his course.

The mountain he wanted to climb is called the Mountain of the Heart. It was steep and discouraging, yet beautiful and inviting. It was near at hand, yet far away. He set a course for a far-off ridge and cried for the memory of home.

Presently he came to a dark cave framed by a jumble of rocks and boulders. He entered the cave, and the darkness of the place took away his eyes and gave him blindness by which to see. In the midst of the confusion of his blindness, the image of his mother appeared to him, radiant, dressed in her wedding dress. She seemed forever beautiful and forever young.

"Here is your heart," she said. "I gave it to you when you were born. You must have it for your journey. Without it you cannot complete your quest. It is a seed," she said, "to be planted in the earth of your body." She held the heart out to him and beckoned him to take it. "This is your spiritual food," she said.

176

He realized suddenly that he was to eat his heart. The idea was not greatly abhorrent to him. The heart was of his own substance and yet seemed insubstantial. He took the glowing, living thing in his hand and crushed it to his mouth. He swallowed. He swallowed again. He could not swallow it down. Suddenly he felt choked and hysterical. He could not swallow his heart. It was caught in his throat.

He clutched at his throat, as if to squeeze his heart from it. He called for his mother, but her image had faded into the blindness.

Against the velvet walls of unseeing he began to weep. And as he wept he felt a keen sensation at the core of his throat, a feeling of pain and joy, as though his throat were welling up with the tears of humankind.

When he finally reappeared at the mouth of the cave, light was falling into the darkness of the west. The evening star tolled in a deep blue sky. Now, more than ever in his life, he felt alone. His mother was gone. An old life was fading into the curtain of memory. Come what may, he was alone.

In his loneliness, he tried to call out a prayer to the west, the prayer his children had taught him: "Have mercy on me. I am starving and have nothing to eat." But he could not utter the words; his heart was stuck in his throat. The mountain he had to climb was stuck in his throat.

He sank to his knees in dismay. The cool dusk and its first smattering of stars offered scant consolation. He looked up into the shadowy bulk of the mountain that was stuck in his throat. How could he ever climb that mountain?

He was able to see his life with greater clarity then: the women he had loved, the friendships he had forged or forsaken, the dashed hopes, the thwarted ambitions, the self-pity. His life heaved in on him, a dark heavy burden of *karma*. The mountain looming up defied his skill and challenged his little faith. "You are but a scrap of meat to be pecked to pieces by the raven of Death," said the mountain to him. "How have you made yourself worthy to climb me?"

The moon rose, a horned owl perched on a bough of darkness. He looked up at the mountain and sighed. He could not, would not, separate himself from his quest. The wind blew fresh and a little cool. He resumed his climb, as the twilight deepened.

He had not gone far before he came across a rattlesnake. The rattlesnake, who was hunting, had noticed him long before, as a rumble in the earth and an approaching warmth in the air. The snake had curled into a defensive posture, warning the intruder.

It was a Panamint rattler, salmon and dun, a male in his prime. He had been born live and sleek from his mother, who had chosen not to linger with her litter, but had left them to fend for themselves. His enemies were many; his friends were few. Fated to travel without leg, foot, or claw, he had survived by depending on instinct, unable, when on the hunt, to protect himself from the sudden claws from the air that would rivet him to the rock with thorns of steel.

Gifted with an uncanny ability to stalk, paralyze, kill, swallow, and digest, he was also motivated by his soul to shake the rattle fixed to his tail whenever danger lurked on the wind. This self-defeating gesture, this warning to others, even a creature of such infinitely dangerous capabilities as a human being, was both foolhardy and graceful, an unjustifiable act of mercy: the lesser knight bravely standing his ground and waiting in the open, nobly refusing to lurk, or to strike from the back.

The two stared at each other in the night. Neither wanted to harm the other. Each hoped merely to pass by. Impassively noble, the snake rattled louder. "Pass by!"

I have no intention to harm you, thought the man. I am compelled to climb this mountain. Your presence in my path leads me to believe you are here to teach me. I seek to transform myself, to be more than I am, to be new.

"I have shed many skins," said the snake. "I hope to shed many more. I live upon the sand, hiding in the rock, waiting like silence for the appearance of life with which to fill my hunger."

Death will reward your search, the man thought bitterly. Death will stoop on you with a pair of feathered claws. Death will satisfy your hunger, even as it will satisfy mine. You, snake, will die with grace and abandon. What about me?

The snake shifted and drew himself into a tighter circle of power and tested the palpable air. "I shall be neither quick to strike nor slow," he warned. "I shall not hesitate. I am not at war within myself, divided between body and mind. I am what I do, and I do it well."

Sensing a new menace in the snake, the man drew away, though he was by far the stronger, and went on. The waning moon spread a path and the stars pressed him close.

He trudged ahead, the only sounds his panting breath and scrambling footfalls. Above him the mountain was etched in dull silver. The going was not easy. He became hot and sweaty beneath his clothing. The dark wind cooled, then chilled him. He found a small gully and a juniper growing from a projecting ledge, the boughs of the tree spreading down to form shelter. From his knapsack he took a blanket and lay down in the soft, fragrant bed of needles. As he sank into sleep he observed that the stars were becoming obscured by clouds.

He did not awaken to the glow of morning light. He awoke to the flash of a bolt of lightning. He sat upright, ears ringing with the sound of thunder.

A late spring storm was drifting in from the west. The moon and the stars were gone. From dark, massed clouds came a scatter of rain and wind, then down, down around his ears the storm came, sweeping the ridges with its broom of lightning, tearing loose boulders of thunder from the cliffs of the sky.

Alone in his wretched little place the man began to weep from fear and helplessness. Nowhere could he hide. From childhood he had retained a terror of lightning and now he was forced to watch, like a cornered animal, the delicate, probing fingers of death.

The landscape flickered in stark negative. His tree appeared to be the only one for miles, his ledge the most exposed. His scalp began to tingle and his hair to rise. Too easily he imagined his body to be a lightning rod. He tried to pray.

The terror he felt was beyond telling. In the end he had to let go, to surrender to forces incomprehensible to him. The storm raged on, blinding the darkness with livid light. He was but an insect, a mosquito to be smashed against the stone. Faced by the realization of the meager conditions of his existence, he finally could not hold on to his life. When he was ready to die, the storm subsided, the mist fell away. Morning light flooded the east. He was alive, not by intention but by miracle. Aloft on the blue winds a raven greeted the new day.

But something in the man had changed. The storm had shocked him into an extended and heightened awareness of the magnitude of his love for life, which he now felt as extreme exhaustion. It had been an ordeal. He had seen the eyes of death, a blinding white. He had shriveled from fear of those bottomless eyes. He had experienced the frailty of life and surrendered to the element of death.

The morning sun seized him with drowsiness. The animal in him felt a torpid desire to curl up on a warm rock and sleep. He drowsed and slept like any wretch lucky to be alive, sprawled without thought on the verge of nothingness.

When he awoke the sun was high in the sky. He was uncomfortably warm. He took a sip of tepid water from his flask and realized the level was low. He would have to find water.

Directing his gaze along a ridge he saw where rains had cut deep into the flesh of the mother mountain. One canyon appeared dry. The other canyon, though steeper, held more promise. Up the ravine, up a dry wash streaking down from some old wound in the mountain, he could see a patch of bright green.

The way down the ridge and up the canyon, however, proved to be difficult and required great effort. As he had eaten nothing, the man was weak and dizzy. By the time he reached the green area, he was dusty and played out.

He arrived at a mesquite tree and a large growth of willows and reeds, certain signs of the presence of water. The air smelled damp. He got down on his knees among the willow shoots and dug his fingers through the lush intertwining of reeds and shadows, but he was unable to discover more than a small mud hole.

Knowing he must have water or die, he began to scoop out the mud from the hole. Gradually, water began to rise within the depression until the hole was filled with dusky liquid, which, when allowed to settle, turned clear.

He looked long into the tiny pool and saw, at the bottom, flecks of chert magnified in the waterlight, glittering amid the roots and stems of the vegetation. The little bank upon which he leaned was soft and hidden, the color of coolness. Tiny purple flowers no bigger than freckles pushed up from the moss.

He lay down on his belly, in the crush of tall reeds and willows, and drank the water. It was profoundly satisfying water, hinting of mineral from the dark earth. He drank as long as he wished.

When his thirst was quenched and his flask full, the grateful man rested beneath the shade of the mesquite tree and contemplated his world. He looked at his dusty clothes. Dirty and wretched, he felt almost happy. Early afternoon breezes crept up under his shirt and hair. A hummingbird droned in the tops of the mesquite, where long, greenish flowers were blossoming into fruit.

Born of a venerable mother and the earth, germinated by the greedy feet of bees, the soul of the mesquite tree had fallen to the earth in the form of a honey bean. Slowly the bean had deteriorated, eaten away by tiny worms and raindrops, finally releasing its hoard of ironlike seeds. Winter came, and then early spring, with occasional thundershowers scattering the seeds and washing them down the canyon, away from the precious, life-sustaining moisture of the spring.

But one seed escaped the diaspora. One tough little soul unto itself held an obscure purchase, its purpose known only to the Heart of the Universe. And oblivious to all but survival, that hungry, determined little soul held on through a mean, wet winter, and gradually began to gnaw on the soil.

The seed, true to its nature, began to climb the mountain. With the coming of spring it quickened from within, stirred by the presence of another mountain without, a mountain of pure light. Before it had done climbing, it had traveled as far down into the earth as up to the sky. While ascending its graceful, branching ladder of light, it was giving birth to children: long, twisting honey beans. These sunburned beans ripened in the hardwood boughs and hung in the heat of the day and the cool of the night. Wild ambrosia, they beckoned the deer and bighorn sheep and the ghosts of Indians.

Yearning to fulfill herself, the mesquite fulfilled others, among them the human fruit of America, the peoples with names like Paiute, Mohave, Yuma, Cocopa, Pima, Papago, and Seri. In their hands her fruit became meal, gruel, broth, pudding, bread, drink, and joy juice. She was boiled and washed in sore eyes and open wounds. She was smoothed on chapped lips, cracked fingers, open blisters, and sunburn. Her fruit was ground down into a fine powder and applied to the navels of newborn children. For this and so much more she was revered and worshipped. How many could not have lived without her!

And so gracefully and guilelessly did she assume her purpose, that the man who reclined beneath her did not give one thought to the truth that grew above and beneath him. But something of her soul, something beneath ordinary awareness passed into him—perhaps it was nothing more than her dappled coolness, the whisper of early afternoon wind in her leaves, her staunch yielding to the sun. He partook of her and felt, intermingled with his compulsive yearning, a sense of calm and unjustified, unmerited favor.

It was deeply pleasant to lie in the shade and indulge his exerted body. It seemed he had been climbing the mountain for years. The blue sky soothed him with a vast indifference. How unimportant in the scheme of things he was, tucked away in a tiny, forgotten pocket of the mountain.

Glancing idly around, he saw that his foot had dislodged a stone, beneath which an earthworm lay in the moist indenture, half concealed. He plucked the worm from the soil and held its small coolness in the palm of his hand.

"Lowly earthworm," he addressed the creature, "I am no more important in the scheme of things than you." He said this in mock drama, not realizing that the common creature he thus addressed was, in fact, a being of great consequence. And though the worm neither saw nor heard him, it certainly sensed him—with an ancient wisdom of its kind that no human could ever fathom.

For this worm was hundreds of millions of years old, with an innate method of survival instilled in its nervous system long before there were humans on Earth. This common earthworm was a near-perfect evolutionary adaption: the *Annelida* ("rings"), who stands out through history as the single creature most responsible for the survival of all living things. A master alchemist, the earthworm performs the magical function by which death and decay are transformed into fertile earth, the sacred womb of seeds. This it does by eating, digesting, and excreting its food in the form of castings. These castings have buried the Earth many times over in richness.

A body of interconnected rings, or *somites,* makes the earthworm a veritable pile driver, able to move obstacles up to sixty times its own weight. A denizen of the underground, the worm has blue, photosensitive cells in its head to bend its course always away from the sunlight and down into cool, moist, dark, ravenous byways, where, starving and with nothing to eat, it performs its ceaseless, sacred, magical quest.

182

Of course the man did not know or think of this, or he would not have absentmindedly tossed the earthworm beyond the lifesaving shade of the mesquite. There, in the full sunlight, it died within sixty seconds.

It might have died forgotten. But the man, deciding finally to resume his quest, spied the lifeless form of the creature on a rock. He saw that it was dead and realized that he had killed it.

He picked it up again. The corpse had begun to smell. He had murdered the worm while it was on a quest. It had begun to form a cocoon around the clitellum (sex organ). In a short while it would have given birth to twin young. Of this the man was also largely ignorant. He knew only a moment of self-annoyance. He had not intended to kill an innocent creature and thus spoil the perfection of the place where he had found peace. He had kicked the door ajar and was now powerless to close it.

"How many times have I done this?" the man thought wearily. "How many times have I destroyed life around me?" His heart throbbed in his throat. It seemed as though his children were stuck there, with a host of others whom he had hurt through his preferred ignorance. It was this he had hoped to escape by embarking on his quest. But it had come back to remind him, in the form of a lowly worm.

An earthworm did not mean much to him, except as a symbol of how he had fallen short of his own expectations, perhaps, and for this the worm had died. Was it a fair exchange, the worm's life for the man's momentary self-reproach? He threw the corpse back to the earth. He did not think that other worms would feed someday on his own body. He thought with a sigh, "I must go on."

But as he continued upward through the afternoon sun, sweating, straining always upward, he began to realize just how difficult it would be to attain the transformation he sought. Such a transformation did not come as a gift. It would not occur merely because he desired it. Even the act of leaving all and putting his body on the upward path did not suffice. Something else had to happen, something he did not yet know about. Vaguely, that something else tugged at him in the wish to die, to end it all, to finish this chapter forever, to come full circle.

But the mountain was there, in his throat, under his feet. And the higher he got, the fuller his heart beat in his throat. Perhaps he would never learn the secrets of self-transformation. Perhaps his life would be a life of trying, trying, finally consummating itself in a death untried for.

Sometime during the afternoon he reached the point of no return. It came to him, as he rested in the shade of an outcropping and looked out over the valley below, that he could not go back. Home was too far away. The only way to get back home was to climb the mountain.

He watched the afternoon shadows stride across the distant valley and the mountains beyond. Through the sweat stinging his eyes the landscape seemed to shimmer and dance, its ruddy face beguiling the sun. It seemed alien to him.

Something had gotten into his blood. Perhaps it was the rigor and adventure of the quest itself. Perhaps it was desperation. Whatever it was, he found himself preferring to be lost for the time, to be scarred by the rock and blistered by the sun. He preferred the dust and the glare, the sharp, hot smell of sage and the terror of distance. He preferred the barren, eroded soil, the shape of cactus and stone, the shadow of the blue-black raven that hovered above him, reminding him that death itself was also on a quest, that it was starving and had nothing to eat. His belly cried out to be filled. His throat cried out to be emptied. His being cried out to be transformed. Above him the raven circled, clacked its beak and hoarsely croaked.

Nightfall found the tired man on a shoulder of the mountain. For the last few hours he had followed what seemed to be a faint trail that headed in the general direction he wished to travel. The trail terminated amid a pile of basalt that appeared to have been placed there by human hands, forming a rough semicircle against the northwest. Down on the ground he found faint traces of ash from an old fire. It seemed a good place to spend the night.

Close by he found fuel: pungent sage and fragrant juniper. With his hands he dug a firepit, scooping the sandy soil into his lap. The simple ritual of building it gave him pleasure—the placement of stone into a sculpture to serve his need.

As night fell, his fire climbed. Hungry light leaped for the darkness, for his eyes. Again, he experienced a sense of deep satisfaction. Below his hunger for a new life there was a deeper hunger, symbolized by the sinuous flames of his fire. Ceaselessly he burned, perched in the pyre of his crumbling bones. To do what? To give off warmth and light.

He sat back against a boulder and watched the evening star bathe herself in reflected light. He longed for the source of the reflection. The small fire carved a cave in the darkness. Save for the sputtering flame, silence was absolute.

He must have dozed off. When he opened his eyes again, a humanlike figure was silently sitting opposite him.

The man gave a start of surprise, leaping suddenly to his feet, scattering the fire. An involuntary exclamation exploded from his lips. But the figure did not move or speak or look up from its lap. Closer attention revealed that the sudden guest was a male Indian of indeterminate age with long, black hair and a broad-brimmed, silver-banded black hat. Despite a pair of rabbit skin moccasins, he was not otherwise dressed as a native American, but as a white man, in blue jeans and a rough, white workshirt.

More cautious than frightened now, the man returned to the fire. "Who are you?" he asked the dark figure staring at his hands in his lap. "Why are you here?"

"My name is The Cutter. You camp in my camp by my fire," said the form, looking up without a trace of malice. "You are welcome to sit here and be warm."

The man realized his visitor was incorporeal. What passed as a human figure was a bright mass of fleshy pools and shadows that shifted and flowed. Glittering, dark, rainbow eyes measured him. The man fought an intense desire to flee; but the terms of his own quest again compelled him to remain and to learn whatever the apparition's presence in his life required of him.

"Forgive me for intruding," he said. "I had hoped to spend the night here and in the morning to resume my quest."

The apparition wavered, then held steady. The fire sputtered. Finally the dark form spoke. "This mountain belongs to The People."

"Who are The People?"

"My people are The People," the apparition replied. "Your people will pass away when the winter is past. I wait here for the return of spring and The People." A screech owl trembled the night air. The Cutter looked away, into the night and said nothing.

The man ventured another question of the ghost. "Why do you call yourself The Cutter?"

"My white name is Jack Wilson. I am also called The Christ. When I was a grown man I was taken up into the heart of heaven. I was there forever. I learned the secret of bringing The People back. I learned how to cut, to split apart, to sever. I brought back peace and I brought back an axe, with which to cut away, to make clear and ready. I live to make a way for The People to return."

There was a long pause. The Cutter took from his belt a circular, flat, polished, black object. He held it up to the light of the fire. It was an obsidian mirror. "It cuts away lies. Look," he commanded, and passed the object to the white man.

In the dull light of the fire the wondrous mirror softly glowed. The man looked into the black, lustrous reflection. He saw a little boy who was starving and had nothing to eat. His body was frail, his soul was innocent. A shock of blond hair topped a guileless face holding a tentative smile. "Do you like me?" he seemed to be asking. The little boy was none other than the man himself, when he was a boy. Astonished, the man turned to the apparition.

"You are a man growing older," The Cutter said. "You are really a little boy growing younger. Soon the little boy will die."

For a long time the man could not speak. He experienced a great sadness. The heart of his childhood that his mother had given him mourned in his aching throat and made it impossible to speak. He was afraid. He wanted to be with his mother. He did not understand death. He did not want to be set adrift on the sea of life. His boat was frail. Inevitably it would sink. He did not want to accept the responsibility of death.

"I will tell you a story," said the apparition. A great sensation of pain, like a wave, seemed to overwhelm him. "It is the story of the Ghost Dance."*

"When I returned from Heaven I saw far and clear. I became a prophet and a teacher among my people. I sent out messages to all the Nations. I said, Come and meet me here at Walker River where the white man has put me. I sent out my message: Salvation is at

*The apparition is a real personage, and the tale that follows is derived from historical accounts of the Ghost Dance Religion, a late nineteenth-century messianic movement founded by the Paiute prophet Wovoka, sometimes called the Indian Christ. See *Bury My Heart at Wounded Knee*, Dee Brown. The sequence of Ghost Dance songs that follow are quoted or adapted from *Technicians of the Sacred*, Jerome Rothenberg, ed.

hand. We will be delivered from the white man. Come and dance the dance of salvation. Come and learn to dance the Ghost Dance.

"From everywhere Indians came to hear and to see. Many Nations came, for many were living by the hand of the white man instead of the hand of God, and they were starving and had nothing to eat. The buffalo were gone. Birds fell from the sky, too rotten to be eaten. The snows came. The Indian's tongue was frozen to the white man's axe.

"I said, Everyone come. Learn to dance the Ghost Dance. Indians everywhere must dance and keep on dancing. Pretty soon, when spring returns, God will return. God will bring back the fish and the game. I said, If you keep on dancing your mothers and fathers and grandmothers and grandfathers will return and the Earth will be young again.

"I said, The white man will be cut down like grass in the fire. Rains will tear his house into the oceans. Fire will rain from the sky and burn his bones to ash. I said, The white man will be eaten by the forest; the Earth will swallow him. All Indians must keep on dancing and the white man will die, chopped and burned as if by a stroke of lightning. O my People, I cried, the winter is cold. Let us dance so that spring will come!

"These things I taught, and the Nations came and listened, and believed. They learned to dance the Ghost Dance. They went back to their people and taught them also how to dance the Ghost Dance. Soon many people of many Nations were dancing the Ghost Dance.

"But the white man saw. First he was disturbed. Then he was frightened. He saw Indians dancing. In the terrible dead cold of winter he saw Indians dancing.

" 'No!' said the white man. 'You cannot dance here. You disturb my dreams; you disturb my conscience. I am afraid of you because I took your land away from you by force. You cannot, you *must not* dance this dance.'

"The Indians went away to another place and kept on dancing. In his dreams the white man heard the drumming of their feet and he was afraid for his life. He came with many big guns and soldiers and ordered my people to stop dancing. But my people would not stop dancing. They were dancing to make the white man go away. He could not allow them to dance. With his soldiers and big guns he killed my people. He slaughtered them in cold blood, even the women and children. Even the dogs. They died like the rabbit, like the fish, trapped, hunted down. The snow was stained with the blood of my people.

"And every bullet that found its mark was a nail that crucified me to the white man's cross. With every bullet that found its mark I died again.

"But let me tell you, white man," the ghost said with a curiously warm and gentle intonation, "I am not dead. I am risen. And the Ghost Dance goes on."

The wind stirred the fire, the stars cast their cold brilliance. All was silent. The flame died into coals. The man reached to throw more wood on the fire, suddenly afraid of the darkness. He had felt, more than heard, what the apparition of The Cutter had said to him and now he was empty and cold.

The ghost resumed. "You ask me what is the meaning of your life. You ask me to teach you how to let go of one world so that you may attain a better one. You ask me to be your guide to the sacred mountain. I tell you that you must learn to dance the Ghost Dance and to keep on dancing, for winter is hard and you are starving and have nothing to eat. Come, white man. You will learn to dance the Ghost Dance."

The apparition of the man who taught the Nations how to die by dancing shifted from the fire and became seemingly corporeal off to the side where there was room to move about. Then he began to dance in a circle, shuffling his feet in a coherent, rudimentary rhythm. And as he danced he sang a song. The song was simple and powerful.

> We shall live again.
> We shall live again.

Something within the questing man responded, something that was deeply sorrowing, something that was full of joy. The little boy in the mirror tugged at the heart in his throat. Let us dance, said the little boy, so that the evil of the world will go away. Let us dance, proud in ourselves and sure that spring will return, that we shall live again. Let us dance with the heat of the sun, for I am afraid of the dark and my mother's breasts are cold.

In a twinkling, spring had yielded to summer, summer to fall, and fall to winter. The world was dying, smothered in chilling, deadly white, the color of the white man. The springs were frozen, the pinyon were rotting, the eagle had no hope, the rabbit was sick, The People were starving. There was a man who had been to Heaven who said the only hope for all was to dance the Ghost Dance, and to keep on dancing, for surely spring would come.

The white man arose and began to dance. And after a while he sang his song, the song his children and the rattlesnake and the worm had taught him, the song of his heart yearning for spring.

> Great Spirit, have mercy on me.
> I am starving, I have nothing to eat.

And the two danced on, as the fire grew dim and the cold numbed the darkness. The white man felt his body become the body of humankind. His heart, as it pounded and whirled in his throat, caused him to moan and cry out, to reach God, to be God.

And then the night was pierced again by the ghost, who sang a new song in a ringing voice that sounded like the rush of water from beneath a snow bank.

> In the great night
> My heart will go out
> Toward me the darkness comes rattling
> In the great night
> My heart will go out

The firelight faded. Darkness surrounded and took possession of the dance. The presence of the two dancing forms became measureless, invisible. All that mattered was the pounding of the darkness through the feet of the earth, the whirling of stars in the mind of the night sky. From the darkness of this ecstasy came a voice that spoke through the heart in the throat of the white man.

> The earth will tremble
> Everyone will arise
> Stretch out your hands.

Something was stirring in the darkness, in the hoarse panting, in the letting go, in the insensate knowing of the dance. Was it a seed of perfect silence sown to the winds of motion? Was it a moment of undying truth? In the dead of darkness, light was singing. And it was this light that took the form of the dance. The same light shone from the hearts of all peoples and drew them together into the One Dance, which was being danced by the earth, the night, and the light of the stars.

Light stirred in the heart of darkness, in the tomb of the seed, in the dung of the beetle, in the fang of the rattlesnake, in the pumping hearts of man and ghost until neither could be distinguished from the other, until their substance received the darkness and the earth and stars and their spirits were born as one and a voice sang one last endless song.

> This earth too old
> Trees too old
> Our lives too old
> All will be new again
> All will be new again

When the white man could no longer dance he fell lengthward, toward the unrisen dawn.

When again he opened his eyes he was not sure he had ever closed them. No time had elapsed. He was still dancing the Ghost Dance to the light of the fire in his veins.

Gradually he became aware that he was lying in the hard dust. Morning had broken in upon the night. In the morning light all perspective had changed. The Cutter was gone. The ashes of the fire lay inert and cold. But the earth on which the white man lay was pounded into a circular groove, apparently by dancing, shuffling feet. All the footprints belonged to him.

The white man felt alert, at ease and ready for what must surely come. The terms of his dream of quest had brought him to a final reckoning. From the start he had known, deep inside, that he must face it.

A croak from above reminded him, as if he should forget, that the raven was still sitting up there, waiting on the air. He hoisted his pack to his shoulders and began the last day of his climb.

He felt amazingly whole, strong enough to look his mountain in the eye. His body moved with ease and freedom, accommodating gravity. Details of the landscape stood out with peculiar clarity, every stone and bush, every tree and gully, every new perspective on the valley below—the habitations of the white man, the life he had left behind.

His feet lifted him steadily. At noon he stopped to rest in the shade of a pinyon. He had been climbing an arroyo punctuated by intermittent springs. Patches of maidenhair fern clung to wet rocks. Willows were budding and thistles putting out their purple and yellow stars. Bees and hummingbirds sang on the air. Once he startled a doe, coming downwind of her. He was surprised at how silently he had been able to approach her. Heavy with child, she was sleek and wide-eyed.

He basked for a while in the sweet wind, looking ahead. The outer curve of the shoulder of the mountain obscured the peak. The way continued to be steep. Ahead lay barren highlands, with an occasional pinyon or whitebark pine, twisted and scoured by the winds. This was no country for faint hearts. The uplands were bare and exposed. Nowhere was there shelter. Trees could not grow here without paying the awful price of slow, agonized adaption and growth. The air was thin, rarefied. The sky had turned a deeper blue. Ahead lay pockets of snow and the wind-besieged heights.

Sinking into the shade of the pinyon, he lay his head on his arm and heaved a sigh. Always the upward pull against the current. The factor of work. Surely, there was a joy to this work. For a long time he listened to the beating of the heart in his throat, steady and hot. His very blood seemed to be answering his weariness with a resolute energy. Tired as he was, he knew he would gain the summit before nightfall.

A small object on a branch caught his eye. He looked closer. A small, ruby-throated hummingbird, silent and still as any pebble. Was it asleep? He went closer. No, it was dead.

To the man who stroked it, the feathered little shell was a symbol of the way of all life. In the corpse he saw mirrored his own body and recognized that there is something in beauty that lives on, that survives, that is born again in a higher, transcendent dimension. Thus his dying heart pulled him forward, to some hoped-for death or culmination at the summit of the mountain, to the unveiling of the treasure.

By evening he had reached the summit. It was barren, crusted with ancient, wind-scoured dolomite. There were no trees here. There were no bushes, no boulders among which to find shelter. There was only the bulge of the mountain and the surrounding sky.

The view was magnificent. To the east he could see a hundred miles: desolation and wilderness, expanse, *las sierras desiertas,* the crests of the ranges of the Great Basin. To the west, in the rays of the setting sun, lay a composition of dark angles and contours and shadowed hulks: *La Sierra Nevada,* the saw-teeth of snow. Slowly the sun was quitting the habitations of day.

Out there somewhere were his wife and children, his parents and friends, his people, his work, his life. He pictured that universe and loved it with great feeling, from a great distance. What are they doing now? he wondered, and pictured them sitting down to dinner or driving home along the highway. He longed to be with them. He longed to be without them. He loved them for themselves; he loved them for who they wanted to be. He felt their presence in him, strong and warming in the darkening wind.

From his lofty purchase he contemplated for a moment the human condition, the beauty and the tragedy of it, the aching and throbbing in the heart of humanity. But quickly he became bored with his own philosophy. His quest required doing, not contemplation.

He set about the task of constructing a circle of stones to protect himself from the night wind. Somewhere in a book he had seen pictures of circles made by primitive peoples for the same reason. Carrying and placing the rough dolomite proved to be hard work, but he was pleased with the results. He would lie curled up inside his circle of stones, like a baby, like an old man, hugging himself and the earth, and wait for what the night would bring him. Darkness was coming and darkness was starving and had nothing to eat.

The last light hung to the western horizon like a purple curtain. The silhouettes of mountains higher than the one he had climbed etched the distance like great stepping stones. And then from the east night came, climbing the mountains as silently and effortlessly as light, until it had conquered all.

He entered the circle and lay against the stony soil. Still the wind blew cold. He huddled up tight, covered himself with a blanket, his back to the wind. He had not realized it would be so cold, that he would be miserable. Where was the triumph?

He shut his eyes tight against the shivers and tried to unclench the core of himself. He felt tired and sick and afraid. Yet in the extremity of his exhaustion he could not sleep or overcome his fear of exposure and the cold. He realized that he was panting, that his heart was beating faster than normal, distending his throat with an ache, a desire to cry endlessly.

He looked up at the stars. Familiar and alien, menacing and compelling, the stars gripped his body with their ancient spell and told him a tale he would never understand. His bones ached, his feet were cold. He was a long way from home, lonely and alone. He had taken himself beyond the hearing of any other human. He was lost.

He began to question his actions. What am I doing here? I climbed this mountain—for what? I left my wife and children behind—for what? Here I am, cold and miserable, atop the illusory dream. I have worked hard to get here. It has been a lifetime. Where is the fulfillment of the promise? Where is the precious treasure? Where is God? Where is the Great Spirit? The stars watched impassively.

What a fool I am, he thought bitterly, to believe that those who hunger shall be filled. He pitied and belittled himself, and for a long time stared vacantly at the newly risen moon, overwhelmed by a sense of failure. What had his life amounted to? When he was young he had entertained dreams of greatness. He was going to be somebody, a servant of humanity, a hero, a Great Teacher. As he grew older his dreams had faded into the obscurity of his lived experience. There might be heroes, but he was not one of them.

But even in the midst of his average, day-to-day existence, even when he knew all too well his imperfection and impotence, he had hoped that someday he would be more complete, more fulfilled by his life. That hope had brought him to the summit of the Mountain of the Heart. But now that he was here, where was *here*? He felt no joy in having successfully climbed the mountain. Night was upon him. He feared the meanness and smallness of his own life. Whatever gain he had won on the approach to the mountain was lost to him now, swept away by the winds of self-doubt.

A poignant solitude pervaded the universe of the great mountain atop which crouched a tiny figure encircled by stones. Was this the meaning of life, this unquenchable, empty loneliness? Was this the gift of life, this separation from the mother, this freedom to be filled with despair and longing for what one can neither know nor express?

Perhaps the universe heard him. The chill wind subsided. Silence and deep darkness pervaded the mountain. He lay in his grave of stones and fell into a profound reverie, punctuated only by the sound of his heartbeat and heavy breathing. For a long time he ceased to think or feel and went away to a place where Nothing ruled. He became invisible to the cold, indifferent to himself and the night of stars. He forgot the dimension of time. Neither asleep nor awake, he existed as if he were suspended in no space, no time. He was somewhere. He was nowhere.

But the wind spoke again and startled him from his eternity. The wind was starving, starving for his body, starving for his attention. It seethed between the stones of his circle and shook him from his Nothing Dream, saying: "Here we are, you and I. Here we are."

The wind spoke so clearly that he might even have heard it in his mind's ear. He groaned back at it, from his numbed and aching body.

"I want to die."

"Then die," sang the wind.

"How?"

"Let go, let go," moaned the wind.

"But I *have* let go."

"Let go of it all. Let go of yourself," cried the wind.

"How?"

"Mother, mother, mother," whispered the wind. "Go to your mother."

"But my mother is dead."

"Your mother is not dead. Your mother lives forever."

So sang the gentle, cruel, wise, impatient spirit of the night wind. And the man heard. In his cold misery of wanting to die he heard the wisdom of the wind and knew what he had to do there in the brooding darkness.

Ignited by the keening of the starving, desolate wind, an aching longing to go home, to go home to mother, seized him. If only he could curl up against her breast and feel her holding him up, warm and steady. He could not endure their separation any longer. He would go back to the source, to the place from whence he had come, for he was sick of himself, sick of his life, sick of his incompleteness, sick of being separate from that which he desired deep in his earthen body.

It seemed for a moment the image of his mortal mother passed before him again, as she had in the cave. His father also appeared and the two of them were young and vibrant. It was their wedding day. She was in a bridal gown and held a wreath. He was in a dark suit and held her hand. The two of them appeared so innocent of any knowledge of what they later became: old and tired and ailing.

He loved them with the longing of one who would never see them again. He wanted to tell them that he loved them, that he wished them well, that he hoped they would find their life treasure. "I was one of their treasures," he thought, "their first born son." The thought made him want to be worthy of them, to do what he was to do with bravery and grace, to live this one night perfectly atop the mountain of his dreams.

The two images remained, silent, before him, symbols of foreverness, symbols of change and death. He did not speak to them. His heart throbbed in his throat, contending with feelings too deep for words. And then they were gone. He let them go. Somehow, they lived in him already, were married in him. The force of their spiritual vow he carried in his bones and blood and in the fiber of his soul.

He said good-bye to them, as if for the last time, and sat upright in his circle, looking into the nothingness. Then his wife and children came to him, his life as a husband and father.

He had loved many women before he loved his wife. But he had loved her best and finally. It had not been she, or any other person, who was responsible for his restless searching for a vision. She trusted him and gave him courage, took him for what he was and gave him to his dreams.

Remembrance of the richness and the beauty of his life with his wife and children suffused him. He could not recall the depression and anxiety that had led him to the top of the mountain. Surely I am incomplete, he thought, not to have seen the completeness of my life. Certain moments he had spent with them would let any man die happily. He wondered: Why was I unable to enjoy my life, to see the beauty in it?

But down inside he knew why. Because he had been unhappy with himself. He had carried his life around like a burden. Why did he climb the mountain? Not because he wanted to be more than who he was, but because he wanted to lose himself so that he could find himself. If losing himself meant that he must die, then he would die.

Suddenly he was struck by an extraordinary truth. Dying does not mean leaving loved ones behind, for all are united in the great Mother Heart. "I cannot leave those I love behind, for all are bound together by love and love is stronger than death." He thought this thought and trembled with fear; he had so little faith.

Outside the circle of his laboring thoughts the substance of things held steady, as it does without beginning or end. The night persisted. The darkness of the grave, the crypt, the vault, the hidden and secret, the mysterious and fecund, pervaded the night. Out across the Great Basin and west to the Ocean of Peace the night *was.* And somewhere in it was the feeble spark of consciousness that was the man who wanted to lose himself and go home to his mother.

That spark of consciousness was a seed—a seed that could not break forth from its corpse until it had gone back to the dark, star-filled vulva of the Mother Heart. The rattlesnake, the worm, the mesquite tree, the hummingbird, the prophet Wovoka, were they not all seeds that hungered to return to the Mother Heart and shared with him the hope of being united with her? And did these seeds not obey, with thousands of years of obedience, the heartbeat of the source that conceived and sent them forth into an outwardness that was always and eternally a returning, a coming home?

Whatever strength he had won by being weak, whatever hope he had salvaged from a heap of broken dreams, whatever faith he possessed from a life of doubt, whatever love was left in his bitter cup of breath, began to fill his heart. But the reservoir would never be filled, nor would it ever run dry. And his heart's cry unto the Mother Heart continued to pierce the night: "Have mercy on me. I am starving and have nothing to eat."

His being went out to all the creatures and spirits of the Earth, in a flood of empathy: We are all separate and alone and yet we share the same origin, the same flesh, the same mind, the same destination. Our hearts beat in unison. We have all endured the painful labor of separation and growth. Severed from our mother, we wander the Earth, starving, looking for our home. Lonely, we seek oneness with our kind, and though we wake apart and die apart, in waking we take root in our Mother; in dying we sow our seeds to the wind and go back to her.

He let go of his life and let the wind carry him out into the darkness across the moonlit crags and crests of the eastern mountains. His heart was a seed winging its way to the meadowlands of the mountain of the heart. The wind pierced him with cold, bright song. It buoyed him up, as though his soul were a boat setting forth on an unknown journey. For a moment he felt a twinge of regret, a nostalgia for the beauty of the life that had been. But then he yielded his heart to his Mother and the little boy, free of his aging, tired flesh, ran home.

Like the rustle of wings, the light of dawn began to beat its heart against the east. The moon paled. The mountain in the desert reared up to the rosy sky, and a tiny form atop its summit stirred and looked up. As the clear water of dawn cleaved the stone of darkness, so the man came forth from the night, wide-eyed and fresh, eager to see and know. The treasure he had come for lay shimmering just below the edge of the horizon. He knew it. His crystal-cold body could feel it: the stirring of life. A cosmic upwelling of emotion filled and then overflowed him. He tried to sing, but his heart was still in his throat. Is this the treasure? he wondered, and laughed. Then he cried, like a baby.

For abruptly, illuminating his red, grizzled, bawling face and casting the first shadow as far as eternity, thundered the sun, throbbing light into the world like a beating, bursting heart. As it consumed the night with its thunder-arrows of desire, it sang a song. The song was: "Great Mother have mercy on me. I am starving. I have nothing to eat."

BOOK 7

THE MOUNTAIN OF THE HEART

This mountain situated in the midst of the Earth, or center of the world . . . is both small and great. It is soft, also above measure hard and stony. It is far off, and near at hand, but by the providence of God, invisible. In it are hidden most ample treasures, which the world is not able to value. This mountain . . . is compassed about with very cruel beasts and . . . ravenous birds, which make the way thither both difficult and dangerous; and therefore hitherto, because the time is not yet come, the way thither could not be sought after or found out. But now at last the way is to be found by those that are worthy, but notwithstanding by every man's self-labor and endeavors.
—*Eugenius Philalethes,* Lumen de Lumine, *1651*

He had to return. Even before he left he knew he would come back. He would not have climbed the mountain in the first place if he had not planned to confront his past and the terms of his life. With the mountain in his heart and his heart in his throat he returned to his home and to his wife and children. They were waiting for him.

While he was away, they had gone about their life, but they had

201

missed him. Every thought of him had been a prayer that he would return. When he crossed the threshold of his home he saw the love mirrors of their eyes and knew the joy of belonging to someone. He had gone to be alone in order to discover that he was not alone. Now he was theirs and they were his. They were what his life and deeds had given him. They flung their arms around him and he was glad.

His wife kissed him and held his strange-familiar body against her. She felt the wild wind sweeping across the dark ridges of his bones. He smelled of ashes, dirt, and sweat. His lips were cracked, his cheeks bewhiskered and sun stained. His eyes caressed her with fingers of green tourmaline. Her man had returned but he was something more than a man. There was a freshness and an animalness to him. His grin devoured her. All her fears that he would never come back melted in the reality of his presence. Were those tears in his eyes? He wiped his face with a grimy sleeve and told her he loved her, that he was mated to her for life. Her heart leapt up like a rabbit from cover and ran into the wildness of him. There had never been troubles. He had never frightened her with his deathwarding words. All was new again.

He looked at her and saw all the women of the world in her face. How strange and beautiful she was! She who could have loved many men had chosen to love him. For the first time he did not feel unworthy of her choice. The darkness had coiled and rattled at him but he had passed by. He had said goodbye to his mother and gone to his Greater Mother. Nature had fashioned him into a man-child to her own liking. Then she had sent him back to his woman with a fresh desire. However, he felt more than desire. For the first time he truly appreciated her commitment to him. He was deeply moved. In his childhood he had been taught that God's love had preconditions, that love would be withdrawn if he turned away. But all along, this slender, graceful being had been teaching him that there were no conditions.

Her faithfulness only made him want her more, not just to possess her but to give her back to herself. A daring thought came to him: The more she grew into herself the more their lives would intertwine, engraft, and meld. The more he set her free, the more she would be his. The stronger their union, the more they could share. The deeper their sharing, the wider their sphere of life exploration. Nothing should be forbidden to the freedom of their love. He laughed and told her he wanted her. When she said yes, he came to her with the Ghost Dance drum beating in his blood.

When they were finished making love he lay with her and looked around at the walls and ceiling of the bedroom. "A comfortable lion's den," he thought, recognizing the pictures and bookshelves with new eyes. She stirred and moved against him. Her breasts clasped his arm, her breath stirring the hair on his chest. He kissed the top of her head. How unlike the top of the mountain his bedroom was! He heard the gurgle of the plumbing. The kids were watching TV and talking in the other room. Outside their window, cars swished down the street like noisy shadows. "What are your plans, my love?" his wife whispered, stroking his face.

He tried to think about the reasons why he had gone away. But his mind seemed reluctant to go back. Was it because there was too much pain there? He remembered that he had quit his job. Or had he been fired? It all amounted to the same thing. He had no means of earning his family's survival. This fact did not greatly disturb him at the time. At least the pain and self-loathing were gone. Instead, he waxed optimistic about the future. Somehow they were going to be all right. His wife might have to keep working for a while longer until he got on his feet, but he was ready to give it a try. "I'm not sure," he replied to her question, "but it's growing in me. Give me a little time."

Later, he went into his study. It was just as he had left it. The books, desk, and typewriter were in their customary places. The plants had been watered by his wife. He sat down and sighed at the unanswered letters and bills that had piled up on his desk. How could he have imagined that he was leaving it all behind? He chuckled under his breath and felt within himself the strength to tackle this smattering of unfinished business.

But there was something else he was supposed to do. What was it? He caught a glimpse of himself in the glass face of a framed picture. An aging man, wrinkles around his eyes, sagging cheeks, a shadow of his youthful self. He smiled ruefully and rubbed the stubble on his chin. "You might as well accept yourself, you old scarecrow," he advised. A fear of death momentarily seized the nape of his neck. At that same instant a tincture, a gleam, a glance of invisible light, fell from a pocket of his heart and landed on his inner eye. He looked up and saw the sun rising from the jagged teeth of the mountains of the east. He heard the dawn humming in the heart-lodge of his throat. Yes, there was something he had to do. He saw it clearly now.

He would lead others to the foot of the mountain he had climbed. No, it would not be the same mountain. Each would have his or her own mountain to climb and every person's mountain was different. Still, it would be the same mountain—for every mountain range had been uplifted by the same Great Mother. He saw himself from a great distance, bending over the tiny spring he had found in the vagina of the mountain. Greedily, he was drinking. With each swallow he grew stronger and more aware. The water would distill into words that came from the heart in his throat. His hunger would be filled with the purposes of truth.

He looked out the window of his study at the trees. It was early fall. The leaves were turning gold, the color of death, the color of the rising sun, the color of his vision. Soon winter wind would strip away all but the sap of incipient spring. It was time to break the mesquite bean apart and scatter its iron seeds to the ground, before the soil froze.

Sitting there at his desk he fell into a reverie. He remembered the thunder of the storm, the silent footfalls of the lightning, the impassive deadliness of the rattlesnake, the purity of the little spring, the quiet death of the murdered earthworm. He felt the upward pull of the mountain, the bright coldness of the stars, the steady pressure of the wind in his face. The mountain had fed him when he was starving with nothing to eat. Now it was his turn to feed the mountain. He would make it grow with his vision.

The sun was setting on another day. The failing light shafted through the window and fell on the pile of unanswered letters. In the other room the vacuum cleaner was roaring. But the man did not hear or see. He had come to the edge of a great precipice and was looking off into the distance. The walls of his study had dissolved into the rarified air at the top of the mountain. Once again he was back in his circle of stones, trying to shield himself from the cold wind. The wind was singing, "Mother, mother. You must go back to your Mother."

His daydream was interrupted by a call from the other room.

Something had come up. His presence was needed. Their son needed a ride. "No, it's nothing, really," said his wife. "If you're busy I'll do it."

With a slight sense of irritation he got up and went to his family. In his absence his wife had taken care of all the domestic duties. Now it was time for him to shoulder his part of the load. Wasn't it true that he had chosen to accept the conditions of his life, to make the most of his remaining years? No longer was he alone in the wilderness. He was back in the place that boredom, frustration, and disappointment had once rendered intolerable. Now he had to make it work. This was no time for dreaming.

As he drove his son downtown he thought about his role as a father. He knew he had not done his best. Many times he had sought to escape his responsibilities through work or by otherwise holding himself apart. Absorbed in his own Odyssean journey, he had neglected his home island and the uprearing of his children. Now he returned to face the troubles he had caused by his own absence. He assessed his abilities to be a nurturing father. Could he trust this new perspective he had brought back from the mountain? Could he trust the newly found feeling that he was, in fact, made of the right stuff for parenthood?

He realized his son had been talking and that he had not heard a word. The boy had been going on about what had happened while he was away. He forced himself to concentrate on what the boy was saying. The subject matter was of little import. But the exchange was. The son was trying to touch his father. He was seeking signs of his father's respect and regard. The man relaxed and assumed the rhythm of his son's thoughts. Dreams, fears, anxieties, and hopes all contended in his words. The father saw himself reflected in his boy. "What am I doing to prepare him for manhood?" he wondered.

For a moment he allowed himself to detest the culture into which the boy was growing. How could children develop well when always there was the threat of nuclear annihilation? How could his son grow into manhood when those held up as models and heroes were themselves like little boys? No wonder his son still played with toy soldiers and miniature war machines. As he grew older would he cope with this same fear of death by allowing others to build real weapons that would "defend" him? He determined that his son would never grow up accepting the warlike conditions of his culture as givens.

As he drove they talked about school and what was happening in the boy's life. Traffic lights winked green and red. Cars whistled by like guided missiles going someplace to explode. Reflexively, the man kept the car within the relative safety of the white lines. A driver cut dangerously in front of them, forcing him to brake in order to avoid a collision. His muscles tensed. He cursed under his breath. His son was chattering on about a bully at school who wanted to fight him. But how could the man think clearly in such traffic? He tried to formulate a meaningful answer to the implied fear in his son's words. Ahead, flashing red lights signaled the presence of a patrolman. He eased up on the gas pedal. He did not want to get stopped. He had forgotten his wallet.

As the days passed he lost track of them. There was so much to do at home. In the morning the kids would go to school and his wife would leave for work. After doing the breakfast dishes he would shop or clean house or do the laundry or go down to the unemployment office or pay the bills or answer letters or the phone. At noon, his daughter, who was in kindergarten, came home. He would make her lunch, spend time with her, take a short nap, read the morning newspaper, make a few phone calls, and then his son was home from school. He would touch in with his son, get him started with his homework, and then his wife was home from work. Then, if it was "my night," he would start dinner. After dinner and dishes he would go for a walk. Sometimes he walked down by the park, sometimes by the grammar school, sometimes through the shopping center. When he returned, it was his daughter's bedtime. Then his son retired. Finally, he and his wife had a couple hours of blessed peace.

At first, he found the routine a challenge. But before long he got bored. His boredom was only a sign of deeper anxiety that he was not doing what he came back to do. His newfound love for his family and home and his energy to devote himself to them was apparently not enough. He had always known deep in his heart that he had been born, as his parents had put it, to "amount to something." This sense of mission had driven him through the work of his former life. That work was gone. He was glad, for it had not been work that healed him. Now there was other work to do. His neighbors were starving and had nothing to eat but their television sets and the dreams their culture dreamed for them.

His wife noticed it first—the vacant stare, the creased brow, the absent-minded attempts to stay abreast of current events at home. "Why don't you go for it?" she urged him. "You're not getting any younger. Now is the time." At her words, he felt a deep sinking in his stomach and a choking sensation in his throat. Was he actually afraid to get started? That evening, as he walked through the park, a chill wind sprang up and stirred the fallen leaves of the chestnut and poplar trees. A deep shiver ran up his spine. He had to do something. Winter was coming.

Later that night, as he lay in bed sleeping, he was awakened by a desperate dream. He had traveled to a foreign country to meet with the king. But customs would not allow him into the country unless he passed the "manhood test." With great fear he agreed to the trial. Whereupon he was stripped of his clothing and dropped into a deep shaft in the earth. He fell out of control, screaming. He landed in deep water and sank like a stone. After what seemed an eternity he arose to the surface and caught his breath. "What now?" he wondered, expecting that his trial was over. Minutes passed. No one came to rescue him. He began to tire of treading water. "Is anybody there?" he yelled, reasoning that surely there was some person accountable for his welfare. But there was no response to his cries. He looked back up the hole down which he had fallen. At the very end there was a tiny pinprick of light.

He jolted awake and lay there, listening to his wife's soft breathing. Everything was still. The bedside clock read 3:30. He was bathed in sweat. Grateful to be alive, he turned against his wife's backside and snuggled against her. The early morning breeze of the bay freshened the pillow. He closed his eyes, determined to dream more optimistically. He was just going under when he heard it—and his eyes opened wide.

It was a low moaning sound, like nothing he had ever heard. It seemed to be distant, to come from the direction of downtown. He listened, straining against the darkness. It sounded like the voice of a gargantuan woman trying to say something. He could almost hear her despite the low background of intervening noise: the barking of a dog, the passing of a distant car, the whisper of his wife's breath, the far-off drone of a jet plane. The sound of her voice, in pain or travail, rose and fell against the darkness like the heaving coils of a great serpent. "Haya ... no ... wanna ... yanna ... oyo ... uhna ... no ... haya ..." the voice droned, the sounds moaning from deep in her throat.

"It is the spirit of the city!" thought the man, not knowing how he knew. She was revealing herself to him. She was telling him she was trying to give birth to a child. But she had been horribly abused. She badly needed his help. In his imagination he saw her, lying on splinters of broken glass in a parking lot in the financial district. Her eyes were as blue as the day, her body green as the dark. Her wild, dark hair was streaked with tar. Her dress was spangled with electric light. Toxic waste oozed from her open vagina. Semen from countless rapes glistened on her thighs. Her swollen, distended belly, branded with neon and scarred by sirens, concealed the mystery of something vast, precious, and alive.

"Wake up!" he called to his wife. "Wake up and listen to this!" She stirred and opened her eyes. She was still far away in dreamland. "Listen to what?" she mumbled. "The voice of the city!" She smiled and struggled up from her sleep to listen. "I don't hear anything." "Listen!" There was a long silence while she tried to hear. "Sounds like an old man snoring," she said finally, and lapsed back into sleep.

The next day, the man set forth on the trail of his vision. He made an appointment with a man who directed a school. He thought perhaps he could offer a kind of course at the school, a course for people who had come to the end of their rope and needed to go to the wilderness to be alone and fast and seek meaning for their lives.

The director received him courteously, listened to his plan, and then asked for his credentials. Although the man had plenty of credentials, he did not have the required ones. "Come back when you are certified to do this," said the director. The man reviewed what he would have to do to obtain the proper credentials. It would take him years. Besides, there existed no officially recognized means of obtaining those credentials. He pondered on this and decided to try again at another institution.

The middle-age lady was imposing, pompous, and articulate. She knew all the ins and outs of writing grants, getting funding, and running community health programs according to the book. She said, "If you didn't have such impressive recommendations I would consider you to be insane. As it is, your plan is not only ill-conceived and naive, it is positively dangerous."

Troubled, the man refused to give up. He went to a charitable foundation with a painstakingly written proposal detailing the rationale, methodology, expected outcome, and long-term benefits of his program among people in the midst of life crises. The secretary referred him to another secretary who listened to him briefly and then cut in. It was lunchtime in the factory. She assured him his proposal would be considered by "appropriate members of the foundation staff" and that he would hear from them by a certain date. Long before then the foundation informed him by letter that his proposal had been rejected. He was not encouraged to try again. He was told that the foundation had only limited funds and that they could not be allocated for programs such as his.

No self-pity, the man told himself, and sent the proposal to another foundation. Again, the answer came back no. So he sent his proposal to forty other foundations. Not a single one nibbled.

With some of his wife's hard-earned money he hired a professional "consultant" for an hour. The consultant heard him out and then opined, "Quite frankly, in terms of how foundations and other institutions think, your program is a total loser."

The man began to doubt his vision. Although he would not admit it to anyone, he had even begun to entertain thoughts about going back to his old vocation. He knew how tired his wife was working at a demanding job. But every day he was feeling more useless. The meager amount he was getting from unemployment had stopped when he had formed his "corporation." He had nothing to give his family but the proceeds of his frustrated dreams.

The problem was not simply the lack of money. It seemed to him he was losing contact with the vision. His memory of the great wilderness mountain had faded into a few vivid details. Now that winter was here, he spent most of his time indoors. Sometimes it was so cold he did not take his customary walk. Nowadays he was hardly aware of the natural world. He celebrated the setting of the life-giving sun by flipping on the light switch. He celebrated the matchless beauty of the stars by brushing his teeth and going to bed. Sometimes he was only too aware of the discrepancy between the natural world and his daily affairs. He kicked himself for being so insensitive to the Great Mother. Then he poured himself a drink.

Failure after failure at actualizing his vision finally brought him to the edge of despair. He stopped working at it. Instead, he did nothing. When his wife went off to work and his kids went off to school he did nothing. He sat around the house, numb as an icicle, thinking about what he was going to do next. But he never did it. Instead, he watched the soap operas on TV. Instead, he drank himself into a stupor and was worthless the rest of the evening. Instead, he ate and ate until he was sick as a bloated cow. His jaw became slack, his eyes vacuous and clouded. He no longer cared which clothes he wore. He might go all day in his bathrobe.

Those who were closest to him, who were fully aware of what was happening to him, suffered most. The beautiful father who had returned from the mountain had gradually become a sullen, unresponsive, uninteresting man. Though his children loved him, they avoided him. They had seen him this way before. To his wife, he was a painful reminder of how difficult it was to care for him. His drinking was getting to be a real problem. He was not keeping the household properly. As a lover, he was a shadow of his real potential. As a friend, he was morose and unsympathetic. He left his messes behind for her to clean up. He was fast becoming a parasite.

"Why don't you go back to your mountain for a while?" she suggested, her meaning evident. She wanted to get the family back on an even keel again, to heal some wounds. Though she loved him unconditionally, she harbored few illusions about what might happen to her marriage.

Of course, the man had thought many times about going back. But the idea smacked of retreat. "What kind of a man am I?" he wondered bitterly, "if I cannot live with my wife and children and my neighbors? Am I destined to be a hermit, a recluse, who lives a simple, natural life apart from the concerns of my people, including those I helped bring into this world? Am I going to refuse to be my brother's keeper?" Anyway, it was winter. His mountain was buried in snow.

The man had caught himself in his own snare. He had propped up the boulder of self-loathing with a deadfall trigger of self-pity. Then he hungered for the bait of failure, tripped the trigger, and the boulder fell on him. He did not die immediately. He died by degrees, by suffocation, by inability to let in fresh air. He closed off every escape, every ventilation vent, except for the sewer.

Not that he enjoyed being under that boulder, sweating alone in the darkness, tiredly treading water, waiting for God knows what to come and rescue him. There were cruel beasts crowded in with him there, familiar monsters to be sure, which his self-pity convinced him he could not fight. One monster was anger, the anger of a man pointing an accusing finger at himself. This monster was perhaps the most dangerous to others around him, for it often bounced off the mirror of his perceptions and hit innocent persons.

Another monster was inwardness. The man was a prisoner of the dark forces of his psyche. Fascinated with shadows, tricked by daydreams, paralyzed by awareness of his own ugliness, he was preyed upon by his masochistic side. Inwardly, he beat himself to a bloody pulp with guilt and self-hatred.

Another monster was his rational mind, coldly, scientifically describing to him every nuance of behavior, every shard of emotion, every sign of stupidity. His mind clenched his heart, the heart that was too painful to swallow and too painful to vomit up, and squeezed out every drop of spontaneous love. The rabies of cynicism infected his brain. Even when led to the verge of life-giving water, he baulked, certain that it was simply another illusion, another defeat, another false promise.

Still another monster was his imagination, which would not be satisfied with images of survival or the everyday maintenance of reality. He pursued will-o'-the-wisps, titillated himself with visions of swamp gas. He built grandiose schemes and set them on foundations of clouds. He pursued bright butterflies through his reveries and occupied his awareness with vagaries and diversions. Determinedly, he stalked the muses of the sacred mountain with wishes and empty hopes. He had forgotten how to suit action to his prayers.

Down there under the rock with the ravenous beasts he raked the muck back and forth, but it always stayed muck. After a while, he got to where he enjoyed the swamp. He did not want to come out and wash off. He reveled in it, beating his breast with a perverse kind of pride. At least it was his muck. Smelling so offensively like himself, he was bound to lose friends. Who was going to care about a man who so thoroughly liked to hate himself, who was so convinced his life had been a failure?

The erosion of friendships only convinced him more of the unworthiness of others. He started disliking other people for one reason or another—the way they talked, the way they dressed, the way they betrayed, the way they embraced stupidity. They seemed so shallow with their love for material things and their foolish quests for whatever they could not take with them. "People are past saving," he declared, and ceased to entertain the possibility of his own salvation. His dislike for people extended to the city they lived in. He forgot to listen to the voice of the city's spirit, calling to him for help.

He refused to reach out to his wife. Though she loved him with a desperate love and was gifted with a healing heart and a lovely body, he drew apart from intimacy with her. Though he did not cease to care, he despaired of being vulnerable with her. The despair became a reality. It was impossible to go to her. He had forgotten the language of lovemaking. And why would she ever want him anyway? A has-been lover, a would-be man, a drunken bum, a self-pitying failure?

Thus the winter passed. One day the man hit rock bottom. His wife informed him that she was going to take the kids and go live with her mother. She did not want to do this. She pleaded with him to show by his behavior that he wanted her to stay, that he wanted to keep his home and family. But the man was unable to see the situation clearly. His response was to go on a drinking binge. He drank until he got sick. When he awoke from his stupor, they were gone.

He found himself in an empty house with a strangled heart. He was starving and had nothing to eat. Everything around him mirrored his emptiness back to him. The truth was finally told: His life mission was to fail. From the beginning he had been given nothing. He cursed the Great Mother then. He cursed the illusion of his rebirth on the mountain. He cursed the vision he had been given. He cursed the man who had carried it. He cursed the universe for contriving to birth him. He beat his empty fists against the walls of the empty house and swore he would not live beyond the coming night.

That afternoon the phone rang. He picked it up. It was his six-year-old daughter.

"Hello, daddy."

"Hi, honey. How're you doing?"

"Fine. . . . I miss you."

"I miss you too. How's school?"

"All right. I don't like it at grandma's house. I want to come home. Mommy wants to come home too, only she doesn't want to say it."

"Well, I want you to come home too."

There was a long pause. "Daddy? Why aren't you happy?"

"I don't know. I guess I just don't know what to do with my life."

"Daddy? Will you promise me something?"

"Sure."

"It's such a nice afternoon. Why don't you take a walk in the park? And then when you're done, you can call me and tell me about it?"

The man promised he would, though he did not feel like walking. But then he looked outside. The sun was shining. A couple of kids were skateboarding down the sidewalk. He realized he had not gone walking in a long time. He rummaged under the bed for his walking shoes. Out on the back porch he found his walking jacket, freshly laundered and hanging on its customary peg. The jacket pocket bulged with his old walking cap, the one he had worn for his trek on the mountain.

He walked out of the house. The air was cool. A slight breeze was blowing. But in the sun it was warm. He walked the long mile down the street to the corner and turned his feet toward the park. It was a Sunday, and one of the first warm days of the year. People of all ages were out in the street. A few greeted him as he passed. He must have looked a sight. He had not shaved in days. His face had taken on the palor of shadows, his gait the uncertainty of an invalid. He passed the news stand. Stacks of newspapers blared the latest disheartening headlines. This time he ignored them. He was so sick and tired of being reminded of how ugly the human world was.

He crossed the street that fronted the park and entered it. It was a large park, with many walking trails and open areas. He kept to the sunlight, preferring it to the afternoon shade cast by the bushes and evergreen trees. Though deciduous trees were still bare, their white branches were outlined with the barest suggestion of green. The man compared his mood to the sunny day. His heart wrenched painfully in his throat. "Why can't there come a spring renaissance to my soul?" he wondered.

He watched a stray cat lolling in the vicinity of a trash can. The cat was skinny and starved looking. He identified with it. "The garbage can of my dreams," he thought. He walked on until he came to a playground area surrounded by benches. There he sat down and watched the children playing on the slides and swings. A young father was there, horsing around with his little boy, pushing him back and forth on the swing. The two were roaring with delight. He remembered the days when he had taken his children to the park and played with them. How could he have known that his life would come to this? He wanted to go over and warn the man, to say, "It will all amount to nothing some day." But a voice inside told him that it was not true, that he was indulging himself.

Usually, the thought that he was indulging himself in self-pity would only generate a deeper self-loathing. This time, there was a subtle shift. Instead, he said to himself, "Well, you don't have to be that way if you don't want to." Though many times he had entertained this thought, for the first time it seemed to register, with a subtle shock. "No!" he said out loud, "You don't have to be that way!"

The father who was playing with his son stopped and looked around. Overhearing, he thought the remark was addressed at him. The man was embarrassed. "Excuse me," he apologized, "I guess I was thinking out loud." The younger man laughed back. "I know what you mean. I sometimes do that too."

Suddenly, the man's heart filled with affection for this young father. His heart twisted and his eyes started with tears. He turned to the side so that his distorted face could not be seen. How could he explain this sudden burst of feeling? Was it that all at once he had realized life was too short and that was a reason to live it? The very idea that life was worth living struck him down like any baby. He began to sob with great wracking sobs.

In the man's tears was a tincture so rare that philosophers have spent a million fruitless years looking for it. This same tincture had trembled in the wings of dawn that last morning on his mountain. It was found in a pocket of the Mother Heart, the same heart that chocked his own throat. Now this priceless essence ran down his nose and splashed in a puddle at his feet.

After a while, the man looked up, and everything had changed. His eyes had been opened. He could see again, with the vision of his heart. The trees were burning with green fire in the setting sun. Daffodils and narcissus etched the green with golden exclamation points. As the children swung on the bars and climbed the jungle gym, light sprang from their little bodies like wings.

"You allright, buddy?" inquired an anxious voice next to him. It was the father who had been swinging his little boy.

"Spring is here!" sobbed the man.

"Yeah, it sure is," agreed the father, folding his arms and watching his son climbing on the jungle gym. He was a bit uncomfortable. Did he have a nut here? Nevertheless, he was determined to be friendly. His concern was like a revelation to a dying pilgrim.

Together they watched the little boy climbing on the bars. "He's a strong little guy," the man observed, between sobs. He was trying to get hold of himself.

"Yeah," said his father proudly. "He thinks he's climbing a mountain."

The little boy was nearing the tip of the apparatus. "Look daddy!" he called. He grunted and puffed as carefully, sure-handedly, he attained the top.

"Good for you!" called the man. "Good for me!" echoed the boy, sitting on the summit, waving his arms. Then he got scared and grabbed hold again. For a moment it looked like he might slip. His father ran over to help.

All at once the man *knew*. With preternatural clarity he saw his life. Like the little boy, he was climbing the mountain. He had never really descended from it. For as long as he had lived the mountain had been there. Many times he had fooled himself into thinking he had climbed it. But these, like the jungle gym, were only minor versions of the *real mountain*.

The *real mountain* was very small. It was the heart in his throat that gestated within him like a shrinking crystal, like a grain of sand. The *real mountain* was also very big. It loomed outside him and was steeper and higher than any Rill Mountain of Mars. This mountain he was climbing was hard, sharp, arduous, and stony. It was faulted, folded, eroded, and endlessly layered; it was a jumble, a chaos. It was also soft as the breeze and invisible as air, for it was composed of emotions, feelings, thoughts, dreams, and imaginings that came and went like the fleecy clouds.

The mountain was made of many things. It was the city and its spirit voice. It was his body and its soul. It was his wife, his family, his home, the everyday routines, his work. It was the rattlesnakes, the hummingbirds, the earthworms, the trees, the flowers, and the stray cats. It was concrete, steel, electricity, TV, gasoline, computers, fast food restaurants, penitentiaries, ghettos, corporations, nuclear bombs, toxic waste, and fried ice cream. It was will, faith, love, hope, myth, conviction, karma, and value. His mountain was as big as the universe. But it was small enough to fit into a chromosome. The mountain was his heart and it was the Mother Heart. It was his voice and it was the voice of the Muse.

"All the time I have been climbing the mountain," he thought with awe. He saw his struggles from a new perspective. He had not been stagnant, dead on the water, a failure to himself and others. He had been climbing a particularly difficult stretch. He had come up Inconsolable Canyon to Despair Gulch. Then he attempted Wrong Way Ridge and got caught in Alcohol Sink. But he had not succumbed to the muck of Self-Pity Swamp, nor did he expire on Anger Mesa. He kept climbing toward Heartbreak Ridge. See? He was still climbing! He was not lost! He had made it finally to Park Bench!

He laughed out loud. A few children were left. The rest had gone home. It was getting cold. The father and his little son were nowhere to be seen. He decided to go home and call his daughter. He started to get up but was arrested by a familiar voice at his elbow.

"You are sitting by my camp, but you are welcome to stay here and get colder." There was laughter in the words.

"The Cutter!" exclaimed the man.

"Yes," said the apparition. "I am walking about my land. I have come to tell you that the mountain you are climbing belongs to The People."

216

"I think I understand now," said the man.

"You *think* you understand. Someday you will not think. You will understand. 'We shall live again!' "

The man's heart tugged at his throat. Words from many languages filled his mouth. He wanted to utter them all, for they were all saying the same thing: "Have mercy on me. I am starving and I have nothing to eat."

He said, "I am not a strong, wise, or understanding man. I am just a man afraid of his own shadow. But I will live for the understanding you speak of."

The Cutter replied, "I am your guide to the Sacred Mountain. Now that you have seen the winter you know the truth that I speak. Again, I say, you must learn to dance the Ghost Dance, and to keep on dancing, for you, like The People, are starving and have nothing to eat. Come, white man. You will learn to dance the Ghost Dance."

The apparition vanished. The playground was still. It was dinner time in the city. The cold, moist air from the bay crept along the ground and enshrouded the bushes. The man shivered with dread and anticipation. What did The Cutter intend to show him? He waited as the chill crept into his bones. But the ghost did not reappear. Finally he got up and called out, "Be with me Cutter! Help me find my way up the mountain!" Still there was no answer. A horn honked along the boulevard.

The man did not feel disappointed. A curious elation crept into his shivering bones. He was determined to return to his house and begin the processes of knitting up his unraveled affairs. He said a silent thanks to the father and his little boy, then started home in the cold dusk. As he walked, a little rhyming song came to him. It went with the rhythm of his footfalls.

> We go now where we go now
> And we do what we must do.
> Remember all the people
> In the world like me and you.

It was a simple ditty, but it warmed him. He sang it under his breath as he walked back through the park. He felt a lightness to his body, a firmness to his step. In celebration he did a hop, step, and jump. Then it came to him, "Why, I'm dancing up my mountain!"

He came to the boulevard. As he waited for the light to change he realized he would not reach the top of the mountain he was climbing until he died. Until then he would be a ghost, a ghost dancing up the sacred mountain in the wilderness of his heart. A middle-age woman joined him at the traffic light. Apparently she had been taking in the air in the park too. He felt a rush of feeling for her. A compadre. An afficionado of park walking. He tried to think of something to say to her. All he could manage was, "Nice evening." "A little cold," she replied. "But wasn't it a glorious day?" Before they had reached the other side he discovered that she walked in the park every day and that she lived only a few blocks away.

At the corner they separated. Thought the man, as he continued on his course, "I will find beautiful treasures on the mountain. Surely, the way will not always be as steep as it has been." He began to name places on the mountain that sooner or later he would reach: Love Spring, Miracle Creek, Peaceful Meadow, Second Wind Ridge, Heart's Desire Canyon—and finally Life Ends Peak, the highest summit of the range. He stopped to buy a bouquet of daffodils for his wife. The girl who sold them was lissome and talkative. She was the kind who actually took interest in her customers. Talking with her the man felt the old stirrings of sexual desire. The girl reminded him of his wife. He imagined his wife without her clothes and remembered the pleasure she took in lovemaking. He took the flowers and went whistling up the street. "Remember all the people/In the world like me and you."

Suddenly he felt hungry, for the first time in ages. He did not want to go home and eat alone. He stopped in the little sandwich shop at the next corner. "Gateway Cafe" read the sign. He laughed. "Even now I am at the mouth of Gateway Canyon." He went in and ordered a sandwich and a glass of milk. As he waited for his order he struck up a conversation with a man about his own age who said he was an architect working for the city. It turned out the man was unhappy with his job and on the verge of a marital breakdown. The two must have talked for an hour or so, hunched over the little table, drinking coffee. As they shared their experiences, the man spoke of the time he had spent on his wilderness mountain and the trouble he had subsequently endured trying to make his vision of benefit to the people.

With fascination the architect listened to his story. At the end he asked, eagerly, "When can I go to the mountain? I'm ready!"

The man was taken aback. Up to now, he had encountered only incomprehension and criticism. Those he had hoped would help him had called him crazy. But here was a respected man who did not consider him insane. In a flash he saw what The Cutter meant when he said, "The mountain you are climbing belongs to The People."

All that time he had been attempting to reach the people through established institutions and organizations that "represented" the values and needs of their constituents. Now he could see that the bureaucracies he placed so much hope in were only ossified cultural means of keeping the status quo and protecting the people from helping themselves. Their very existence was premised on the need to perpetuate ignorance and poverty, without which they would not operate. He realized there was no further need to approach these individuals. They were frightened for their jobs and wedded to the security of narrow-mindedness. It was time to take his vision to the people themselves, to his neighbors and friends, to those whose complacency had shaken their eyes open.

As for him and his vision, it was now or never. He looked the architect in the eye and said, "Are you really serious? Do you realize what you are getting into? Think about what happened to me after I returned from the Sacred Mountain. Are you prepared to face the consequences of the vision you bring back from the mountain? You too will find that if you do not use the treasures you discover there you will die a living death." The architect returned his look, from an anxious, aging face. "I'm ready to leave everything behind," he said.

But the man's ghost dancing was not over. It had just begun. He said goodbye to his new friend and made an appointment to see him again. He paid his bill, left a tip, and started up Gateway Canyon. The song sang in his blood: "We go now where we go now/And we do what we must do." A black dog came up for a pat on the head. An elderly couple walked past so that they could get a good evening from him. A little girl just learning how to ride her bike

gave him a chance to do fancy footwork. Then the street lamps
went on. He might have preferred that they hadn't, but they always
did. He thought how necessary it was to accept that which, in the
long run, could not be changed with benefit to all. Two adolescent
boys passed by in leather jackets and green hair. They were chew-
ing gum, their eyes darting nervously everywhere—even for an
instant at the man. They did not greet him, but he felt the restless-
ness and the random power of their search cling to him as they
sauntered by. "Remember all the people/In the world like me and
you."

Now he was walking up Hillside Drive. An ambulance came
screaming past, lights pulsating, siren wailing. "Aegis Ambulance"
was painted on its door. "We shall live again," he thought. "But
that doesn't mean I won't be afraid of shadows." It seemed to him
that he had reached a more realistic understanding of his own
abilities. He was thankful he had a guide, a "water guardian" of the
sacred mountain. "Speak to me, Cutter," he prayed under his
breath, experimenting with his new source of help. He was walking
past a women's clothing shop. "Small World" sang the name above
the door. "Thank you, Cutter." he breathed.

He reached the corner of his street: Dry Creek Road. One more
mile to go, up the winding drive. By God he was going to dig down
into that dry creekbed and find the water lurking there! He would
dig with the pick and shovel of hunger, for his people were starving. He would spoon the water into channels of words and actions,
gifts from the Great Mother to his people.

Determined, he began that last mile. It grew darker as he left the
street lamps behind. He passed a house on his left, unlit except for
the luminescence of a TV screen. Who lives there? he wondered,
and stopped for a moment to see if he could hear what program
they were watching. But it was commercial time. Above quiet
violins a velvet voice was saying, "Unexpected. Unconventional.
Undoubtedly like you." It was an ad for cognac. Then another
came on: "For those who view responsibility not as a burden but
as one of the most prized credentials of all. . . . Responsibility has
its own rewards. . . . American Express." He laughed. Two days
ago those commercials would have enraged him. He must never
again make the mistake of taking culture too seriously. Anger was

purifying but it could lead to self-victimization. Helpless anger took one up Despair Gulch.

He started walking again, his breath blowing halos of steam. Ideas came in quick pants as he walked. "Starving and nothing to eat . . . the Ghost Dance . . . climbing the mountain. . . ." As he rounded a corner, a car whirled down the road, its headlamps blinding him. It thundered past, radio blaring rock-and-roll. Without warning, he was jogged into a prescient state. He *saw* himself in the future, climbing the mountain of his heart.

He was stunned at the heights he would attain. Yet it seemed he had hardly made headway on the mountain. It had been ten years since he took the architect to the foot of the mountain. Many people were coming to him now. In fact, he was far too busy to deal with all of them. He had found others who were pursuing a similar vision, some who had been at it for a lifetime. But there were not enough to do the work. The people were starving and had nothing to eat. How would they be fed?

He could not answer this question. He could only fill his heart with faith and give himself to the joy and despair of the Ghost Dance on the mountain of his heart. In time he had learned to take courage from those who went with him to the mountain. He saw the truth in their eyes and guided his steps toward it. The Great Mother had been faithful through the years. Never again had she allowed him to ignore her. She revealed herself to him in "civilized" things. Then she drew him to the birthplace of all matter, into the deepest, darkest folds of her earthly vagina.

The Cutter never abandoned him, but he never reappeared, a solid apparition, before the man's eyes. Instead, he walked in the man's shoes, looking with his eyes through the man's own eye sockets, and showed him signs of winter. He cut away lies. He split experience into cords of fuel. He kept the man honest and human so that he could live to make a way for The People to return. He lived in the man as a symbol of his ancestry, the sacred ones from the beginning of time. Some might say The Cutter became something in the man's genes, a dance the sacred ones wanted transmitted through the body of his life.

But what of his wife and family? What became of them? They were also a part of the mountain the man was climbing. Try as he might, he was not allowed to see them ten years from now. They were a question mark, an unknown, a deepest matter of his heart. He knew he loved them too much to ever allow himself to fall into Alcohol Sink again. Oh how he burned for his wife, not only for her body but for her love, for the ordinary, omnipotent god that existed between them and made them one! He would do anything to get her back, to win her peace of mind and respect.

The prescience faded. He was back on Dry Creek Road, just below his home. He started up the walk. Something moving in back of his house caught his eye. It was an animal of some sort—a dog maybe. He walked around the house to the back and suddenly came face-to-face with a raccoon.

The lid to the garbage pail was lying in the dirt. Trash was scattered everywhere. Mr. Raccoon was inching into the shadows, his clever finger-paws holding the core of an apple. The man choked back a yell of outrage. The raccoon was a sign. He watched as the big fellow with the bandit face withdrew into the relative safety of the bushes in the backyard. Only his wary, yellow eyes were left, gleaming in the dark.

"Hey, Raccoon, what are you looking for?" called the man.

"I was in the process of getting into your garbage," answered the raccoon, in a sophisticated voice. "But then you came along and I decided that since you are bigger than I, discretion would be the better part of valor."

"What makes you think I like you getting into my garbage?"

"What makes you think I like living in two worlds? It isn't easy, you know."

"O yeah? What makes it so hard?"

"You should know. You haven't exactly been a success at it. Now you get to pick up your garbage."

This stumped the man for a while. Then he said, "Well, I'm not a failure either."

"Neither am I," said raccoon, with a trace of self-congratulation. "But it isn't easy, what with kids and all."

There was a silent moment of assent. Raccoon and man were starving and had nothing to eat. Their people were also starving. Would they ever be filled?

Raccoon spoke up. "You're lucky I wasn't a skunk."

"Yeah."

"Look. I'll keep the skunks away if you'll leave something nice for me every once in a while."

"Like what?"

"O, a big bowl of chocolate pudding would be fine."

"How about a swift kick in the seat of the pants?"

"No way. We're two of a kind."

"And what would you leave out for me?"

Raccoon thought for a while. "A turd," he said.

The man laughed uproariously. He had finally come home. He went into the house. First, he would call his daughter. Then he would whip up a big batch of chocolate pudding.

What we look for beyond seeing
And call the unseen,
Listen for beyond hearing
And call the unheard,
Grasp for beyond reaching
And call the withheld,
Merge beyond understanding
In a oneness
Which does not merely rise and give light,
Does not merely set and leave darkness,
But forever sends forth a succession of living
  things as mysterious
As the unbegotten existence to which they return.
   —*Lao Tzu,* The Way of Life

Contributors in Order of Appearance

Errol: Errol Shubot, Grapevine Mountains, Death Valley

Creosote: Dr. Mark Stillman, Last Chance Mountains, Eureka Valley

I'd Pick a Daisy: Gerry Goodwin, Inyo Mountains

Companion of the Wind: Eric Baker, White Mountains

Free Bird: Jennie Oppenheimer, Starvation Canyon, Death Valley

Weak Stomach, Strong Heart: Annette Wire, Starvation Canyon, Death Valley

Moon Song Crying: Eric Knudson, Upper Reese River, Nevada

Lone Stone Among the Rest: Sue Amons, Black Mountains, Death Valley

Linda: Linda Gregory, Cerro Colorado, Baja California Sur

Keenan: Keenan Foster, White Mountains

Fire Stick: Rich Kerkorian, White Mountains

Gift Bearer: Virginia Hine, Saline Mountains, South Warner Wilderness

Solo: Natalie Rogers, Funeral Mountains, Death Valley

Mark: Mark O'Neill, Panamint Mountains, Death Valley

Ruth: Sister Ruth Wallin, Panamint Mountains, Death Valley

Listens With the Heart: Sister Patricia Burke, Panamint Mountains, Death Valley

Looking Into the Fire: Marilyn Riley, Hunter Mountain, Death Valley

Lonely Heart Outreaching: Meredith Little, Saline Mountains, Inyo Mountains

Broken Heart Laughing: Willie Stapp, *La Bahia de la Concepción*, Baja California Sur

Rock: Howard Voskuyl, Saline Mountains

Trisha: Trisha Bishop, Starvation Canyon, Death Valley

Turtle Dreamer: Rusty Kavendak, Last Chance Mountains, Eureka Valley

Little Warrior: Steve de Martini, South Warner Wilderness

Glowing Mountain in the Dawn: Claudia Dunlavy, Black Mountains, Death Valley

Silence: Jack Crimmins, Caribou Wilderness

Select Bibliography

Abbey, Edward. 1971. *Slickrock.* San Francisco: Sierra Club.

Blake, William. 1966. *The Complete Writings.* Ed. Geoffrey Keynes. London: Oxford University Press.

Bridges, William. 1980. *Transitions: Making Sense of Life's Changes.* Reading, Mass.: Addison-Wesley.

Brown, Dee. 1971. *Bury My Heart at Wounded Knee.* New York: Bantam.

Brown, Joseph Epes. 1971. *The Sacred Pipe: Black Elk's Account of the Seven Rites of the Oglala Sioux.* Baltimore: Penguin.

Buber, Martin. 1966. *The Way of Man.* Secaucus, N.J.: Citadel Press.

Campbell, Joseph. 1970. *Hero with a Thousand Faces.* New York: World Publishing.

———. 1972. *Myths to Live By.* New York: Viking Press.

———. 1986. *The Inner Reaches of Outer Space.* Toronto: St. James Press.

Castaneda, Carlos. 1972. *Journey to Ixtlan.* New York: Simon & Schuster.

Cavendish, Richard. 1977. *Visions of Heaven and Hell.* New York: Crown Publishers.

Daumal, Rene. 1959. *Mount Analogue.* New York: Viking Press.

Eliade, Mircea. 1967. *From Primitives to Zen.* New York: Harper & Row.

———. 1958. *Rites and Symbols of Initiation.* New York: Harper & Row.

Faraday, Ann. 1976. *Dream Game.* New York: Harper & Row.

Foster, Steven, and Meredith Little. 1983. *The Vision Quest: Passing from Childhood to Adulthood.* Big Pine, CA: Rites of Passage Press.

———. 1985. *The Sacred Mountain: Vision Quest Handbook for Adults.* Big Pine, CA: Rites of Passage Press.

———. 1986. *The Roaring of the Sacred River: Modern Apprenticeship to the Ancient Vision Fast.* Big Pine, CA: Rites of Passage Press.

———. 1987. *A Wilderness Rite of Passage for Youth (teacher's edition) and Technical Guide to Threshold Safety.* Big Pine, CA: Rites of Passage Press.

Garfield, Patricia. 1976. *Creative Dreaming.* New York: Ballantine.

Godwin, Joscelyn. 1981. *Mystery Religions in the Ancient World.* San Francisco: Harper & Row.

Greene, T. A. 1967. *Modern Man in Search of Manhood.* New York: Association Press.

Hall, Manley. 1928. *Secret Teachings of All Ages.* San Francisco: Philosophical Research Society.

Harding, Esther. 1976. *Women's Mysteries.* New York: Harper & Row.

Harner, Michael. 1980. *The Way of the Shaman*. New York: Harper & Row.

Henderson, Joseph. 1967. *Thresholds of Initiation*. Middletown, CT: Wesleyan University Press.

Jung, C. G. 1958. *Psyche and Symbol*. Garden City: Doubleday.

————. 1974. *Dreams*. Princeton: Princeton University Press.

La Chapelle, Dolores. 1978. *Earth Wisdom*. Los Angeles: Guild of Tutors Press.

Lakoff, George, and Mark Johnson. 1980. *Metaphors We Live By*. Chicago: Chicago University Press.

Levine, Stephen. 1982. *Who Dies: An Investigation of Conscious Living and Dying*. Garden City: Doubleday.

Luke, Helen. 1981. *Woman, Earth and Spirit: The Feminine in Symbol and Myth*. New York: Crossroads.

Mahdi, Louise, Steven Foster, and Meredith Little, eds. 1987. *Betwixt and Between: Patterns of Masculine and Feminine Initiation*. Illinois: Open Court Press.

Millman, Dan. 1984. *The Way of the Peaceful Warrior*. Tilburon, CA: H. J. Kramer, Inc.

Neumann, Erich. 1974. *The Great Mother*. Princeton: Princeton University Press.

Perera, Sylvia Brinton. 1981. *Descent of the Goddess: A Way of Initiation for Women*. Toronto: Inner City Books.

Roethke, Theodore. 1962. *The Collected Poems*. New York: Doubleday.

Rothenberg, Jerome. 1968. *Technicians of the Sacred*. Garden City: Doubleday.

Sheehy, Gail. 1977. *Passages: Predictable Crises of Adult Life*. New York: Bantam.

————. 1981. *Pathfinders*. New York: Morrow.

Snyder, Gary. 1980. *The Real Work*. New York: New Directions.

Storm, Hyemeyohsts. 1972. *Seven Arrows*. New York: Harper & Row.

Strong, Emory. 1969. *Stone Age in the Great Basin*. Portland, OR: Binford and Mort.

Szekely, Edmond, ed. and trans. 1970. *The Gospel of Peace of Jesus Christ by the Disciple John*. Berkeley: Shamballa Press.

Turner, Victor. 1967. *Forest of Symbols*. Ithaca: Cornell University Press.

Van der Post, Laurens. 1961. *Heart of the Hunter*. London: Penguin Books.

Van Gennep, Arnold. 1972. *The Rites of Passage*. Chicago: Chicago University Press.

Waters, Frank. 1972. *The Man Who Killed the Deer*. New York: Ballantine.

Wilhelm, Richard, ed. and trans. 1950. *I Ching*. Princeton: Princeton University Press.

About the Authors

STEVEN FOSTER, PH.D. and MEREDITH LITTLE have combined their talents on other books including *The Roaring of the Sacred River* (to be published by Prentice Hall Press), *The Sacred Mountain* and *The Trail Ahead: A Wilderness Rite of Passage for High School Graduates* (Rites of Passage Press), and *Betwixt and Between: Patterns of Masculine and Feminine Initiation,* edited with Louise Mahdi (Open Court Press).

For sixteen years they have guided individuals through wilderness passage rites such as the vision quest and are directors of The School of Lost Borders, a ceremonial and training facility of wilderness initiation form and process in the Eastern Sierra.